THE NEURODIVERSITY OF CONSCIOUSNESS:

Exploring Psychic Abilities, Indigo Children, and the Future of Human Potential

Aurealia Nelson

Staten House

S

Staten House

ISBN-13: 979-8-89686-649-7

*To the extraordinary individuals who have bravely shared
their unique experiences, challenging conventional
boundaries and illuminating the vast spectrum of human
consciousness. This work is dedicated to those who embrace
their neurodiversity, celebrating their gifts and inspiring a
more inclusive and understanding world. It is also dedicated
to the memory of those who suffered from misunderstood
mental health challenges, reminding us of the urgent need
for compassion and a paradigm shift in how we perceive and
address human potential, both extraordinary and seemingly
challenged. Their journeys, both luminous and shadowed,
have illuminated the path towards a more compassionate and
enlightened future for all. May this exploration contribute
to breaking down stigmas and fostering acceptance of
the full spectrum of human experience – a spectrum
that is both breathtaking in its diversity and profoundly
interconnected. This work is a testament to the resilience and
strength of the human spirit in all its magnificent forms.*

INTRODUCTION

For too long, the realms of neuroscience and parapsychology have existed as separate islands, their approaches seemingly irreconcilable. Neuroscience, with its meticulous focus on the physical brain and measurable neurological processes, often dismisses phenomena such as clairvoyance and clairsentience as unsubstantiated or illusory. Parapsychology, on the other hand, frequently lacks the rigorous methodology required to convince the scientific community. This book proposes a radical shift in perspective, arguing that these two seemingly disparate fields are intrinsically linked and that a deeper understanding of one illuminates the other. By exploring the neurological underpinnings of both "normal" and "exceptional" cognitive abilities, we can begin to unravel the mysteries of consciousness itself. The concept of neurodiversity offers a powerful framework for understanding the extraordinary experiences reported by individuals who identify as Indigo children, Starseeds, Lightworkers, or who report having psychic abilities. It suggests that what is often categorized as "mental illness" may, in some cases, represent a form of exceptional cognitive processing, a deviation from the neurotypical norm that opens up access to alternative modes of perception and experience. This book doesn't advocate for dismissing rigorous scientific methods; rather, it calls for a more expansive and inclusive approach, one that acknowledges the limitations of our current understanding and embraces the possibility of phenomena that lie beyond our current explanatory models. We will explore the neurological basis of clairvoyance and clairsentience, investigate the potential genetic and epigenetic influences on these abilities, and examine the similarities and differences between "psychic" experiences and those reported by individuals diagnosed with certain forms of psychosis. Through detailed case studies, scientific literature reviews, and a respectful consideration of spiritual perspectives, we hope to pave the way for a new paradigm in understanding the full spectrum of human consciousness and to advocate for a future where neurodiversity is not only accepted, but celebrated.

PREFACE

This book represents a culmination of years of research at the intersection of neuroscience, parapsychology, and spiritual practices. My journey began with a rigorous scientific training, grounded in the principles of empirical evidence and controlled experimentation. Yet, alongside this, I have always held a deep fascination with the seemingly paranormal and the potential of human consciousness to extend far beyond the currently accepted boundaries of scientific understanding. This exploration isn't about dismissing scientific rigor, but about embracing the possibility that our current models of the brain and consciousness may be too narrow, too limited to encompass the full range of human experience. The individuals I've had the privilege of meeting – those who identify as Indigo children, Starseeds, Lightworkers, or who exhibit unusual sensory perceptions – have profoundly impacted my perspective. Their unique experiences, often misunderstood and marginalized by conventional frameworks, challenge us to broaden our understanding of human potential. This book is an attempt to bridge the gap between these seemingly disparate worlds – the rigorous world of neuroscience and the often-spiritual landscapes of psychic abilities and New Age perspectives. I hope it encourages a deeper dialogue, fostering greater understanding and acceptance of the diverse expressions of human consciousness, whether perceived as paranormal, neurodiverse, or a manifestation of a currently unknown dimension of human capacity. The goal is not to provide definitive answers, but to pose important questions and encourage further exploration of this fascinating and multifaceted area of study.

CHAPTER 1: INTRODUCTION: THE CONVERGENCE OF NEUROSCIENCE AND PARAPSYCHOLOGY

For centuries, the realms of science and spirituality have existed in seemingly separate universes, often viewed with mutual suspicion, if not outright hostility. Science, with its emphasis on empirical evidence and measurable results, has traditionally dismissed spiritual experiences as subjective and unverifiable. Spirituality, on the other hand, often relies on faith, intuition, and experiences that lie beyond the scope of conventional scientific instruments. This chasm has created a significant barrier to understanding certain aspects of human experience, particularly those involving what are often termed "psychic abilities" or phenomena that defy easy categorization within established scientific frameworks. However, a growing number of researchers and thinkers are beginning to bridge this gap, recognizing the limitations of purely materialistic explanations of consciousness and the potential for integrating scientific rigor with spiritual insights.

The historical divide between science and spirituality stems partly from the limitations of past scientific methods. Early scientific approaches, rooted in a mechanistic worldview, tended to reduce complex phenomena to simpler, more easily quantifiable components. This approach, while effective in many areas, proved inadequate when attempting to explain subjective experiences such as intuition, empathy, or mystical encounters. Moreover, the very nature of scientific inquiry, with its focus on repeatable experiments and controlled environments, struggles to accommodate unique or rare occurrences, leaving little room for the seemingly exceptional or anomalous events often associated with parapsychology. This methodology, while valuable for studying predictable phenomena, often overlooks the subtle and nuanced aspects of human consciousness.

Spiritual traditions, on the other hand, often emphasize subjective experience and personal revelation as pathways to understanding reality. While valuable in providing frameworks for meaning and purpose, these traditions often lack the rigorous testing and peer review processes inherent in scientific inquiry. This lack of rigorous methodology can lead to unsubstantiated claims and a vulnerability to biases, making it difficult to evaluate the veracity of spiritual experiences in a way that meets scientific standards. This lack of a common language and methodology has historically created an impasse, hindering any genuine dialogue between these two perspectives.

However, the tide is turning. Advances in neuroscience and the growing awareness of the limitations of reductionist science are paving the way for a more integrated approach. Neuroimaging techniques, such as fMRI and EEG, are providing unprecedented insights into the brain's activity during various mental states, including those associated with altered states of consciousness, intuition, and empathy. These techniques offer the possibility of objectively measuring subjective experiences, potentially bridging the gap between the qualitative data gathered through spiritual practices and the quantitative data sought by scientific researchers.

Furthermore, the burgeoning field of quantum physics is challenging the fundamental assumptions of classical physics, suggesting that reality may be far more complex and interconnected than previously thought. The concepts of entanglement and non-locality, for example, hint at the possibility of connections between consciousness and the physical world that were previously considered impossible. This challenges the purely materialistic view of the universe and opens the door to considering the potential for phenomena that appear to defy conventional scientific explanations.

The integration of science and spirituality isn't about abandoning one for the other. It's about recognizing the strengths of each approach and combining them to create a more complete understanding of the human experience. Scientific rigor provides a framework for testing hypotheses, verifying findings, and establishing credibility. Spiritual insights offer a rich source of qualitative data and alternative perspectives that might otherwise be overlooked by purely reductionist approaches. By employing a blend of quantitative and qualitative research methods, we can move toward a more nuanced and holistic understanding of phenomena that lie at the intersection of science and spirituality.

For example, consider the concept of intuition. Traditionally viewed as a purely subjective experience, neuroscience is beginning to shed light on the underlying neural mechanisms. Studies have shown that certain brain regions, such as the anterior cingulate cortex and the insula, are particularly active during intuitive decision-making. These findings suggest that intuition, far from being a mystical ability, may represent a sophisticated form of unconscious processing that draws on vast amounts of information that are inaccessible to conscious awareness. This scientific understanding doesn't diminish the value of intuition; instead, it provides a more profound appreciation for its complexity and the potential benefits of cultivating intuitive abilities.

Similarly, the exploration of altered states of consciousness, such as those experienced during meditation or near-death experiences, offers valuable insights into the nature of consciousness itself. Neuroimaging studies show distinct patterns of brain activity during these states, often associated with increased activity in areas associated with self-awareness and emotional processing. This scientific data supports the subjective reports of individuals who have undergone these experiences, lending credence to the validity of their accounts. Furthermore, these findings can help inform the development of therapeutic interventions utilizing these altered states to address a variety of mental health challenges.

The integration of science and spirituality also necessitates a shift in our understanding of neurodiversity. The traditional medical model of viewing neurological differences primarily as deficits or disorders needs to be replaced with a more inclusive model that embraces the full spectrum of human experience. Individuals who exhibit exceptional abilities, such as those often associated with "Indigo children" or other groups described in the New Age movement, may not simply be experiencing a form of mental illness; instead, they might represent a different way of experiencing and interacting with the world. A comprehensive understanding of neurodiversity requires acknowledging this potential, moving beyond simplistic diagnostic labels, and exploring the unique strengths and capabilities that these individuals bring to society.

The task of integrating science and spirituality is complex and challenging, demanding a commitment to open-mindedness, intellectual humility, and rigorous methodology. However, the potential rewards are immense. By overcoming the historical divide and fostering interdisciplinary collaboration, we can unlock a new era of understanding, embracing the full spectrum of human potential, and fostering a future where science and spirituality work together to enhance the human condition. This integration is not a simple merging of two opposing forces, but rather a holistic synthesis that recognizes the limitations of both while leveraging their unique strengths to advance our understanding of consciousness, human experience, and the nature of reality itself.

The exploration of psychic abilities necessitates a nuanced approach, acknowledging both the subjective experiences reported by individuals and the objective need for scientific scrutiny. While the term "psychic" often evokes images of fortune tellers and stage magicians, the phenomena under consideration here demand a more rigorous, neuroscientific lens. Clairvoyance, for instance – the purported ability to perceive information beyond the known senses – presents a fascinating challenge. From a neurological perspective, we must ask: what brain regions, networks, or processes might be involved in such an experience? Are there specific neural correlates that distinguish clairvoyant experiences from other cognitive phenomena?

One avenue of exploration lies in comparing clairvoyance to certain aspects of psychosis. Conditions like schizophrenia, for example, sometimes involve hallucinations and delusional beliefs that share some superficial similarities with clairvoyant experiences. However, it's crucial to emphasize the crucial difference: while hallucinations in schizophrenia are generally considered pathological, rooted in neurological dysfunction, clairvoyance, as reported by proponents, is often described as a conscious and controlled ability, even a form of enhanced perception. This distinction highlights the need for careful differentiation and rigorous investigation, preventing the dismissal of potentially genuine phenomena simply due to their apparent association with mental illness. Instead, a comparative analysis of brain activity during both experiences could potentially unveil critical differences in neural patterns, offering valuable insights into the underlying mechanisms. Perhaps the same brain regions are involved, but their activation patterns, the interplay of neurotransmitters, or the involvement of specific genes might dramatically differ. This could potentially identify biomarkers associated with genuinely perceived extra-sensory input, differentiating it from psychotic distortions of reality.

Clairsentience, the alleged ability to sense the emotions or feelings of others, presents a similarly compelling challenge. Empathy, a well-established human capacity, involves mirroring the emotional states of others, activating corresponding brain regions within the observer. However, clairsentience is typically described as extending beyond simple empathy, involving a sense of direct access to another's emotional state, regardless of physical proximity or sensory input. The neural basis of such an experience remains largely unexplored, yet it opens avenues for investigating the limits of our understanding of interconnectivity and consciousness. Are there subtle neural mechanisms, perhaps involving quantum entanglement or currently unknown forms of electromagnetic communication within the brain, that could explain these experiences? Functional magnetic resonance imaging (fMRI) studies could offer valuable data by comparing brain activity during empathetic responses and what individuals describe as clairsentient experiences. Furthermore, exploring genetic predispositions and epigenetic factors could reveal a potential inherited component, offering new perspectives on the heritability of traits previously considered solely within the realm of the paranormal.

Beyond clairvoyance and clairsentience, a vast array of purported psychic abilities exist, each demanding its own neuroscientific investigation. Precognition (the ability to predict future events), psychokinesis (the ability to influence physical objects with the mind), and telepathy (direct mind-to-mind communication) all challenge our current understanding of brain function and the nature of reality. While these abilities remain largely outside the mainstream scientific paradigm, their consistent reporting across cultures and throughout history suggests the possibility of underlying neurological mechanisms yet to be understood. The challenge lies in developing methodologies capable of reliably measuring and quantifying these phenomena, while simultaneously avoiding the pitfalls of confirmation bias and the inherent difficulties of replicating subjective experiences in a controlled laboratory setting. This requires not just innovative experimental designs, but also a shift in mindset, acknowledging the possibility of phenomena that transcend our current scientific framework.

The exploration of psychic abilities should not be limited to controlled laboratory settings. Ethnographic studies of cultures that traditionally incorporate psychic abilities into their worldview offer valuable insights. Shamanic practices, for example, often involve altered states of consciousness and purported interactions with spirits or other unseen entities. Analyzing these practices through a neuroscientific lens, investigating the neural correlates of altered states of consciousness and the potential for accessing information through non-ordinary states of awareness, could provide crucial data. Similarly, studying individuals who report spontaneous psychic experiences can be highly informative. These individuals often possess unique neurological profiles or life experiences that might shed light on potential predisposing factors. These case studies, while not providing definitive proof, can offer valuable hypotheses for further investigation.

It's important to acknowledge the inherent limitations of current neuroscientific tools and methodologies when exploring these phenomena. Our understanding of brain function is far from complete, and many of the processes underlying human consciousness remain shrouded in mystery. However, this should not be a reason for dismissing potentially valid data, but rather a catalyst for developing more sophisticated tools and approaches. Advances in neuroimaging techniques, such as advanced fMRI and magnetoencephalography (MEG), offer the potential for more precise mapping of brain activity, while novel computational modeling techniques can help us understand complex neural networks. Furthermore, the integration of quantum physics with neuroscience offers a tantalizing possibility for explaining certain aspects of consciousness that appear to defy conventional classical physics.

The integration of neuroscientific and parapsychological perspectives is not without its challenges. The subjective nature of many psychic experiences, the potential for fraud and misinterpretation, and the skepticism of the mainstream scientific community all pose significant hurdles. However, a growing number of researchers are embracing a more open-minded and interdisciplinary approach, recognizing the limitations of purely materialistic explanations of consciousness and the potential for integrating scientific rigor with spiritual insights. This approach necessitates a commitment to rigorous methodology, while simultaneously acknowledging the possibility of phenomena that may currently lie beyond our scientific grasp. The exploration of psychic abilities is a journey into the unknown, requiring a combination of scientific skepticism and intellectual humility. It's a quest to unravel the mysteries of human consciousness, potentially leading to a revolutionary understanding of our place in the universe and the untapped potential of the human mind.

The possibility of genetic or epigenetic influences on psychic abilities also deserves consideration. Twin studies, family histories, and genome-wide association studies (GWAS) could help identify potential genetic markers associated with these abilities. This research could not only provide valuable insights into the biological mechanisms involved, but also could potentially lead to the development of new diagnostic tools and therapeutic interventions for individuals experiencing both mental illness and extraordinary mental capabilities. Furthermore, exploring the interplay between genetics and environmental factors, including early childhood experiences, could unveil crucial information about the development and manifestation of these abilities.

The exploration of psychic abilities requires a paradigm shift, moving away from a purely materialistic view of consciousness and embracing a more holistic approach. This approach acknowledges the potential for experiences that transcend our current scientific understanding, yet maintains the rigor and objectivity required for scientific inquiry. By integrating neuroscientific research with parapsychological studies, while carefully considering the ethical implications of such research, we can potentially unlock new avenues of understanding human consciousness, ultimately promoting a deeper appreciation for the diversity of human experience and the untapped potential of the human mind. This broader understanding can foster a more compassionate and inclusive approach to mental health, recognizing the spectrum of human experience and avoiding the stigmatization of individuals who exhibit abilities that lie outside the norm. The future lies in bridging the gap between science and spirituality, embracing the full spectrum of human potential, and harnessing the power of diverse minds to create a brighter future for all.

The exploration of exceptional human abilities, particularly those traditionally categorized as "psychic," requires a framework that moves beyond simple labels of "normal" and "abnormal." This is where the concept of neurodiversity becomes profoundly relevant. Neurodiversity is not merely a fashionable term; it's a paradigm shift in understanding the human brain and its vast spectrum of functioning. It posits that neurological differences, rather than being deficits, are natural variations representing diverse cognitive styles, strengths, and weaknesses. This reframing allows us to consider individuals with atypical neurological profiles not as "broken" or "deficient," but as possessing unique cognitive architectures that may lead to exceptional abilities, including those often associated with parapsychology.

Consider, for example, the reported experiences of individuals who claim to possess clairvoyance or clairsentience. These abilities, often dismissed as fanciful or delusional, might be understood within the neurodiversity framework as manifestations of unusually sensitive or interconnected neural pathways. While psychosis, particularly in conditions like schizophrenia, can involve hallucinations and delusions that bear some superficial resemblance to psychic experiences, the underlying neurological mechanisms may differ significantly. Rather than viewing these similarities as evidence of a singular pathology, a neurodiversity perspective suggests that both psychic abilities and certain aspects of psychosis might arise from variations in brain structure and function, some of which might confer advantages in certain contexts.

The neurodiversity model encourages us to explore the strengths associated with these variations. For instance, atypical patterns of brain connectivity might enhance intuitive abilities, leading to a heightened sense of environmental awareness or an increased capacity for pattern recognition that could be interpreted as clairvoyance. Similarly, heightened emotional sensitivity, often observed in individuals with certain neurological conditions, might underlie clairsentience, enabling the individual to perceive the emotions and experiences of others with unusual acuity. The key is to recognize that these heightened sensitivities, while potentially challenging in certain environments, can also be sources of significant strength and unique insight. It's not about pathologizing these variations but understanding the potential benefits they offer.

This necessitates a shift in research methodologies. Instead of focusing solely on identifying deficits, researchers should also actively investigate the cognitive strengths and unique abilities associated with specific neurological profiles. This requires the development of new assessment tools and experimental designs that are sensitive to the diverse ways individuals process information and experience the world. Traditional neuropsychological tests, often designed to detect impairments, may not be appropriate for identifying the exceptional abilities that may be associated with certain neurological conditions. A more holistic and person-centered approach is needed, one that allows individuals to showcase their unique strengths rather than simply highlighting their weaknesses.

The connection between neurodiversity and the New Age concepts of Indigo, Crystal, and Rainbow children, as well as Starseeds and Lightworkers, becomes particularly interesting in this context. These groups, often characterized by their purported heightened spiritual sensitivity, intuitive abilities, and empathy, could be viewed as exemplars of neurodiversity. Their reported experiences, often dismissed as mystical or metaphorical, might be understood as arising from specific neurological patterns that enhance certain cognitive abilities. These individuals frequently report unusual sensory experiences, altered states of consciousness, and heightened emotional intelligence. These experiences, while sometimes overlapping with aspects of mental illness, also represent a different expression of human potential.

The challenge lies in discerning the crucial differences between genuine variations in cognitive ability and pathological conditions. This requires a nuanced and multi-faceted approach, integrating neurological data with detailed qualitative studies of individuals' subjective experiences. Advanced neuroimaging techniques, such as functional MRI (fMRI) and electroencephalography (EEG), can provide valuable insights into the neural correlates of these unusual abilities. However, these techniques must be complemented by in-depth interviews and qualitative analyses to gain a fuller understanding of the individuals' lived experiences. Moreover, self-report measures must be critically analyzed, as subjective experiences can be influenced by a variety of factors, including cultural beliefs and expectations.

A further crucial element in understanding this convergence is the consideration of genetics and epigenetics. While a simplistic gene-for-ability model is unlikely to be accurate, genetic factors may predispose individuals to certain neurological profiles that increase the likelihood of experiencing what might be classified as psychic abilities. Epigenetic modifications – changes in gene expression without altering the underlying DNA sequence – may also play a role in shaping these traits. Environmental factors, such as exposure to trauma or significant life events, could also interact with genetic predispositions to influence the development and manifestation of these abilities. Therefore, a comprehensive investigation would need to account for the complex interplay of genetic, epigenetic, and environmental influences.

The implications of this neurodiversity framework are far-reaching. If psychic abilities, or what might appear to be such, are viewed as variations within the spectrum of human neurological functioning, then the stigmatization and pathologization associated with these experiences need to be critically examined. Instead of assuming that these abilities are inherently pathological, we should consider the possibility that they represent untapped human potential. This reframing could lead to the development of new therapeutic interventions that focus on nurturing and supporting these unique abilities, rather than suppressing or attempting to "cure" them.

Furthermore, understanding the neural mechanisms underlying these abilities could have significant implications for education and personal development. By acknowledging and respecting neurodiversity, we can create educational environments that cater to diverse learning styles and cognitive strengths. This approach would move away from a "one-size-fits-all" model of education, fostering environments that embrace diverse talents and support individual growth and creativity.

The integration of neuroscience and parapsychology within the framework of neurodiversity opens up new avenues for research and understanding. It challenges us to re-evaluate our assumptions about normality and abnormality, recognizing that human consciousness exists on a vast and richly diverse spectrum. The potential benefits of embracing this perspective are immense. By shifting our focus from identifying deficits to recognizing and celebrating unique abilities, we can unlock new pathways toward personal growth, societal progress, and a more holistic understanding of the human mind and its boundless potential. This approach calls for a radical reimagining of our relationship with mental health, recognizing that what may appear unusual or even anomalous can represent untapped human potential waiting to be cultivated.

Finally, the acceptance of neurodiversity in relation to psychic abilities necessitates a profound shift in ethical considerations. Any research involving individuals reporting such experiences must prioritize their well-being and avoid any form of exploitation or stigmatization. Informed consent is paramount, ensuring that participants understand the research process and have the autonomy to withdraw at any time. This ethical approach, combined with a rigorous scientific methodology, will be critical in unlocking the mysteries of human consciousness and harnessing the potential of neurodiversity for the betterment of society. The path forward demands a commitment to scientific rigor while maintaining a compassionate and inclusive approach that values all forms of human experience.

This book embarks on a journey to bridge the seemingly disparate fields of neuroscience and parapsychology, a quest driven by the conviction that a deeper understanding of the human mind necessitates the integration of both conventional and unconventional perspectives. We will move beyond the limiting dichotomy of "normal" versus "abnormal," a framework that often serves to marginalize and misunderstand individuals with extraordinary experiences or abilities. Instead, we will explore the potential for a unifying model that encompasses the spectrum of human consciousness, from what might be considered typical neurological function to those experiences and capacities traditionally labeled as "psychic."

Our exploration begins by delving into the neurobiological mechanisms that may underpin phenomena such as clairvoyance and clairsentience. While these abilities often reside outside the realm of accepted scientific explanation, a rigorous examination of the relevant neurological pathways and brain regions can illuminate potential connections and correlations. This investigation will not shy away from comparisons with neurological conditions like schizophrenia, where altered perception and unusual experiences are well-documented. The goal is not to pathologize these abilities, but rather to identify potential shared neurological substrates or genetic predispositions. We will examine the possibility of epigenetic factors playing a crucial role, considering that environmental influences can modify gene expression, potentially triggering or enhancing certain neural pathways. This comparative approach allows us to consider whether "psychic" abilities represent an extreme of human potential, a natural variation within the broader spectrum of neurodiversity, or perhaps even a misunderstanding of certain neurological processes.

The subsequent chapters will introduce the concepts of Indigo, Crystal, and Rainbow children, and the related notions of Starseeds and Lightworkers. These concepts, often associated with the New Age movement, posit the existence of individuals with unique spiritual gifts and heightened intuitive abilities. While these descriptions may seem far removed from the clinical observations of neuroscience, our approach will be one of careful consideration. We will explore the potential for these concepts to be understood through the lens of neurodiversity, examining whether these individuals might exhibit unique patterns of brain activity or utilize different neural pathways to process information. Are these reported abilities merely self-reported experiences, or do they reflect actual variations in cognitive function? The examination will delve into the reported experiences, attempting to discern the core neurological underpinnings and potential commonalities with the abilities previously discussed. We will review anecdotal evidence and explore any attempts at scientific investigation of these individuals, searching for potential bridges between subjective experiences and objective measurements. Furthermore, we will critically analyze the claims surrounding these concepts, acknowledging the prevalence of confirmation bias and the need for rigorous empirical research.

A key element of this book is the proposition that a fundamental interconnectedness exists between abilities typically categorized as "psychic" and neurological conditions. This is not to suggest an equivalence, but rather a recognition of shared underlying mechanisms. It is conceivable that the genetic and epigenetic factors influencing "psychic" experiences may also play a role in susceptibility to certain mental illnesses. Conversely, some individuals with neurological conditions may exhibit unusual cognitive abilities that are overlooked or misunderstood within a traditional medical framework. This perspective requires a significant shift in our understanding of mental health, moving beyond a solely deficit-based model to one that embraces the full spectrum of human potential, including exceptional abilities.

The implications of this integrated approach extend far beyond the realm of theoretical understanding. By embracing neurodiversity and acknowledging the potential of exceptional human abilities, we can foster a more inclusive and supportive society. We can move towards a future where individuals with diverse cognitive profiles are empowered to utilize their unique strengths and contribute their gifts to the world. The stigmatization associated with both "psychic" experiences and certain mental illnesses will be challenged, replaced by a compassionate and accepting approach to human difference.

This book is not intended as a definitive answer to all the questions it raises. Instead, it serves as a starting point for a broader dialogue, an invitation to reconsider our assumptions about the human mind and its potential. We will explore existing research, highlighting the gaps in our knowledge and proposing directions for future investigation. The focus is on facilitating critical thinking and promoting a paradigm shift towards a more holistic and inclusive understanding of consciousness. We will evaluate current research, acknowledging its limitations and pointing out the need for more rigorous and multifaceted methodologies. There is a clear need for studies with larger sample sizes, more sophisticated neuroimaging techniques, and a deeper integration of subjective reports with objective measurements.

Ethical considerations will remain at the forefront of our discussion. The exploration of exceptional human abilities must prioritize the well-being and protection of individuals involved. We will examine the potential risks and benefits of research in this area, emphasizing the importance of informed consent and the avoidance of any exploitation or stigmatization. Any research must adhere to the highest ethical standards, ensuring the safety and dignity of all participants.

Moreover, the cultural context of these experiences is crucial. Throughout history and across different cultures, many abilities currently viewed as "paranormal" have been integral parts of spiritual and religious practices. A thorough understanding necessitates a comparative study of the ways different societies have perceived and interacted with these unusual phenomena. Exploring these diverse cultural lenses provides a more nuanced perspective, enriching our appreciation for the spectrum of human experience.

The book will further discuss the potential practical applications of understanding the link between neurodiversity and exceptional abilities. Could these abilities be harnessed for positive societal change? Could therapies be developed that help individuals cultivate or enhance these abilities for personal growth and development? Exploring such applications is not about commercializing or exploiting these abilities but about fostering a society that supports and encourages the unique potential of all its members. This includes the possibility of neurofeedback techniques, targeted interventions, and supportive environments that encourage the development and use of these abilities for personal well-being and positive societal contribution.

Ultimately, this book aims to contribute to a paradigm shift, moving beyond the traditional, reductionist models of the brain and towards a more integrated and holistic understanding of human consciousness. By acknowledging the interconnectedness of neuroscience and parapsychology, we can unlock a deeper appreciation of the incredible diversity and untapped potential within the human mind. The exploration is not solely about unraveling the mysteries of unusual abilities; it's about creating a future where all forms of human experience are valued, understood, and celebrated. This future requires a concerted effort from scientists, spiritual practitioners, and the wider community to embrace neurodiversity and unlock the extraordinary potential residing within every human being.

The persistent skepticism surrounding parapsychology stems, in part, from a rigid adherence to established scientific methodologies that often struggle to accommodate phenomena outside the realm of currently accepted physical laws. This isn't to say that rigorous scientific inquiry should be abandoned; on the contrary, it remains the cornerstone of any credible investigation. However, the current paradigm often defaults to dismissing anomalous experiences as artifacts, hallucinations, or outright fraud, without adequately exploring the potential for genuine, albeit currently unexplained, phenomena. This closed-mindedness hinders progress and prevents us from fully understanding the vast potential of the human mind.

A truly scientific approach demands open-mindedness, a willingness to question established assumptions, and a commitment to exploring all avenues of inquiry. The exploration of psychic abilities, for instance, requires us to move beyond the limitations of solely materialistic perspectives. Neuroscience, with its focus on the physical brain and its measurable activities, offers invaluable tools for understanding the neurological correlates of consciousness. Yet, reducing consciousness solely to neuronal activity ignores the subjective experience, the rich tapestry of thoughts, feelings, and perceptions that constitute the individual's reality.

The investigation of neurodiversity provides a compelling parallel. Conditions like autism spectrum disorder (ASD) and attention-deficit/hyperactivity disorder (ADHD) were once viewed solely as deficits, deviations from the "norm." However, a growing body of research highlights the unique strengths and talents often associated with these conditions. Individuals with ASD, for example, may exhibit exceptional abilities in areas like pattern recognition, memory, or mathematical reasoning. Similarly, those with ADHD may demonstrate heightened creativity and innovative thinking. Recognizing these strengths requires us to abandon the pathological lens and embrace a more nuanced understanding of neurodiversity, appreciating the diverse ways the human brain can function and contribute to society.

The parallels between neurodiversity and purported psychic abilities are striking. Many individuals who report psychic experiences – whether clairvoyance, clairsentience, precognition, or psychokinesis – often display unusual cognitive patterns, enhanced sensory perception, or heightened intuition. While these abilities may manifest differently, and the experiences may differ dramatically in intensity and frequency, the underlying neurological mechanisms may share some common ground. Rather than dismissing these experiences as pathological, we might instead consider them as expressions of a broader spectrum of human potential, a unique form of neurodiversity that extends beyond the currently established categories.

The challenge lies in bridging the gap between the rigorous methods of neuroscience and the often subjective and anecdotal evidence associated with parapsychology. This requires a multidisciplinary approach, involving researchers from neuroscience, psychology, physics, and even philosophy and spiritual studies. It necessitates a commitment to developing new methodologies that can effectively capture and analyze subjective experiences while maintaining scientific rigor. This might involve exploring advanced neuroimaging techniques, such as magnetoencephalography (MEG) or functional near-infrared spectroscopy (fNIRS), to investigate brain activity during psychic experiences. Furthermore, quantitative analysis of subjective reports, employing methods from psychometrics and qualitative research, can help establish reliable patterns and correlations.

Furthermore, embracing a holistic approach is crucial. While the physical brain undoubtedly plays a significant role in consciousness, it's likely not the sole factor. Factors such as epigenetics, the environment, and even subtle energy fields might interact in complex ways to shape consciousness and influence the emergence of what might be termed "psychic" abilities. A purely reductionist approach, focusing solely on the material aspects of the brain, risks overlooking these subtle yet potentially powerful influences.

The inclusion of spiritual perspectives, though often eschewed in mainstream science, offers valuable insights. Spiritual traditions across cultures have long recognized and cultivated forms of consciousness that extend beyond the conventionally perceived limits of the physical world. Practices like meditation, mindfulness, and energy healing have been shown to affect brainwave activity, emotional regulation, and overall well-being. Integrating this knowledge with neuroscientific findings could lead to a deeper understanding of the mechanisms underlying both the purported psychic abilities and the beneficial effects of spiritual practices.

Open-mindedness doesn't imply a naïve acceptance of all claims. Rigorous investigation remains paramount. However, it requires a critical evaluation of evidence, not a preemptive dismissal based on pre-conceived notions. The scientific community should not fear exploring the unknown. Indeed, its exploration is crucial for advancing our understanding of human consciousness and its extraordinary potential. The rejection of parapsychological phenomena without proper investigation perpetuates a self-limiting paradigm that hinders progress in both neuroscience and our understanding of human capabilities. By integrating rigorous scientific inquiry with a willingness to consider unconventional perspectives, we can unlock a deeper understanding of the human mind, its capacity for extraordinary experiences, and its potential to positively transform our world.

The study of psychic abilities and neurodiversity presents a unique opportunity to revolutionize our understanding of human consciousness. It demands a radical shift from a paradigm focused on defining "normality" to one that celebrates the remarkable diversity of human experience. By accepting the possibility that there are aspects of human consciousness that currently elude scientific explanation, we open ourselves up to a wealth of unexplored possibilities. We need to acknowledge that what is currently deemed "paranormal" may simply represent a currently misunderstood facet of human potential, a manifestation of neurodiversity that remains largely untapped.

This shift in perspective requires a collaborative effort

involving scientists, spiritual practitioners, and individuals with firsthand experience of psychic phenomena. A critical and open dialogue is essential to foster trust, encourage transparency, and generate the much-needed empirical data that will allow us to move beyond speculation and into a deeper, more holistic understanding. This inclusive approach is not merely a matter of intellectual curiosity; it has profound ethical implications. By embracing neurodiversity, we create a more equitable and compassionate society, one that values and supports individuals regardless of their unique abilities and experiences.

Moreover, this integrated understanding has the potential to inform novel approaches to mental health treatment. Many individuals who experience intense psychic phenomena also grapple with psychological distress or mental health challenges. By recognizing the potential connections between seemingly "paranormal" experiences and neurodivergent states, we may develop more effective and personalized interventions that cater to the unique needs of these individuals. This holistic approach should consider both the potential strengths and challenges associated with these experiences, fostering a supportive environment where individuals feel safe to explore their abilities and manage any associated difficulties.

The pursuit of understanding the convergence of neuroscience and parapsychology is not a quest to prove or disprove the existence of psychic phenomena in isolation. It's a quest to understand the nature of consciousness itself, the vast spectrum of human potential, and the rich diversity that makes us human. It's an invitation to expand our scientific frameworks, embrace the unknown, and embark on a journey of discovery that promises to revolutionize our understanding of ourselves and our place in the universe. This journey requires courage, open-mindedness, and a willingness to challenge long-held assumptions. But the rewards – a deeper appreciation of human consciousness, a more inclusive society, and a better understanding of our own potential – are immeasurable. The call for open-minded inquiry is not merely a suggestion; it's a necessity for the advancement of knowledge and the betterment of humanity.

CHAPTER 2: THE NEUROLOGICAL BASIS OF CLAIRVOYANCE AND CLAIRSENTIENCE

The exploration of clairvoyance and clairsentience necessitates a deep dive into the intricate workings of the human brain. Understanding how sensory information is processed and integrated is crucial to even begin to consider the possibility of extrasensory perception. While the very concept of ESP remains controversial within mainstream science, exploring the neurological mechanisms behind sensory processing offers a framework for potential parallels, however tenuous they may seem at first glance.

The primary sensory cortices, located in the posterior region of the brain, are the initial processing centers for visual, auditory, tactile, gustatory, and olfactory information. The occipital lobe houses the primary visual cortex (V1), responsible for processing basic visual features such as edges, lines, and colors. Damage to V1, for instance, can lead to cortical blindness, a condition where the eyes function normally but the brain fails to interpret the visual input. This stark demonstration of the brain's crucial role in sensory experience underscores the importance of neurological integrity in any discussion of enhanced or altered perception.

Moving beyond basic sensory processing, the parietal lobe plays a pivotal role in integrating sensory information from multiple modalities. It's involved in spatial awareness, attention, and the perception of body position. Lesions in the parietal lobe can lead to a range of impairments, including neglect syndrome, where individuals fail to acknowledge one side of their visual field or body. This highlights the parietal lobe's crucial role in creating a cohesive sensory experience, a process that may be significantly altered in individuals reporting clairsentience, where the perception of emotions and feelings from others seems to bypass conventional sensory pathways.

The temporal lobe, encompassing the primary auditory cortex (A1), plays a crucial role in auditory processing, memory, and language. Damage to A1 can result in hearing loss or auditory agnosia, the inability to recognize sounds. However, the temporal lobe's function extends far beyond simple auditory processing. It's heavily involved in higher-level cognitive functions, including the interpretation of sensory information within a contextual framework. This contextual understanding is paramount in distinguishing between sensory hallucinations (as seen in some mental illnesses) and the potentially more nuanced experiences reported by individuals claiming clairaudience – the ability to hear voices or sounds from sources not physically present.

The frontal lobe, often considered the executive center of the brain, plays a significant role in higher-level cognitive functions, including attention, decision-making, and working memory. While not directly involved in primary sensory processing, the frontal lobe is crucial for integrating sensory input with prior knowledge, expectations, and beliefs. This integrative function is potentially critical in the interpretation of sensory experiences. For instance, an individual experiencing a strong emotional "sense" (clairsentience) might interpret this feeling within a specific framework, perhaps attributing it to a particular person or event based on prior experience and belief systems. The frontal lobe's role in shaping our interpretation of sensory input highlights the critical interaction between sensory processing and higher-level cognitive functions.

Beyond the primary sensory cortices, several subcortical structures play a critical role in sensory processing and integration. The thalamus, often described as the brain's relay station, receives sensory information from the peripheral nervous system and transmits it to the appropriate cortical areas. Damage to the thalamus can lead to profound sensory disturbances. The amygdala, a key component of the limbic system, is heavily involved in processing emotions, particularly fear and anxiety. Its close proximity to the sensory processing pathways suggests a potential interplay between sensory experiences and emotional responses, a critical factor in understanding the reported experience of clairsentience, where emotional information appears to be perceived without conventional sensory input.

The hippocampus, another crucial part of the limbic system, plays a critical role in memory formation and retrieval. The hippocampus's interaction with sensory processing pathways suggests a potential link between sensory experiences and memory, raising questions about the possible role of memory in shaping and interpreting experiences that may be classified as extrasensory. For instance, a previously experienced event might be recalled and intertwined with a current clairsentient experience, leading to a complex and potentially ambiguous interpretation.

Neuroimaging techniques, such as functional magnetic resonance imaging (fMRI) and electroencephalography (EEG), provide invaluable tools for investigating brain activity during sensory processing. fMRI studies have revealed complex patterns of activation across different brain regions during various sensory tasks, demonstrating the intricate interplay between sensory processing and higher-level cognitive functions. EEG studies, on the other hand, provide insights into the electrical activity of the brain, allowing researchers to investigate the temporal dynamics of sensory processing and potentially identify unique brainwave patterns associated with exceptional sensory experiences. However, the application of these techniques to the study of psychic abilities presents significant methodological challenges. The subjective nature of these experiences makes it difficult to establish objective measures and control for confounding factors, such as expectation and suggestion.

Genetic and epigenetic factors also play a potentially significant role in shaping individual differences in sensory processing and susceptibility to unusual experiences. While research in this area is still in its nascent stages, studies exploring the genetic basis of sensory perception and neurological conditions may eventually shed light on potential genetic predispositions to enhanced or altered sensory experiences. Epigenetic factors, including environmental influences on gene expression, may also play a significant role. For example, early childhood experiences, exposure to trauma, and even cultural beliefs might influence the development and expression of genes related to sensory processing and the interpretation of sensory information.

The study of sensory processing in the context of psychic abilities is complex and fraught with challenges. The subjective nature of these experiences makes it difficult to establish objective measures, control for confounding factors, and replicate findings. Nevertheless, a thorough investigation of the neurological mechanisms underlying sensory perception can provide a framework for understanding the potential parallels, albeit tenuous, between conventional sensory experiences and experiences typically associated with extrasensory perception. Further research, utilizing advanced neuroimaging techniques and rigorous experimental designs, is crucial to move beyond speculation and develop a more nuanced understanding of these phenomena. The convergence of neuroscience and parapsychology, while challenging, offers a potentially groundbreaking path towards expanding our understanding of the human brain and consciousness. The ongoing exploration of these complex interactions, through a blend of scientific rigor and open-minded inquiry, promises a more comprehensive understanding of the vast spectrum of human experience.

The exploration of potential neurological underpinnings of clairvoyance and clairsentience necessitates a closer examination of synaptic plasticity – the brain's remarkable ability to reorganize itself by forming new neural connections and strengthening or weakening existing ones. This dynamic process, crucial for learning, memory, and adaptation, offers a compelling avenue for investigating how heightened perceptual experiences might arise. Consider the profound changes in brain activity associated with meditation or deep trance states. These altered states of consciousness, often characterized by reduced sensory input and heightened internal awareness, demonstrably affect synaptic connectivity. Neuroimaging studies, employing techniques such as fMRI and EEG, reveal shifts in brainwave patterns and activity in regions associated with self-awareness, introspection, and sensory processing. These changes are not merely temporary fluctuations; prolonged practice of meditative techniques has been shown to induce structural and functional changes in the brain, including increased grey matter density in areas linked to attention and emotional regulation.

This neuroplasticity, the brain's capacity to reshape itself in response to experience, suggests a mechanism through which extraordinary perceptual abilities might emerge. Imagine, for instance, an individual with an unusually high degree of synaptic plasticity. Their brain might exhibit a greater capacity for forming and strengthening connections between brain areas not typically associated with sensory processing, potentially leading to the integration of information from unconventional sources. This could manifest as an enhanced ability to perceive subtle energy fields or receive information outside the usual sensory channels. This isn't to suggest a direct causal link, but rather to posit a potential neurological substrate upon which such experiences might be built. Furthermore, the very act of attempting to access information through clairsentience or clairvoyance, even if unsuccessful, could lead to repeated activation of certain neural pathways, reinforcing connections and making future attempts easier. This is analogous to learning a new skill, where repeated practice leads to strengthened neural networks and improved performance.

The role of altered states of consciousness in facilitating such experiences is equally significant. During these states, the brain operates under a different set of rules, characterized by reduced activity in the default mode network (DMN), a brain system associated with self-referential thought and internal monologue. The reduced DMN activity can be interpreted as a dampening of the internal "noise" that typically filters and interprets sensory input. This reduction in filtering could potentially allow for the processing of information that would otherwise be ignored or suppressed. This is analogous to turning down the volume on background noise to hear a faint whisper. In states of deep relaxation, meditation, or even under the influence of certain psychoactive substances (though the latter requires extreme caution and ethical consideration), this "noise reduction" allows for a heightened sensitivity to subtle stimuli, both internal and external.

Consider the anecdotal reports of individuals experiencing vivid precognitive dreams or intuitive insights during periods of intense stress or altered emotional states. These states are often associated with significant shifts in neurotransmitter levels and brainwave activity. While lacking rigorous scientific validation, these accounts highlight a potential connection between intense emotional experiences, altered brain states, and heightened perceptual awareness. The link between emotional arousal and heightened sensory perception is well-established. The release of stress hormones, like cortisol and adrenaline, significantly alters brain activity, potentially sharpening sensory processing. This effect, while demonstrable in conventional sensory modalities, might extend to forms of extra-sensory perception in some neurologically predisposed individuals.

It is important to acknowledge that the exploration of altered states and heightened perception is fraught with methodological challenges. The subjective nature of these experiences makes them difficult to objectively measure and replicate. The potential for bias, both in self-reporting and in experimental design, needs careful consideration. Moreover, the complex interplay of various neurochemical and physiological factors involved makes isolating the specific contributions of synaptic plasticity and altered states challenging. However, advances in neuroimaging techniques, along with more sophisticated statistical methods for analyzing subjective data, are gradually improving our capacity to investigate these phenomena.

The comparison with certain aspects of mental illness, specifically psychosis, is essential, but must be approached with extreme sensitivity and caution. Conditions like schizophrenia, while often involving hallucinations and delusional beliefs, share some common ground with reported experiences of clairvoyance and clairsentience in terms of altered perception. However, this similarity doesn't imply equivalence. The crucial distinction lies in the context, interpretation, and associated distress. While a person experiencing psychosis may interpret their altered perceptions as symptoms of a severe mental illness leading to significant impairment, individuals reporting clairvoyance or clairsentience typically do not experience such distress or functional impairment. Furthermore, the qualitative nature of the experiences differs; the hallucinations in psychosis tend to be vivid, uncontrolled, and emotionally charged, whereas reported experiences of clairvoyance and clairsentience are often described as more subtle, controlled, and integrated with the individual's worldview.

The investigation of possible genetic or epigenetic factors contributing to both heightened perception and susceptibility to psychosis requires a multi-faceted approach. Studies comparing the genetic profiles of individuals reporting psychic abilities to those with and without mental illness could shed light on the possible overlapping genetic vulnerabilities or protective factors. Epigenetic research, exploring modifications to gene expression without altering the underlying DNA sequence, could reveal environmental factors that might either enhance or suppress the manifestation of such abilities. This might involve the study of early childhood experiences, stress levels, and exposure to various environmental factors, all of which could impact gene expression and brain development.

Ultimately, it is crucial to refrain from drawing simplistic conclusions. The relationship between synaptic plasticity, altered states of consciousness, and the reported experiences of clairvoyance and clairsentience is intricate and multifaceted. While increased synaptic plasticity and altered states might create a neurobiological landscape conducive to such experiences, they do not inherently

cause them. Furthermore, the presence of these neurological factors does not automatically equate to psychic abilities. Many factors – genetic predisposition, environmental influences, individual experiences, and cultural contexts – likely play a complex and interwoven role.

Furthermore, it's essential to remember that the very definition of "clairvoyance" and "clairsentience" remains elusive and culturally influenced. What one culture might categorize as a supernatural ability, another might view as a form of heightened intuition or a sophisticated pattern recognition skill. This ambiguity necessitates a rigorous, cross-cultural approach to the study of these phenomena, avoiding culturally biased interpretations. The very terminology itself reflects our limited understanding; perhaps future research will reveal more precise and accurate descriptions.

Therefore, the exploration of this fascinating intersection of neuroscience and parapsychology requires a cautious yet open-minded approach. We must strive to integrate rigorous scientific methods with a sensitivity to the subjective nature of experience, acknowledging the limitations of current knowledge while remaining committed to expanding our understanding of the remarkable plasticity of the human brain and the multifaceted nature of consciousness. The path ahead is challenging, but the potential rewards – a deeper understanding of human consciousness and the limits (or lack thereof) of human potential – are profound. The journey requires patience, rigorous research, and a willingness to challenge existing paradigms. Only through this integrated approach can we hope to unlock the secrets of the human brain and its extraordinary potential.

Building upon the established link between synaptic plasticity and altered states of consciousness, we must now delve into the genetic and epigenetic factors that might predispose individuals to experiences of clairvoyance and clairsentience. While the field remains largely unexplored, promising avenues of research are emerging, intertwining the seemingly disparate realms of genetics, epigenetics, and parapsychology.

The human genome, a vast and complex blueprint, holds the instructions for building and maintaining our bodies, including our brains. Variations within this genome, known as single nucleotide polymorphisms (SNPs), can subtly alter gene function, potentially influencing an individual's susceptibility to certain traits or conditions. While no specific "clairvoyance gene" has been identified, research into related neurological conditions offers clues. For instance, studies investigating the genetic basis of schizophrenia, a condition sometimes associated with heightened sensory experiences, have identified several candidate genes. These genes often play roles in neurotransmission, impacting the intricate balance of neurochemicals that underpin brain function. Interestingly, some of these genes are also implicated in conditions characterized by altered states of consciousness or heightened sensitivity to subtle environmental cues.

This doesn't suggest that schizophrenia and clairvoyance are directly comparable. Rather, it highlights the possibility that genetic variations influencing neurotransmitter systems might contribute to both the aberrant perceptions seen in schizophrenia and the heightened perceptual acuity potentially associated with clairvoyance. The critical distinction lies in the context and interpretation of these heightened perceptions. In schizophrenia, these experiences are often distressing, disordered, and disconnected from reality. In contrast, individuals reporting clairvoyant experiences frequently describe them as meaningful, insightful, and potentially even beneficial. This suggests that the interaction between genetic predispositions and environmental factors plays a crucial role in shaping the manifestation of these experiences.

Epigenetics adds another layer of complexity to this picture. Epigenetics refers to heritable changes in gene expression that do not involve alterations to the underlying DNA sequence. Instead, these changes are mediated by chemical modifications to DNA or associated proteins, influencing how genes are "read" and translated into proteins. Environmental factors, such as stress, diet, and exposure to toxins, can trigger epigenetic modifications. This is where the intriguing possibility of a link between early childhood experiences and the development of psychic abilities arises.

Imagine a child growing up in a highly sensitive or spiritually-focused environment, regularly exposed to practices like meditation, energy healing, or spiritual development. Such consistent exposure could potentially induce epigenetic changes, influencing the expression of genes related to sensory perception, consciousness, and brain plasticity. These epigenetic changes might enhance synaptic plasticity, making the brain more responsive to subtle energy fields or information sources that remain largely inaccessible to most individuals. Conversely, a traumatic childhood could also leave its mark epigenetically, perhaps leading to altered states of perception that manifest differently, potentially resembling symptoms of mental illness rather than psychic ability. The exact mechanisms are still largely speculative, but the concept warrants further investigation.

Furthermore, consider the possible role of ancestral inheritance. Certain traits, predispositions, or abilities might be passed down through generations, not necessarily through the direct transmission of genes, but through epigenetic marks accumulated over time. This idea aligns with some narratives within New Age spirituality, suggesting that psychic abilities are inherited or activated through lineage. While the scientific evidence for such intergenerational epigenetic inheritance is still evolving, the possibility remains an intriguing subject of inquiry, particularly when considering the reported clustering of psychic abilities within families.

The investigation into the genetic and epigenetic basis of clairvoyance and clairsentience requires sophisticated approaches, combining genetic sequencing, epigenetic profiling, and detailed psychological assessments. Such studies should take into account the individual's life history, including early childhood experiences, cultural background, and spiritual practices. This interdisciplinary approach, incorporating insights from both neuroscience and parapsychology, is essential for moving beyond simplistic genetic determinism and toward a more nuanced understanding of the complex interplay between genes, environment, and the emergence of extraordinary human experiences.

The challenge lies in designing research protocols that can objectively and rigorously assess subjectively reported experiences. Self-reported accounts of psychic abilities are inherently susceptible to bias and suggestibility. Therefore, any research in this area must employ robust methodologies, such as double-blind studies, controlled sensory deprivation experiments, and advanced neuroimaging techniques to minimize subjective bias and enhance the reliability of the findings.

The ethical considerations are equally paramount. Any research involving individuals claiming psychic abilities must be conducted with utmost respect and sensitivity. It's crucial to avoid stigmatizing individuals or reinforcing negative stereotypes about mental health. The goal is to foster a collaborative and supportive environment that encourages open dialogue and the exploration of these extraordinary human experiences without pathologizing them.

The study of the genetic and epigenetic factors underpinning purported psychic abilities is in its infancy. However, the potential implications are vast. Understanding the interplay between genes, environment, and consciousness could revolutionize our understanding of the human brain, not only in terms of paranormal phenomena, but also in the treatment and prevention of mental health conditions. A future in which we integrate the study of "paranormal" abilities into mainstream neuroscience could usher in a new era of understanding human potential and mental well-being. This would involve a paradigm shift in our approach to mental health, embracing neurodiversity and recognizing the spectrum of human consciousness. It's a journey requiring patience, rigorous research, and a willingness to move beyond the constraints of current paradigms, acknowledging that the potential rewards – a richer comprehension of the human mind and its capacity – are significant.

This requires a significant shift in societal perspectives, moving beyond a reductive model focused on pathology to one that acknowledges the vast spectrum of human experience. Instead of viewing perceived psychic abilities as aberrations or symptoms of illness, we need to explore them within a broader framework of human potential. This approach embraces the possibility that certain neurological configurations, potentially influenced by both genetics and environment, might lead to heightened perceptual experiences, creativity, and intuitive abilities.

One crucial aspect to consider is the influence of cultural and spiritual beliefs. The very concept of "psychic ability" is shaped by cultural frameworks and interpretations. What might be seen as a psychic experience in one culture could be attributed to other factors in another. Similarly, spiritual beliefs and practices can influence how individuals interpret and experience such phenomena. Therefore, any thorough investigation must account for this cultural and spiritual context, avoiding imposing preconceived notions or interpretations.

Moreover, the field necessitates a critical evaluation of existing research and methodology. Many studies on parapsychological phenomena have suffered from methodological flaws, resulting in inconclusive or questionable findings. The advancement of the field depends on the adoption of rigorous scientific standards, transparent data collection, and robust statistical analysis. A collaborative approach, involving researchers from diverse disciplines, is crucial to addressing the methodological challenges and fostering a cumulative body of knowledge.

In conclusion, while the evidence for a direct genetic basis for clairvoyance and clairsentience is currently limited, the exploration of related neurological conditions, particularly those involving altered sensory perceptions, offers intriguing clues. Similarly, the emerging field of epigenetics provides a framework for understanding how environmental influences and life experiences might shape the development of these abilities. Further research, employing rigorous scientific methods and embracing interdisciplinary collaboration, is essential to unravel the complexities of this fascinating interface between neuroscience, genetics, and parapsychology. The goal is not necessarily to prove or disprove the existence of psychic abilities, but rather to deepen our understanding of human consciousness and the remarkable plasticity of the human brain. The journey ahead is challenging but potentially transformative, promising to expand our understanding of the human mind and its seemingly limitless capacity.

The exploration of clairvoyance and clairsentience, while challenging within the confines of conventional neuroscience, can benefit from a comparative neurological approach. Examining animal behavior that suggests extrasensory perception (ESP) offers a unique perspective, allowing us to move beyond the limitations of solely human-centric studies. While acknowledging the inherent challenges in definitively proving ESP in animals, the observation of seemingly anomalous behaviors warrants investigation. This comparative approach can illuminate potential neurological underpinnings that might also be present, albeit perhaps more subtly or differently expressed, in humans exhibiting similar abilities.

One of the most compelling areas of research involves the study of animal communication and seemingly precognitive behavior. Consider the well-documented instances of companion animals exhibiting distress or anticipatory behavior prior to the arrival of their owners, even when no conventional cues, such as sound or scent, could account for their response. These anecdotal accounts, while not offering rigorous scientific proof, suggest a potential for a form of remote sensing or precognitive awareness that transcends our current understanding of sensory perception.

Further fueling this line of inquiry are studies on animal navigation and homing behavior. The remarkable ability of certain animals, such as birds and sea turtles, to navigate vast distances with seemingly uncanny accuracy continues to challenge researchers. Some argue that these animals may utilize a form of "magnetoreception," sensing the Earth's magnetic field to guide their movements. However, even this explanation doesn't fully account for the precision and apparent intelligence involved in some navigation feats. Could an element of ESP, a form of remote sensing beyond known physical mechanisms, contribute to their navigation prowess?

Beyond navigation, consider the reported instances of animals seemingly responding to impending disasters, such as earthquakes or tsunamis, well before any detectable seismic activity. Numerous reports detail animals exhibiting unusual behavior—restlessness, fleeing from their habitats, or displaying unusual levels of distress—hours or even days before such events. While possible explanations exist, involving subtle changes in the environment or heightened sensitivity to infrasound, the consistency and timing of these reported events in various animal species warrant further investigation. Could a form of precognitive ability allow these animals to sense impending danger through a mechanism not yet fully understood?

The exploration of animal models should not be limited to anecdotal reports. Rigorous scientific studies, utilizing controlled environments and quantitative measures, are needed to further explore these phenomena. These studies could involve training animals in tasks that require seemingly extrasensory abilities, for example, tasks that require them to detect events occurring outside their immediate sensory range. While the design of such studies presents numerous challenges—control for confounding variables, establishing objective measures of ESP—the potential rewards justify the effort.

Comparative neuroanatomy also plays a crucial role in this investigation. By comparing the brain structures and neural pathways of animals that exhibit seemingly ESP-related behaviors with those of animals that do not, we can potentially identify neurological correlates of these abilities. This involves exploring different brain regions, such as the hippocampus (associated with memory and spatial navigation), the amygdala (involved in emotional processing and fear responses), and the pineal gland (associated with melatonin production and circadian rhythms, and sometimes linked to intuitive abilities). The use of advanced neuroimaging techniques, such as fMRI and EEG, can further refine this comparative approach.

Furthermore, the application of genetic and epigenetic analyses to animal models opens up exciting new possibilities. By examining the genetic makeup and epigenetic modifications of animals displaying ESP-related behaviors, we can potentially identify genetic predispositions or environmental factors that might contribute to these abilities. This interdisciplinary approach, integrating neuroscience, genetics, and parapsychology, can help us unravel the biological basis of what we currently perceive as "psychic" abilities. The focus here is not to necessarily prove or disprove the existence of ESP, but to understand the potential neurological mechanisms underlying these behaviors.

One can draw parallels between certain animal behaviors and human experiences of clairvoyance and clairsentience. For instance, the uncanny ability of certain animals to detect impending threats mirrors the reported experiences of some individuals who claim to experience precognitive dreams or intuitive warnings. Similarly, the seemingly inexplicable ability of some animals to find their way home over vast distances resonates with human accounts of remote viewing or psychic navigation. By exploring these parallels, we can potentially identify common neurological substrates that underpin these abilities in both humans and animals.

However, it's crucial to acknowledge the methodological challenges inherent in this line of research. The subjective nature of many of the observations, the difficulty in controlling for confounding variables, and the inherent skepticism within the scientific community make this a complex area of investigation. The risk of anthropomorphism, assigning human-like qualities to animal behavior, also demands careful consideration. Any conclusions drawn must be based on rigorous scientific evidence, avoiding subjective interpretations and unsupported speculations.

Nevertheless, the potential benefits of exploring animal models of ESP are immense. By embracing an interdisciplinary approach, combining rigorous scientific methods with open-mindedness and a willingness to consider alternative explanations, we can potentially unlock new insights into the complexities of consciousness and the potential for extraordinary abilities within the animal kingdom and, by extension, humanity. The exploration of animal models provides a unique opportunity to move beyond the limitations of solely human-centric studies, allowing us to explore the neurological basis of psychic phenomena from a broader, more comparative perspective. This approach offers the potential for transformative discoveries that could challenge our current understanding of the brain, consciousness, and the nature of reality itself.

The study of animal models also opens up possibilities for developing novel therapeutic strategies for neurological conditions characterized by altered perception and cognitive function. For example, understanding the neurological mechanisms that allow certain animals to exhibit seemingly ESP-related behaviors might offer clues for developing new treatments for conditions like schizophrenia or autism spectrum disorder, which are often characterized by unusual sensory experiences or atypical cognitive abilities. While acknowledging the limitations of such comparisons, the potential for translational research in this area is considerable.

Ultimately, the exploration of animal models of ESP is not about proving or disproving the existence of psychic abilities, but rather about expanding our understanding of the remarkable capacity of the brain and the intricate connection between biology, consciousness, and the wider environment. By approaching this research with scientific rigor, interdisciplinary collaboration, and an open mind, we can potentially unravel some of the most profound mysteries of nature and the human experience. The journey promises to be challenging, filled with both setbacks and breakthroughs, but the potential rewards—a deeper understanding of consciousness, a broader appreciation of animal intelligence, and the development of novel therapeutic interventions —make it a compelling and worthwhile endeavor. The integration of this research with the previously discussed genetic and epigenetic factors provides a more complete picture of the complex interplay of nature and nurture in shaping these extraordinary abilities. The future of this research lies in sophisticated interdisciplinary collaborations that bridge the perceived gaps between rigorous scientific inquiry and the exploration of seemingly paranormal phenomena. Only through such integrated efforts can we hope to gain a truly comprehensive understanding of the remarkable potential inherent within both the human and animal minds.

The inherent difficulty in scientifically investigating clairvoyance and clairsentience stems from the very nature of these phenomena. Unlike more readily measurable neurological functions, such as motor control or sensory processing, psychic abilities are subjective experiences, often lacking objective, repeatable measures. This poses significant challenges for traditional scientific methodologies that rely heavily on quantifiable data and controlled experiments. The variability in individual experiences, the lack of standardized assessment tools, and the potential for confounding factors like suggestion, expectation bias, or outright fraud all contribute to the complexity of the research.

One of the primary obstacles is the reproducibility of results. A cornerstone of scientific validation is the ability to replicate findings across multiple studies and different researchers. In the case of clairvoyance and clairsentience, this replicability is often elusive. What one individual perceives as a clear instance of precognitive awareness, another might dismiss as coincidence or chance. This lack of consistent, objective measures makes it difficult to establish clear cause-and-effect relationships and draw firm conclusions. Furthermore, the very act of attempting to scientifically measure a subjective experience can alter the experience itself, introducing observer effects that complicate data interpretation. The observer's expectations, conscious or unconscious, may influence the outcome, leading to inaccurate or biased results. Double-blind protocols, designed to minimize these biases, are challenging to implement effectively in studies involving psychic phenomena, necessitating innovative and creative experimental designs.

Another major hurdle is the development of robust and reliable assessment tools. Unlike standardized tests for cognitive abilities or neurological functions, there are no universally accepted metrics for clairvoyance or clairsentience. Current methods rely heavily on subjective self-reporting, which, as previously discussed, is prone to error and bias. While some researchers have attempted to create structured questionnaires or scoring systems, these often lack the precision and objectivity required for rigorous scientific analysis. This lack of standardization also makes it difficult to compare findings across different studies, hindering the accumulation of robust evidence. A critical need exists for the development of objective, quantifiable measures that capture the essential characteristics of these phenomena, perhaps employing advanced neuroimaging techniques or sophisticated signal-processing algorithms to identify subtle neurological correlates.

The problem of confounding factors also significantly complicates research. The potential for coincidences, misinterpretations, and even outright deception can easily confound results. For example, a seemingly accurate precognitive prediction might simply be a lucky guess, statistically improbable but not impossible. Similarly, individuals with existing cognitive biases or strong expectations may inadvertently interpret ambiguous stimuli to support their belief in psychic abilities. Furthermore, the possibility of fraud, either conscious or unconscious, cannot be entirely ruled out. While rigorous experimental controls can mitigate the impact of these factors, completely eliminating them remains a significant challenge. Transparency, meticulous record-keeping, and independent verification are crucial to maintaining scientific integrity in this sensitive area of research.

Moreover, the ethical considerations surrounding research in psychic abilities are complex and multifaceted. The potential for psychological harm to participants, especially those who are highly suggestible or vulnerable, needs to be carefully considered. Informed consent, clear communication of risks and limitations, and provision of appropriate support are crucial elements of ethical research practices. Further complicating the issue, societal and cultural beliefs regarding psychic abilities can profoundly influence participants' responses and interpretations of events, leading to subtle biases that are difficult to control for in experimental settings. Therefore, a sensitive and nuanced approach to ethical considerations is vital to ensure the integrity and well-being of all involved.

Despite these challenges, there are promising avenues for future research. Advances in neuroimaging techniques, such as fMRI and EEG, offer the potential for identifying specific brain regions and neural networks associated with clairvoyance and clairsentience. By comparing brain activity in individuals reporting these experiences with that of control groups, researchers might be able to pinpoint neurological correlates, paving the way for a more objective understanding of the underlying mechanisms. Further advancements in signal processing and data analysis techniques may also help to identify subtle patterns and correlations that were previously undetectable.

Furthermore, the integration of different research perspectives is crucial. Combining the rigorous methodology of neuroscience with the insights gained from parapsychology, anthropology, and other relevant fields could create a more holistic and comprehensive understanding of psychic abilities. Interdisciplinary collaborations can help to overcome the limitations of individual disciplines, fostering a more integrated and productive approach to research. This collaborative approach could leverage the strengths of various methodologies and perspectives, providing a richer and more nuanced understanding of the phenomenon.

Beyond neuroscience, the investigation of genetic and epigenetic influences on psychic abilities warrants further exploration. Family studies and genome-wide association studies could potentially identify genetic markers linked to increased susceptibility to these experiences. Epigenetic mechanisms, which involve modifications to gene expression without altering the underlying DNA sequence, might also play a role, influencing how genetic predispositions are expressed throughout an individual's life. This line of research could shed light on the heritability of these traits and help to identify individuals who might be more prone to experiencing such phenomena.

The exploration of potential correlations between psychic

abilities and neurodiversity also presents a promising avenue for future research. Studies examining the prevalence of clairvoyance and clairsentience in individuals with autism spectrum disorder, schizophrenia, or other neurodevelopmental conditions could reveal interesting insights. While these conditions are often associated with challenges, they might also involve unusual cognitive strengths or sensory processing capabilities that could be related to psychic experiences. It's crucial to approach this area with sensitivity and avoid perpetuating harmful stereotypes, focusing instead on identifying shared neurological underpinnings or cognitive mechanisms that could be contributing factors. This research should prioritize the well-being and dignity of all participants.

Ultimately, the future of research into clairvoyance and clairsentience hinges on a paradigm shift. We need to move beyond simplistic dichotomies of "paranormal" versus "normal" and embrace a more nuanced and integrated perspective. This requires a willingness to challenge established paradigms, embrace unconventional methodologies, and collaborate across disciplinary boundaries. By integrating rigorous scientific investigation with a deeper understanding of human consciousness and individual variation, we can potentially unlock profound insights into the nature of reality and the boundless capacity of the human mind. This journey will undoubtedly be challenging, demanding intellectual humility, persistent curiosity, and unwavering commitment to ethical research practices. However, the potential rewards – a deeper understanding of consciousness, the development of novel therapeutic interventions, and a profound expansion of our scientific understanding – make it a pursuit well worth undertaking. The integration of seemingly disparate fields, from neuroscience and genetics to parapsychology and spiritual practices, is essential to unraveling the mysteries surrounding these extraordinary human capacities. Only through a concerted effort, involving interdisciplinary collaboration and a willingness to question established paradigms, can we hope to unlock the full potential of human consciousness.

CHAPTER 3:
PSYCHIC ABILITIES
AND PSYCHOSIS:
EXPLORING THE
OVERLAP

Schizophrenia, a devastating neurological disorder, is characterized by a profound disruption of thought processes, emotions, and perceptions. One of its most prominent features is the presence of hallucinations, often auditory but sometimes visual, tactile, or olfactory. These hallucinations are vivid and compelling, experienced as real by the individual, despite lacking external stimuli. Similarly, individuals reporting psychic abilities often describe experiences of heightened sensory perception, sometimes exceeding the bounds of ordinary sensory input. This raises a compelling question: are the altered perceptions in schizophrenia and the purported extraordinary sensory experiences of psychics fundamentally different, or do they share underlying neurological mechanisms?

The experience of a hallucination in schizophrenia can be deeply distressing. A patient might hear voices that insult, command, or even threaten them, leading to paranoia and fear. Visual hallucinations might involve seeing distorted

THE NEURODIVERSITY OF CONSCIOUSNESS

figures, objects, or scenes that are not actually present. Tactile hallucinations, the feeling of something touching or crawling on the skin, can be equally disturbing. Olfactory hallucinations, the perception of unpleasant odors, can also contribute to a sense of unease and discomfort. These experiences are not simply misinterpretations of sensory input; they are actively generated by the brain, often in the absence of external triggers. The content of these hallucinations often reflects the individual's anxieties, fears, and beliefs, further suggesting a strong internal generation process.

In contrast, individuals claiming psychic abilities, such as clairvoyance or clairsentience, often describe their experiences as being insightful or even helpful. Clairvoyance, the ability to perceive distant events or objects, might involve seeing a scene unfolding miles away or sensing a friend's emotional state at a distance. Clairsentience, the ability to sense emotions and feelings of others, can manifest as an uncanny intuition about people's moods and intentions. While both schizophrenia and purported psychic abilities involve altered sensory perception, the context, emotional valence, and the individual's interpretation differ drastically. A schizophrenic patient might feel overwhelmed, frightened, and even persecuted by their hallucinations, whereas an individual claiming psychic abilities may find their experiences empowering and meaningful.

However, the distinction is not always clear-cut. Some individuals diagnosed with schizophrenia have reported experiences that could be interpreted as forms of psychic ability. For example, a patient might experience a hallucination that coincidentally predicts a future event. This raises the possibility that some individuals diagnosed with schizophrenia may possess unusual sensory abilities which, because of their clinical context, are misunderstood and miscategorized as psychotic symptoms.

The neurological underpinnings of these phenomena are equally complex and interconnected. Research suggests that disturbances in neurotransmitter systems, particularly dopamine, glutamate, and serotonin, play a crucial role in schizophrenia. These imbalances can lead to aberrant neural activity in various brain regions, potentially contributing to the generation of hallucinations and delusions. While much remains unknown about the neurological basis of purported psychic abilities, some researchers propose that they might involve similar brain regions but in a different context. For instance, the heightened sensory awareness described by some psychics might be linked to enhanced activity in sensory processing areas of the brain, perhaps driven by genetic or epigenetic factors. The crucial difference would lie not in the involved brain regions but in the regulatory mechanisms.

Indeed, there is a growing body of research exploring the genetic and epigenetic factors that may contribute to both schizophrenia and purported psychic abilities. Family and twin studies have demonstrated a heritable component to schizophrenia, implicating multiple genes and environmental interactions. Interestingly, some research suggests that certain genetic variants associated with schizophrenia may also be related to creativity, heightened intuition, and even exceptional sensory abilities. This opens the possibility that some genetic variations, while increasing susceptibility to schizophrenia in one context, could enhance certain perceptual capacities in another context, particularly in individuals with resilient or protective genetic and environmental factors.

Furthermore, epigenetic mechanisms—changes in gene expression not involving alterations in the DNA sequence —may play a significant role. Exposure to environmental stressors during prenatal or early postnatal development can alter gene expression, potentially increasing the risk of schizophrenia or influencing the development of unusual sensory abilities. This suggests that the interplay between genetic predisposition and environmental factors might determine whether these genetic variations lead to psychosis or exceptional sensory perception.

Differentiating between psychosis and exceptional perception requires careful clinical assessment. A thorough evaluation, including a comprehensive history, neuropsychological testing, and imaging studies, is essential to distinguish between hallucinations associated with schizophrenia and experiences potentially reflecting exceptional sensory perception. This process requires not only diagnostic expertise but also a critical and open-minded approach to the individual's lived experience. Clinical practitioners should strive to avoid prematurely labeling unusual experiences as psychotic symptoms, as misdiagnosis can lead to unnecessary stigmatization and prevent individuals from receiving appropriate support.

The ethical implications of research in this area are profound. It is essential to prioritize the well-being and dignity of participants, obtaining informed consent and ensuring confidentiality. Researchers must carefully weigh the potential benefits of their work against the risks of perpetuating stigma or causing harm to individuals with mental health conditions. The responsible conduct of research requires a commitment to scientific integrity, respect for human subjects, and a nuanced understanding of the complex interplay between mental illness and exceptional human abilities.

The concept of a "spectrum of neurological experiences" offers a more integrated perspective. Rather than viewing psychosis and psychic abilities as categorically distinct, we can consider them as points along a spectrum of potential neurological experiences. This approach acknowledges the significant overlap in sensory phenomena while emphasizing the contextual factors and individual interpretations that influence the expression of these experiences. It shifts the focus from categorical distinctions to a more nuanced understanding of the complex interplay between brain function, genetics, environment, and individual experiences.

Investigating the potential genetic overlap between schizophrenia and purported psychic abilities requires a rigorous and multidisciplinary approach. This includes genome-wide association studies, epigenetic analyses, and investigations into the interplay of environmental factors and gene expression. The results of such studies will not only illuminate the genetic architecture of these complex phenomena but also contribute to a deeper understanding of the human brain and its remarkable capacity for diverse experiences. Identifying shared genetic markers could lead to novel diagnostic tools, personalized treatment approaches, and a more nuanced understanding of the spectrum of human neurological diversity.

The exploration of the relationship between schizophrenia and psychic abilities is fraught with challenges, not least the lack of a universally accepted definition and reliable methods of assessing psychic abilities. However, viewing this as a spectrum rather than a binary distinction could provide a pathway towards a more integrated understanding of human neurodiversity, consciousness, and mental health. This perspective embraces a future where unique abilities are not only understood but celebrated, where both scientific rigor and open-mindedness work in tandem, to achieve a more comprehensive and humane approach to the human condition. We must move beyond simply classifying and labeling to understanding the underlying neural pathways and to develop approaches that support the holistic well-being of individuals, irrespective of their experiences and abilities. The path forward requires interdisciplinary collaboration, a commitment to ethical research practices, and a willingness to challenge conventional paradigms in the pursuit of knowledge and human well-being.

The line separating psychosis and exceptional perception is undeniably blurry, a challenge that demands a nuanced approach far beyond simple diagnostic categorization. While hallucinations in schizophrenia are often chaotic, disorganized, and distressing, leading to significant impairment in daily functioning, the experiences reported by some individuals claiming psychic abilities are frequently described as focused, insightful, and even beneficial, albeit sometimes unsettling. The crucial difference lies not solely in the content of the experience, but in its context, impact, and the individual's subjective interpretation.

Consider the case of auditory hallucinations. In schizophrenia, these hallucinations might involve persecutory voices, commanding self-harm or violence, or delivering streams of incoherent and distressing messages. This contrasts with the experiences of some individuals who report hearing "intuitive whispers" or "guiding voices," which they interpret as sources of guidance, inspiration, or precognitive information. The

content might superficially resemble each other—a voice heard—but the meaning ascribed to that experience differs profoundly. One is experienced as a symptom of illness, creating significant distress and impairment; the other is interpreted as a talent, potentially even a gift. This highlights the critical role of subjective experience in differentiating these phenomena.

Furthermore, the individual's coping mechanisms and overall mental state play a significant role. Someone experiencing auditory hallucinations in the context of schizophrenia often struggles to differentiate between internal and external reality, leading to paranoia, fear, and social isolation. In contrast, individuals who claim to receive psychic information may develop coping strategies to manage and integrate these experiences into their lives, using them for creative endeavors, decision-making, or even healing practices. The perceived controllability of the experience also plays a vital role. In psychosis, the individual typically feels powerless over the hallucinations, unable to control their onset or content. Those claiming psychic abilities, however, often describe a level of control, or at least a capacity to consciously engage with and interpret the information received.

The clinical evaluation must therefore move beyond a simple checklist of symptoms. A thorough assessment needs to explore the individual's history, their subjective experience of the phenomena, the impact on their daily life, and their coping strategies. It is essential to consider cultural context, as certain experiences deemed paranormal in one culture may be normalized or even revered in another. Neuropsychological testing can help assess cognitive functioning and identify potential areas of impairment, further assisting in differentiating between psychosis and exceptional perception. For example, neurocognitive deficits associated with schizophrenia, such as difficulties with attention, memory, and executive function, would be less likely to be present in individuals with exceptional perceptual abilities. While a neuropsychological assessment is unlikely to definitively prove psychic abilities, it will help in the more critical role of ruling out conditions like schizophrenia or other psychotic disorders.

Furthermore, the intensity and frequency of the experiences are crucial factors. In psychosis, hallucinations tend to be persistent, pervasive, and often increase in intensity over time. Exceptional perceptual abilities, as claimed by some individuals, are often reported as episodic, occurring less frequently, and generally causing less impairment to daily functioning. In essence, the disruption to the person's life should be a significant indicator—a persistent state of fear, paranoia, and inability to function in a normal, day-to-day manner strongly suggests a clinical condition. The ability to maintain relationships, work effectively, and manage daily routines while experiencing these "abilities" significantly reduces the possibility that these experiences are symptoms of a psychotic break.

However, it is essential to acknowledge the limitations of current diagnostic tools. The absence of objective, verifiable measures for psychic abilities makes it challenging to conduct rigorous scientific research. The subjective nature of these experiences necessitates reliance on self-reported data, which can be prone to bias, misinterpretation, and even conscious or unconscious deception. This inherent difficulty emphasizes the importance of utilizing a multi-method approach, including structured interviews, psychological testing, and physiological monitoring (such as EEG or fMRI, to identify neural correlates), to construct a comprehensive clinical picture. The use of projective tests can also uncover underlying psychological issues that may be influencing the reporting of psychic abilities.

The concept of a spectrum is valuable here. Rather than rigidly classifying individuals as either psychotic or psychic, we might consider a continuum of altered states of consciousness. At one end of the spectrum lies severe psychosis, characterized by significant distress, impairment, and a loss of contact with reality. At the other end, we might find individuals with exceptional perceptual abilities who experience heightened sensory awareness, intuition, or precognitive insights without significant impairment. Between these two extremes lie a range of experiences, some of which might overlap with features of both psychosis and exceptional perception. This model acknowledges the complexity of human experience and avoids the simplistic categorization of individuals into mutually exclusive categories.

Genetic and epigenetic factors likely play a significant role in the predisposition towards both psychosis and exceptional perceptual abilities. While research is still in its early stages, preliminary studies have suggested potential genetic overlap between certain psychiatric disorders and traits associated with increased sensory sensitivity or creativity. Further investigation into these genetic and epigenetic mechanisms is crucial for understanding the underlying biological processes involved. Specifically, the study of genetic polymorphisms related to neurotransmitter systems such as dopamine, serotonin, and glutamate could provide critical insights into the neural substrates of both psychosis and exceptional perception. The epigenetic landscape also warrants further investigation, exploring how environmental factors might interact with genetic predispositions to modify the expression of genes related to sensory perception, cognitive processing, and emotional regulation. A nuanced exploration of these areas might reveal common pathways, contributing to the understanding of this often-misunderstood spectrum.

Moreover, the role of neuroplasticity should not be overlooked. The brain's remarkable capacity for change throughout life suggests that experiences, both positive and negative, can shape neural pathways and influence sensory processing. For example, individuals who regularly engage in meditative practices, mindfulness techniques, or other mind-body interventions may experience altered states of consciousness that could be misinterpreted as psychic abilities if not carefully evaluated within a broader clinical context. Similarly, trauma, stress, or chronic illness can also significantly alter brain function and potentially lead to experiences that mimic symptoms of psychosis. Differentiating these effects from true psychic phenomena requires a rigorous assessment of the individual's history and current mental state.

In conclusion, differentiating psychosis from exceptional perception requires a comprehensive, multi-faceted approach.

It's not a simple dichotomy, but rather a complex spectrum of experiences that necessitates a profound understanding of neurobiology, psychology, and the profound influence of individual experiences. A future that accurately assesses these experiences necessitates a departure from rigid diagnostic categories and embraces a more holistic, nuanced, and individualized approach to clinical evaluation. This approach integrates the latest advances in neuroscience with a respectful understanding of subjective experiences and the diversity of human consciousness. Only through such an approach can we truly begin to understand and support individuals across this complex spectrum of human experience, fostering both mental health and the potential for exceptional human capabilities.

The search for a biological basis underlying both psychosis and purported psychic abilities has led researchers down fascinating, albeit complex, paths. One promising avenue of investigation lies in exploring shared genetic markers or epigenetic modifications. While the field is still nascent, preliminary findings hint at intriguing overlaps. A key challenge, however, lies in the heterogeneity of both "psychosis" and "psychic abilities." Psychosis, as a clinical diagnosis, encompasses a wide range of conditions, from schizophrenia and bipolar disorder to brief psychotic episodes stemming from various underlying causes. Similarly, the term "psychic abilities" lacks a standardized definition, encompassing reported experiences as diverse as clairvoyance, clairsentience, precognition, telepathy, and psychokinesis. This inherent variability makes identifying common genetic threads a significant hurdle.

Nevertheless, several research directions offer potential insights. Genome-wide association studies (GWAS) have identified numerous genetic variants associated with an increased risk of schizophrenia. Some of these genes are involved in neurodevelopment, synaptic plasticity, and immune function – processes that are also likely to influence sensory perception and information processing. Intriguingly, some of these same genes have been implicated in other conditions associated with altered states of consciousness, including autism spectrum disorder and epilepsy. This suggests that variations in these genes might not directly cause psychosis or psychic abilities, but rather modulate individual susceptibility to experiencing unusual sensory phenomena, which can manifest as either pathology or heightened sensitivity depending on other factors, including environmental influences and epigenetic modifications.

Epigenetics, the study of heritable changes in gene expression without alterations to the underlying DNA sequence, presents another compelling line of inquiry. Environmental factors, such as stress, trauma, and nutrition, can induce epigenetic modifications that affect gene expression. Individuals experiencing severe childhood trauma, for example, may exhibit epigenetic changes that increase their risk for psychosis later in life. Conversely, individuals with a history of meditation or other contemplative practices may exhibit different epigenetic profiles reflecting altered brain plasticity and potentially influencing their ability to access altered states of consciousness. While direct evidence linking specific epigenetic modifications to either psychosis or psychic abilities remains scarce, this area holds significant promise for future research.

Further complicating matters is the potential role of gene-environment interactions. Genetic predisposition might increase an individual's vulnerability to developing psychotic symptoms under certain environmental conditions, while the same genetic profile might lead to the development of heightened sensory sensitivity under different circumstances. Imagine a scenario where a specific gene variant increases the sensitivity of the visual cortex. In one individual, this might manifest as vivid hallucinations and delusions, leading to a diagnosis of schizophrenia. In another individual, with a different life experience and coping mechanisms, the same gene variant might contribute to heightened visual acuity, possibly leading to exceptional artistic ability or even the experience of clairvoyance. This emphasizes the critical importance of considering individual context and experience in understanding the interplay between genes and environment.

Studying individuals who report both exceptional sensory abilities and a family history of psychotic disorders could provide valuable clues. These individuals offer a unique opportunity to dissect the genetic and environmental factors contributing to both ends of the spectrum. Such research requires a sensitive and ethical approach, ensuring informed consent and avoiding stigmatization. Careful phenotyping – detailed characterization of both the "psychic" experiences and any co-occurring mental health conditions – is crucial for accurate interpretation of genetic findings. Moreover, the reliance on self-reported experiences necessitates rigorous methodological approaches to minimize bias and ensure the validity of the data.

Furthermore, the exploration extends beyond solely genetic factors. Neuroimaging techniques, such as fMRI and EEG, can provide valuable insights into brain structure and function in individuals reporting psychic abilities. Comparing brain activity patterns in these individuals with those exhibiting psychotic symptoms could reveal shared neural substrates or distinct patterns associated with each condition. For example, altered activity in the default mode network, a brain network associated with self-referential thought and introspection, has been observed in both meditation practitioners and individuals with schizophrenia, suggesting a potential overlap in brain states that could underpin both heightened self-awareness and delusional thinking.

Investigating candidate genes involved in neurotransmitter systems, such as dopamine and serotonin, also holds promise. Imbalances in these neurotransmitters are strongly implicated in psychosis, and they may also play a role in influencing sensory perception and consciousness. Studies examining gene expression levels in specific brain regions could offer further understanding of the molecular mechanisms underlying the potential overlap between psychic abilities and psychosis. Furthermore, the emerging field of connectomics, studying the brain's intricate network of connections, could reveal structural and functional differences in brain networks that distinguish these conditions.

Looking beyond the purely biological, we must consider the profound influence of culture and belief systems. The interpretation of sensory experiences is profoundly shaped by one's cultural background and personal worldview. What might be perceived as a hallucination in one cultural context could be interpreted as a spiritual experience or prophetic vision in another. This highlights the limitations of relying solely on Western psychiatric diagnostic criteria in understanding experiences that might be considered exceptional in other cultures.

In conclusion, unraveling the genetic and epigenetic underpinnings of the potential overlap between psychosis and purported psychic abilities requires a multifaceted and interdisciplinary approach. While the current state of knowledge is limited, emerging research methods offer exciting possibilities for future discoveries. The challenge lies not only in identifying shared genetic markers, but also in understanding the intricate interplay between genes, environment, and individual experience in shaping both mental health and extraordinary human capabilities. Only through such a comprehensive approach, embracing both scientific rigor and an open mind to unconventional phenomena, can we hope to bridge the gap between these seemingly disparate realms of human experience, fostering a future where both mental health and exceptional human potential are nurtured and celebrated. A holistic understanding that transcends the rigid boundaries of conventional scientific thought, integrated with perspectives from alternative healing and spiritual traditions, will prove crucial in navigating this fascinating frontier of human consciousness. The exploration continues, and the answers may lie not in simplistic genetic determinism, but in the dynamic interplay between our genes, our environments, and the ever-evolving landscape of the human mind.

The previous chapter laid the groundwork for exploring the potential connections between psychosis and psychic abilities, focusing on the search for shared genetic and epigenetic factors. However, focusing solely on genetics risks overlooking a crucial aspect: the spectrum of neurological experiences. Rather than viewing psychosis and psychic abilities as distinct and opposing entities, it is more fruitful to consider them as points along a continuum of neurological function, a spectrum of consciousness that encompasses both the profoundly challenging experiences of mental illness and the extraordinary capacities sometimes associated with what we call "psychic" abilities.

This broadened perspective necessitates a shift in our conceptual framework. Instead of searching for a single, definitive genetic marker, we should explore a wider range of factors: neurotransmitter imbalances, variations in brain structure and connectivity, and epigenetic modifications influenced by both genetic predispositions and environmental factors. This approach is further supported by the burgeoning field of neurodiversity, which emphasizes the inherent variability of brain function and the recognition of diverse cognitive styles as valuable assets rather than deficits.

Consider, for instance, the case of synesthesia, a neurological condition where stimulation of one sensory pathway leads to automatic, involuntary experiences in a second sensory modality. A person with synesthesia might see colors when they hear music or taste shapes. While not typically considered a "psychic ability," synesthesia shares certain similarities. It involves unusual cross-wiring in the brain, resulting in experiences beyond the typical range of human perception. Could similar neurological mechanisms, perhaps amplified or differently expressed, underlie some reported psychic experiences?

The heightened sensory perception often reported by individuals with certain forms of psychosis, such as hyperacusis (extreme sensitivity to sound) or intensified tactile sensations, provides another compelling example.

While these sensory distortions can be incredibly distressing within the context of psychosis, they also highlight the brain's capacity to process sensory information in unconventional ways. It is conceivable that a similar amplification of sensory processing, but without the accompanying distress and disruption of daily functioning, could contribute to certain clairvoyant or clairsentient experiences.

Furthermore, we need to consider the role of altered states of consciousness. Meditation, deep relaxation, and even certain forms of sleep deprivation can significantly alter brainwave patterns, potentially opening channels to information processing that are usually suppressed under normal waking consciousness. This suggests a possible connection between altered states of consciousness and the emergence of psychic abilities. Interestingly, altered states of consciousness are also a feature of many psychotic episodes. The difference, it could be argued, lies not in the underlying neurological mechanisms, but in the context, the individual's coping mechanisms, and the way the experiences are interpreted and integrated into their conscious awareness.

Intriguingly, recent research on the default mode network (DMN) – a network of brain regions active during mind-wandering, self-reflection, and daydreaming – has illuminated a potential link between this brain network and both altered states of consciousness and potentially even psychic experiences. The DMN is implicated in the generation of internal imagery and spontaneous thoughts, functions that are crucial for many reported psychic experiences. In individuals with certain forms of psychosis, the DMN may function differently, leading to the generation of internally generated experiences that are perceived as reality, while in others, perhaps a similar activation could lead to what are perceived as extra-sensory experiences. It's not a matter of the DMN being inherently "good" or "bad," but rather a matter of how it functions within the wider context of brain activity.

This nuanced perspective challenges the simplistic dichotomy between "normal" and "abnormal" brain function. It suggests instead a rich tapestry of neurological capabilities, some of which are currently perceived as desirable, others as problematic. The key difference may lie not in the presence or absence of specific neurological mechanisms, but in the individual's ability to integrate these experiences into a coherent and functional life. This is where supportive interventions, both medical and spiritual, play a crucial role. For those experiencing distressing psychotic symptoms, appropriate medication and therapy can help manage and alleviate their symptoms, allowing them to live fuller, more meaningful lives. For those who experience what they perceive as psychic abilities, a supportive environment that fosters self-understanding and responsible use of these abilities is critical.

The potential overlap between psychosis and psychic abilities also highlights the limitations of traditional diagnostic categories. The diagnostic and statistical manual of mental disorders (DSM) and the international classification of diseases (ICD), while valuable tools for clinicians, may not fully capture the complexity of human experience. These manuals typically focus on pathology and dysfunction, often overlooking the potential for extraordinary capacities that can emerge even within the context of mental illness.

This doesn't imply that we should minimize or disregard

the suffering caused by psychosis. On the contrary, a more holistic understanding of the spectrum of neurological experiences emphasizes the importance of providing effective treatment and support for individuals struggling with mental illness. However, it does suggest a need to move beyond simplistic labels and toward a more nuanced and compassionate approach that acknowledges the potential for both extraordinary abilities and significant challenges within the same individual.

Furthermore, the exploration of this spectrum requires a willingness to integrate perspectives from diverse fields of study. Neuroscience, psychology, parapsychology, and even spiritual traditions all offer valuable insights that can contribute to a more comprehensive understanding. The rigid boundaries that often separate these disciplines can hinder progress. We need to foster interdisciplinary collaboration, encouraging open dialogue and mutual respect between researchers with varying perspectives.

The research into the neural correlates of psychosis and psychic abilities is still in its early stages. However, the growing body of evidence supports a model that views these experiences as points along a continuum of human potential, a spectrum of neurological experiences shaped by a complex interplay of genetic, epigenetic, and environmental factors. This understanding paves the way for new approaches to diagnosis, treatment, and support, fostering a more compassionate and comprehensive approach to human consciousness in all its wondrous and challenging manifestations. Ultimately, embracing this spectrum allows us to move beyond fear and stigmatization, fostering instead a society that values and celebrates neurodiversity in all its forms, recognizing the potential for both exceptional abilities and significant challenges to coexist within the rich tapestry of the human experience. The future of understanding consciousness lies not in narrow definitions and exclusionary approaches, but in embracing the full spectrum of human potential, acknowledging the intricate connections between seemingly disparate aspects of the human mind, and working towards a more holistic and compassionate approach to mental health and human flourishing. The journey is ongoing, and the answers, I believe, are waiting to be discovered by a courageous willingness to explore beyond the confines of conventional thinking.

The exploration of potential links between psychic abilities and psychosis necessitates a rigorous ethical framework. Our pursuit of knowledge must never come at the cost of the well-being and dignity of the individuals involved in our research. This is particularly crucial given the sensitive nature of mental health conditions and the potential for stigmatization surrounding claims of psychic phenomena. The very definition of "psychic abilities" remains elusive, making informed consent a significant hurdle. How do we obtain truly informed consent from individuals who may themselves be uncertain about the nature of their experiences? Are they capable of comprehending the implications of participating in research that probes into the potentially unsettling depths of their consciousness?

One of the primary ethical concerns revolves around the potential for harm. The act of investigating unusual experiences, especially those bordering on the pathological, could inadvertently trigger or exacerbate existing mental health challenges. A poorly designed study might inadvertently reinforce negative self-perceptions or lead to heightened anxiety and distress. The very act of labeling someone as possessing "psychic abilities" could inadvertently lead to a self-fulfilling prophecy, further entrenching them in beliefs that may be detrimental to their psychological well-being. Conversely, dismissing such experiences as purely delusional could be equally damaging, invalidating their lived experience and potentially hindering access to appropriate support.

Therefore, rigorous safeguards must be in place to protect participants. This includes comprehensive pre-screening processes to assess mental health status and identify individuals who may be at risk of harm from participation. Studies should be designed to minimize potential stressors, with built-in mechanisms for immediate intervention should any participant exhibit signs of distress. This might entail regular check-ins with mental health professionals and the availability of appropriate therapeutic support. Moreover, researchers should be trained in identifying and managing potential triggers and distress, possessing the sensitivity and expertise to address the complexities of human experience with empathy and understanding.

Furthermore, data anonymity and confidentiality are paramount. The potential for stigmatization associated with both mental illness and claims of psychic abilities necessitates rigorous protections of participant privacy. Data must be securely stored and handled according to the highest ethical standards, ensuring that no personally identifiable information is ever disclosed without explicit consent. This includes protecting participants from the potential for public disclosure or misuse of research findings. The ethical responsibility extends beyond the direct participants to their families and communities, who could be impacted by the disclosure of sensitive information.

The publication of research findings also presents significant ethical considerations. Results must be reported in a responsible and nuanced manner, avoiding sensationalism or language that could perpetuate stigmatizing stereotypes. Interpretations of data should be cautious and avoid drawing unwarranted conclusions, particularly those that could be detrimental to individuals experiencing mental health challenges. The findings should be presented within the broader context of scientific understanding, acknowledging the limitations of the research and emphasizing the need for further investigation. Sensationalist reporting could amplify public misconceptions, leading to further marginalization of individuals with mental health issues and those who report extraordinary experiences.

Another significant ethical dilemma arises from the potential for exploitation. Individuals reporting psychic abilities may be particularly vulnerable to manipulation and exploitation, especially if they lack a strong support system or understanding of the scientific process. Researchers must be vigilant in safeguarding participants from any form of coercion, undue influence, or financial exploitation. The research environment must be designed to empower participants, ensuring that they feel respected and valued, and that their experiences are treated with the utmost dignity and respect. This requires a genuine commitment to collaboration and partnership, placing the well-being of participants at the forefront of the research process.

The potential for misinterpretation and misuse of research

findings also poses ethical challenges. For example, research into the neurological basis of psychic abilities could be misinterpreted or misused to justify discriminatory practices or to promote pseudoscientific beliefs. It's crucial, therefore, that researchers engage in proactive efforts to disseminate their findings responsibly and to counter any potential for misuse. This includes actively engaging with the public, educational institutions, and policymakers to promote accurate understanding and to prevent the exploitation of research for harmful purposes.

The ethical dimensions of this research extend beyond the immediate participants and encompass a broader societal responsibility. Our investigations should aim to foster understanding and reduce stigma surrounding both mental illness and claims of psychic abilities. A compassionate and nuanced approach is essential, one that avoids simplistic categorization and acknowledges the complex interplay of neurological, psychological, and spiritual dimensions of human experience. The potential benefits of such research – a more compassionate understanding of consciousness, improved mental health care, and a more inclusive society – demand a commitment to the highest ethical standards. Only through meticulous adherence to ethical principles can we ensure that our pursuit of knowledge contributes to human flourishing and avoids causing further harm. The goal is not merely to understand the mysteries of the mind, but to use that understanding to promote a healthier and more inclusive world for all. This requires a continual reassessment of ethical considerations, a process of critical self-reflection and a commitment to adaptation as our understanding of the complex interaction between mental health and purported psychic abilities evolves.

The responsibility extends beyond the individual researcher. Institutional review boards, funding agencies, and professional organizations have a critical role to play in overseeing ethical practices and setting standards for research involving sensitive populations. Collaboration between researchers, ethicists, and mental health professionals is paramount to ensure that research is conducted responsibly and that participants' well-being is prioritized at every stage of the research process. Ultimately, the ethical challenges inherent in this field underscore the necessity of a holistic and compassionate approach, one that respects the dignity and autonomy of all individuals and strives to promote a deeper understanding of the human experience in all its multifaceted complexity. This integrated approach, blending scientific rigor with a sensitivity to the spiritual dimensions of human experience, is crucial for ensuring the responsible exploration of this fascinating and complex area of research. It is through this careful navigation of ethical considerations that we can hope to unlock the potential for genuine advancement in our understanding of consciousness, while simultaneously safeguarding the well-being of those who generously participate in these vital explorations. The future of this research depends not only on scientific breakthroughs but also on the unwavering commitment to ethical principles and the compassionate treatment of all individuals involved.

CHAPTER 4: INDIGO, CRYSTAL, AND RAINBOW CHILDREN: A NEURODIVERSITY PERSPECTIVE

The New Age movement has introduced a fascinating concept: Indigo children. These children, born predominantly after the mid-1970s, are described as possessing unique characteristics and abilities that set them apart from previous generations. The term "Indigo" itself evokes a sense of mystery and intensity, often associated with deep intuition, heightened sensitivity, and unconventional thinking. While lacking rigorous scientific validation, the characterization of Indigo children has resonated with many parents and educators, sparking widespread interest and discussion.

One of the most frequently cited characteristics of Indigo children is their intense empathy and intuitive understanding of others' emotions. They are often described as highly sensitive individuals, deeply affected by the energy and emotional states of those around them. This heightened empathy can be both a gift and a challenge, as it may lead to emotional overwhelm in environments characterized by conflict or negativity. These children often exhibit a strong sense of justice and fairness, readily challenging authority figures when they perceive injustice or unfairness. They are often described as possessing an unwavering moral compass, pushing boundaries and questioning societal norms in pursuit of truth and authenticity.

Their intellectual abilities are also frequently highlighted. Many proponents of the Indigo child concept suggest these children possess advanced cognitive skills, exhibiting high levels of creativity, problem-solving abilities, and out-of-the-box thinking. They may demonstrate a natural talent for specific areas, such as art, music, or technology, showcasing unique capabilities that surpass expectations for their age. Furthermore, they often display a strong dislike for routine and rigid structures, preferring unconventional approaches and self-directed learning. This preference for autonomy can sometimes be misconstrued as defiance or a lack of discipline, leading to challenges in traditional educational settings.

The spiritual aspects of Indigo children are equally significant within the New Age narrative. Many believe these children are here to bring about positive change in the world, carrying a heightened sense of purpose and a profound connection to spirituality. They may display a keen interest in metaphysical subjects, such as energy healing, meditation, and other alternative practices. These children often report profound spiritual experiences or intuitive insights that transcend conventional understanding. Their inherent connection to the spiritual realm is often viewed as a driving force behind their unconventional behavior and unwavering belief in their own unique path.

It is crucial to approach the Indigo child concept with critical discernment. While the anecdotal evidence and personal experiences shared by parents and proponents are compelling, scientific research remains limited. The lack of objective data makes it difficult to objectively assess the validity of these claims. The attributes often associated with Indigo children, such as empathy, sensitivity, and heightened intuition, can also be observed in other children, suggesting that the characteristics might not be unique to this particular group.

However, viewing the Indigo child phenomenon through a neurodiversity lens offers a potentially fruitful avenue for exploration. Many of the characteristics attributed to Indigo children align with traits found in neurodivergent individuals, such as individuals with autism spectrum disorder (ASD) or attention-deficit/hyperactivity disorder (ADHD). These conditions often manifest in heightened sensory sensitivity, intense emotional responses, and unconventional ways of processing information. The strong sense of justice and moral compass frequently associated with Indigo children might reflect an enhanced capacity for moral reasoning, a trait sometimes observed in individuals with certain neurodevelopmental conditions.

The focus on creativity and unconventional thinking in Indigo children parallels the creative and innovative thinking often found in individuals on the autism spectrum. Many individuals with ASD display extraordinary talent in specific areas, showcasing unique skills and abilities that might be misunderstood or undervalued in traditional educational or social settings. This creative potential, however, frequently requires nurturing and a supportive environment to fully develop and flourish.

Moreover, the challenges faced by Indigo children in traditional settings – difficulty with conformity, resistance to authority, and intense emotional responses – are frequently experienced by neurodivergent children. The struggles they face are not necessarily indicative of a problem with the child but rather a reflection of a mismatch between the child's neurocognitive profile and the demands of the environment. The frustration and difficulties experienced by Indigo children might result from a lack of understanding and appropriate support within the existing social and educational structures.

The spiritual inclination often associated with Indigo children could also be viewed through a neurodiversity lens. Certain spiritual practices, such as meditation and mindfulness, have been shown to benefit individuals with various neurodevelopmental conditions, contributing to improved emotional regulation, reduced anxiety, and enhanced focus. The apparent spiritual depth and heightened intuition observed in some individuals might also stem from an enhanced capacity for introspection and self-awareness, abilities that can be cultivated through supportive and understanding environments.

Therefore, instead of viewing Indigo children as a separate, extraordinary category, it's more productive to consider them as individuals on the broader spectrum of human neurodiversity. This perspective emphasizes the importance of recognizing and celebrating diverse neurological profiles, rather than attempting to categorize individuals into rigid boxes. It encourages a paradigm shift towards inclusive education and social structures that support individuals with diverse cognitive styles and processing preferences, embracing the unique strengths and talents that often come with neurodiversity.

While the term "Indigo children" lacks scientific validation, the underlying concept highlights the need for a more nuanced understanding of human potential and neurodevelopmental variations. The characteristics often associated with these children are not isolated phenomena but rather points along the broad spectrum of human experience. By shifting from an approach that seeks to classify and define to one that embraces individuality and diverse strengths, we can better support and nurture the unique talents and abilities that make each individual remarkable. Furthermore, embracing neurodiversity offers a potentially fruitful lens for exploring claims of paranormal or exceptional abilities, recognizing that neurological differences might influence perceptions of reality and interactions with the world in ways we are only beginning to comprehend.

This shift in perspective is not just about altering terminology or classification; it's about fundamental changes in societal structures and expectations. It means creating educational and social environments that cater to diverse learning styles and sensitivities. It requires a more compassionate and understanding approach to behaviors that might be deemed "difficult" or "disruptive" but are often merely expressions of a neurological profile that deviates from the norm. By embracing this more inclusive model, we create opportunities for all individuals to reach their full potential, regardless of their neurological differences.

The ongoing discussion about Indigo children, while rooted in New Age spirituality, provides a valuable opportunity to reflect on our understanding of human consciousness and neurodiversity. Rather than dismissing the concept entirely, it is crucial to examine the underlying message: that we are a diverse population with a spectrum of capabilities and needs. By moving towards an inclusive approach, that prioritizes understanding and support rather than strict categorization, we foster a more compassionate and supportive society where all individuals can flourish. Future research needs to take a more scientifically rigorous approach, exploring the neurological underpinnings of the characteristics often attributed to Indigo children within the broader context of neurodiversity. This could involve neuroimaging studies, genetic analysis, and extensive behavioral assessments to investigate any potential correlations between reported abilities and neurological markers.

This exploration into Indigo children needs to move beyond anecdotal evidence and embrace a multi-disciplinary approach. Collaboration between parapsychologists, neuroscientists, educators, and social scientists is essential to develop a comprehensive understanding of these phenomena. Furthermore, ethical considerations need to be carefully addressed, particularly regarding the potential for misdiagnosis and the stigmatization of neurodivergent individuals. By employing a respectful and evidence-based approach, we can learn more about both the potential benefits and challenges associated with neurodiversity while avoiding perpetuation of harmful stereotypes or misinformation. The journey toward a more inclusive understanding of human potential is a complex one, but the rewards – a society that celebrates diversity and supports every individual's unique abilities – are immeasurable.

Building upon the exploration of Indigo children, we now delve into the subsequent generations: Crystal and Rainbow children. These classifications, while lacking the same widespread recognition as "Indigo," offer valuable insights into the evolving landscape of perceived neurodiversity and purported psychic abilities. The Crystal children, generally understood to have been born after the 1990s, are often described as possessing even higher levels of empathy and sensitivity than their Indigo predecessors. Their heightened intuitive abilities are frequently cited, along with a strong connection to nature and a deep-seated desire for peace and harmony. Anecdotal accounts portray Crystal children as being exceptionally intuitive, often exhibiting advanced levels of emotional intelligence and a profound understanding of interconnectedness. They are often described as highly sensitive individuals, easily overwhelmed by intense stimuli, yet possessing an inner strength and resilience that enables them to navigate the complexities of the modern world.

The defining characteristic often attributed to Crystal children is their pure, crystalline energy. This metaphor alludes to their perceived clarity of intention and their ability to channel positive energy. Their purported connection to the spiritual realm is frequently described as being more profound and direct than that of Indigo children, leading some to view them as natural healers or conduits of spiritual energy. It's important to note, however, that these descriptions rely heavily on subjective accounts and interpretations, lacking the rigorous scientific backing necessary for definitive conclusions. Further research, employing methodologies such as EEG and fMRI studies, could illuminate the neurological correlates of these purported abilities, helping us to understand the underlying mechanisms.

The Rainbow children, the latest generation in this evolving typology, are portrayed as embodying the culmination of the attributes of their Indigo and Crystal predecessors. Born in the late 2000s and beyond, they are often described as possessing an even more heightened level of empathy, intuition, and creativity. They are envisioned as being highly adaptable and resilient, capable of navigating complex social and environmental challenges with remarkable ease. Their unique perspective is often viewed as a powerful force for positive change, contributing to a more harmonious and sustainable future. Descriptions often portray Rainbow children as possessing a deep understanding of universal consciousness, a heightened sense of compassion, and an inherent ability to connect with others on a profound level.

While the descriptions of Crystal and Rainbow children share common threads with those of Indigo children, certain distinctions emerge. For instance, while Indigo children are often characterized by their rebellious spirit and questioning of authority, Crystal children are frequently portrayed as more collaborative and cooperative. Rainbow children, in turn, are seen as embodying a more harmonious blend of these qualities, showcasing a unique combination of assertiveness and compassion. These distinctions, however, remain largely based on observational accounts and require further investigation.

The conceptualization of these generational distinctions raises critical questions. Are these descriptions accurate representations of developmental differences, or are they simply reflective of societal expectations and evolving cultural norms? Are we witnessing a genuinely novel expression of human potential, or are these classifications merely a reflection of shifting paradigms in child-rearing practices and educational philosophies? These questions underscore the crucial need for rigorous, interdisciplinary research.

One perspective to explore is the influence of epigenetics. The environment, encompassing factors such as diet, stress levels, and exposure to toxins, can alter gene expression without changing the underlying DNA sequence. Could environmental changes since the 1970s have contributed to the observed differences between generations? This avenue of research could reveal whether observed differences are genetic, environmental, or a complex interplay of both. Furthermore, investigating potential correlations between these purported abilities and specific neurological conditions, such as autism spectrum disorder (ASD) or attention-deficit/hyperactivity disorder (ADHD), could shed further light on the complex interplay between neurodiversity and exceptional abilities. This comparative study should be conducted with utmost ethical sensitivity, prioritizing the well-being and dignity of individuals with these conditions.

Another important consideration is the potential for confirmation bias. Parents and caregivers who believe their children belong to one of these categories may unconsciously interpret their behaviors in ways that align with those expectations. This bias can lead to the selective recall of events and the exaggeration of certain traits. Rigorous research needs to account for this inherent bias to ensure accurate interpretation of observations and to avoid self-fulfilling prophecies. Controlled studies, using objective measures and avoiding leading questions, are crucial in minimizing the impact of confirmation bias.

Furthermore, the social and cultural context in which these children are raised must be considered. The growing emphasis on self-expression, mindfulness, and emotional intelligence in modern society may influence how these children are perceived and how their traits are interpreted. The increasing accessibility of information and the rise of alternative spiritual practices may also contribute to the prevalence of these labels.

It is crucial to approach the subject matter with a balanced perspective, recognizing the limitations of the current research and the potential for misinterpretations. While anecdotal evidence may provide a glimpse into potential differences between generations, it is not sufficient to establish definitive conclusions. Future research must employ rigorous scientific methods, including quantitative data analysis and controlled experiments, to gain a more accurate understanding of the phenomenon. This research should incorporate longitudinal studies, following these children from childhood into adulthood, to trace developmental trajectories and assess the long-term implications of these perceived traits.

The focus should not solely be on identifying potential "special abilities," but also on understanding the challenges these children may face. Heightened sensitivity, for instance, can lead to sensory overload and emotional difficulties. The need for empathy and understanding extends to recognizing the potential emotional vulnerability of these individuals, as well as providing support and guidance in navigating social and educational environments.

The exploration of Indigo, Crystal, and Rainbow children offers a unique opportunity to further our understanding of human potential and neurodiversity. By integrating scientific rigor with a nuanced appreciation of subjective experiences and spiritual perspectives, we can develop a more holistic and compassionate approach to understanding the spectrum of human consciousness. The journey is complex, requiring careful attention to ethical considerations and a commitment to evidence-based research. However, the potential rewards —a deeper understanding of ourselves and a more inclusive society—make this a worthwhile endeavor. Ultimately, the goal is to foster an environment where individuals of all neurotypes feel supported, understood, and empowered to live their lives to the fullest. This journey requires moving beyond simplistic labeling and embracing a deeper investigation into the complex interplay of genetics, environment, and personal experience that shapes the development and expression of human potential.

This exploration necessitates a paradigm shift, moving away from a purely medical model focused on pathology to a more holistic framework encompassing the full spectrum of human experience. This includes acknowledging the limitations of current diagnostic tools and categories and the need to develop more sensitive and nuanced ways of assessing human capabilities. A crucial element of this paradigm shift involves recognizing the potential for positive aspects of neurodiversity, viewing it not as a deficit, but as a source of creativity, innovation, and heightened awareness. This requires a conscious effort to move beyond the pathologizing of difference and to embrace the vast spectrum of human experience.

THE NEURODIVERSITY OF CONSCIOUSNESS

Finally, the understanding of Indigo, Crystal, and Rainbow children should not remain confined to academic circles. It should be integrated into educational practices, fostering a more inclusive and supportive learning environment for all children, regardless of their perceived neurotype. This requires a re-evaluation of traditional educational methods and the development of more personalized learning approaches that cater to individual learning styles and needs. By fostering an environment of understanding, empathy, and acceptance, we can help these individuals thrive and contribute meaningfully to society. The goal is to cultivate a future where these purported abilities are seen as assets, not deviations, creating a more compassionate and equitable world.

The descriptions of Indigo, Crystal, and Rainbow children, while often rooted in anecdotal evidence and spiritual beliefs, invite us to explore potential neurological correlates. The claimed heightened empathy, intuition, and sensitivity suggest variations in brain structure or function compared to the neurotypical population. While definitive scientific research is still lacking, several hypotheses can be put forward, drawing parallels with existing neurological research and conditions.

One prominent area of investigation is the mirror neuron system. This network of neurons, activated both when performing an action and observing someone else perform it, plays a crucial role in empathy and understanding others' intentions. It's plausible that Indigo, Crystal, and Rainbow children possess a more robust or differently organized mirror neuron system, leading to their reported heightened empathy and intuitive understanding of others' emotions. Studies have shown correlations between mirror neuron system activity and autistic traits, a condition often associated with heightened sensitivity and empathy, although expressed differently than in the narratives surrounding these child types. Further research exploring the functional connectivity of the mirror neuron system in individuals identified as belonging to these groups could provide valuable insights. Functional magnetic resonance imaging (fMRI) could be used to map brain activity during empathy tasks, comparing these individuals to neurotypical controls. Electroencephalography (EEG) might also offer insights into the temporal dynamics of brain responses during social interactions.

Another area warranting investigation is the default mode network (DMN). The DMN is a collection of brain regions active during rest, involved in self-referential thought, mind-wandering, and introspection. Some researchers suggest that individuals with heightened intuition or psychic abilities might exhibit atypical DMN activity, potentially leading to enhanced access to unconscious information or altered states of consciousness. Individuals reporting strong intuitive insights might show altered connectivity patterns within the DMN or increased activity in brain regions associated with creativity and insight generation, such as the anterior cingulate cortex (ACC) and the anterior prefrontal cortex (aPFC). Again, fMRI studies could be crucial in comparing DMN activity and connectivity in these individuals to control groups. Additionally, exploring correlations between DMN activity and specific abilities reported, such as precognitive experiences or clairsentience, would enrich our understanding.

The limbic system, crucial for processing emotions, is another potential area of focus. The heightened emotional sensitivity reported in these children suggests possible differences in limbic system function or connectivity. The amygdala, responsible for processing fear and other intense emotions, might exhibit heightened reactivity or different connectivity patterns. This could explain the reported sensitivity to environmental stimuli and overwhelming sensations. Similarly, the hippocampus, crucial for memory consolidation, might play a role in the reported heightened intuitive insights, as these experiences could involve accessing and integrating information from various sources subconsciously. Research investigating the structure and function of the amygdala and hippocampus using MRI and EEG in individuals described as Indigo, Crystal, or Rainbow children, compared with controls, could yield valuable data.

Furthermore, research should explore potential genetic or epigenetic factors that might contribute to these purported differences. While the concept of "Indigo," "Crystal," and "Rainbow" children lacks rigorous scientific definition, the characteristics associated with these labels point towards potential neurodevelopmental variations. It's possible that specific gene variants or epigenetic modifications might influence brain development and lead to altered neural circuitry, resulting in the heightened sensitivities and intuitive abilities frequently reported. Genome-wide association studies (GWAS) could be utilized to identify potential genetic markers associated with these traits. Epigenetic studies could explore environmental influences on gene expression that might contribute to the development of these purported abilities. Such investigations require large, well-defined cohorts and rigorous methodological approaches to control for confounding factors.

Beyond specific brain regions, the overall brain connectivity, or "connectome," could play a significant role. A more integrated or efficient connectome might allow for faster information processing and enhanced integration of diverse sensory inputs, potentially contributing to intuitive insights. Advanced neuroimaging techniques such as diffusion tensor imaging (DTI) can map white matter tracts, revealing connectivity patterns within the brain. Comparing the connectomes of individuals identified with these labels to those of neurotypical individuals could reveal important differences in brain organization. Furthermore, research could explore the relationship between connectome features and specific abilities.

It's crucial to acknowledge the methodological challenges in researching these claims. The lack of standardized definitions and diagnostic criteria for Indigo, Crystal, and Rainbow children presents significant hurdles. The reliance on anecdotal evidence and self-reporting poses considerable limitations on the validity and reliability of the data. Future research requires carefully defined criteria for identifying individuals belonging to these groups, utilizing objective measures and standardized assessments of purported abilities. Researchers must also carefully consider potential confounding factors, such as pre-existing mental health conditions, and employ rigorous control groups to rule out alternative explanations for observed differences.

The exploration of these neurological correlates should not be perceived as an attempt to dismiss or pathologize the experiences reported by individuals identified as Indigo, Crystal, or Rainbow children. Instead, it's an attempt to understand the neurobiological basis of human experience, acknowledging the vast spectrum of human potential. A neurodiversity perspective allows for a more inclusive and compassionate approach to understanding these phenomena, recognizing the unique contributions of individuals with different cognitive profiles. It challenges us to move beyond simple dichotomies of "normal" versus "abnormal," embracing the full range of human variation and celebrating the diversity of human consciousness. By employing rigorous scientific methods alongside a respectful and open-minded approach, we can enhance our understanding of these phenomena, potentially unlocking new therapeutic interventions and educational strategies that support individuals with exceptional abilities and sensitivities. This approach aims to empower these individuals, fostering their strengths and helping them navigate the world with confidence and self-awareness. The ultimate goal is not to "prove" or "disprove" the existence of these purported abilities but to understand the intricacies of the human brain and its astounding capacity for diverse experiences. The integration of scientific investigation with a holistic understanding of human consciousness promises to yield invaluable insights into the very nature of being human.

The widespread acceptance of the Indigo, Crystal, and Rainbow Children concepts within certain sociocultural circles underscores their profound impact on individual identities and societal perceptions of difference. These labels, while lacking rigorous scientific validation, provide a framework for understanding and embracing unique experiences, particularly among those who feel marginalized or misunderstood within traditional societal structures. The self-identification with these groups fosters a sense of community and belonging, offering support networks and a shared understanding of often-challenging life experiences.

Online communities and support groups dedicated to these concepts thrive, facilitating connection and mutual support among individuals who resonate with the associated traits and characteristics. This sense of community is crucial, providing a space for validation, understanding, and the sharing of strategies for navigating a world that may not always accommodate their sensitivities and perceived differences.

However, the social and cultural significance of these concepts extends beyond the individuals who identify with them. The very existence of these labels challenges established norms and expectations regarding human development and potential. The emphasis on heightened intuition, empathy, and spiritual awareness encourages a reevaluation of traditional measures of intelligence and success. This shift in perspective can promote greater inclusivity and acceptance of neurodiversity more broadly. By acknowledging the validity of diverse cognitive styles and experiences, we can create a society that values and supports individuals across the spectrum of human potential. This paradigm shift also necessitates a reassessment of educational systems and workplaces, urging them to adapt and accommodate the unique needs and talents of individuals who identify as Indigo, Crystal, or Rainbow children. The inherent challenges they may face – heightened sensitivity to stimuli, difficulty with conformity, and a strong internal compass often at odds with societal expectations – require innovative solutions within the educational and professional contexts.

Furthermore, the focus on spiritual development and connection often associated with these concepts contributes to a broader cultural shift towards mindfulness, self-awareness, and holistic well-being. This emphasis on inner growth and spiritual evolution resonates with a growing segment of the population seeking meaning and purpose beyond material success. The integration of spiritual practices and alternative healing modalities into mainstream culture, fueled in part by the popularity of these concepts, reflects a growing interest in holistic approaches to health and well-being. This trend has the potential to create a more compassionate and empathetic society, one that values individual spiritual journeys and encourages the exploration of inner consciousness. However, this increased focus on spiritual concepts also requires critical engagement. It's crucial to distinguish between responsible spiritual exploration and potentially exploitative practices, ensuring that individuals are empowered to make informed choices based on their own values and beliefs. The rise of spiritual communities surrounding these concepts provides fertile ground for both supportive and problematic practices. It's vital to critically evaluate the information and guidance offered within such communities, ensuring alignment with ethical and evidence-based principles.

The potential for misunderstanding and misinterpretation is significant. The lack of standardized criteria for identifying Indigo, Crystal, and Rainbow children makes accurate classification challenging, leading to potential misdiagnosis and the inappropriate application of labels. This can be particularly problematic if it leads to the stigmatization of individuals who may exhibit behaviors traditionally associated with mental health conditions. Careful differentiation between genuine neurodiversity and potential underlying mental health issues is crucial. A holistic approach, one that integrates psychological evaluation with an understanding of neurodiversity, is vital in providing accurate assessments and appropriate support. Collaboration between mental health professionals, educators, and spiritual advisors could be incredibly valuable in ensuring that individuals receive the appropriate care and guidance.

The economic implications of these concepts are also worth exploring. The growing interest in holistic healing modalities, influenced in part by the beliefs surrounding Indigo, Crystal, and Rainbow children, has created new markets for alternative therapies, spiritual coaching, and related products and services. This burgeoning market necessitates careful monitoring and regulation to protect consumers from potentially exploitative or ineffective practices. The economic opportunities are undeniably present, offering pathways for entrepreneurs and practitioners in the fields of spiritual guidance, holistic health, and alternative therapies. However, responsible development of this market requires ethical standards and consumer protection measures to prevent fraudulent or harmful practices. The potential for both benefit and harm emphasizes the need for a thoughtful and balanced approach to the development and regulation of this economic sector.

Beyond the economic implications, the social narratives surrounding these concepts shape personal identities, community building, and societal perceptions of difference. The emphasis on inherent gifts and unique abilities fosters self-acceptance and empowerment, allowing individuals to embrace their strengths and navigate their challenges with greater confidence. The narrative itself, however, needs critical assessment. While empowerment and self-acceptance are valuable, the emphasis on inherent giftedness can potentially lead to the neglect of appropriate support systems for individuals facing genuine difficulties. The narrative needs to balance the positive aspects of self-discovery and empowerment with the realistic acknowledgment of potential struggles and the need for proper mental health support when necessary.

The evolution of the Indigo, Crystal, and Rainbow Children concepts is a fascinating example of how societal beliefs, spiritual practices, and scientific understanding can interact and influence each other. These concepts challenge us to broaden our understanding of human potential, fostering a more inclusive and accepting society that celebrates neurodiversity in all its forms. However, this requires a responsible and critical approach, one that integrates scientific investigation with a holistic understanding of human experience. Through thoughtful consideration of the social, cultural, and economic implications of these concepts, we can harness their positive potential while mitigating potential risks and ensuring the well-being of all individuals. A deeper understanding of the underlying neurological and psychological factors, combined with respectful engagement with the lived experiences of individuals who identify with these concepts, is crucial for a balanced and ethical approach. The journey to fully understand and appreciate the social and cultural significance of these phenomena is an ongoing process, one that requires constant critical engagement and a commitment to fostering a more inclusive and compassionate society. This process is inherently complex, requiring ongoing dialogue and collaboration between diverse stakeholders, including scientists, mental health professionals, spiritual leaders, educators, and most importantly, the individuals who identify as Indigo, Crystal, and Rainbow children themselves. Their lived experiences and perspectives are fundamental to shaping a truly inclusive and respectful understanding of these complex phenomena.

The current understanding of Indigo, Crystal, and Rainbow Children, while rich in anecdotal evidence and personal testimonials, remains significantly limited by a lack of rigorous empirical research. The very definition of these groups is fluid and lacks standardized criteria, making objective scientific study challenging. Many individuals self-identify based on perceived intuitive abilities, heightened sensitivities, or a strong spiritual connection, often lacking concrete, measurable indicators. This inherent subjectivity poses a significant hurdle for researchers attempting to establish reliable methodologies and statistical analyses. Furthermore, the diverse and often overlapping characteristics associated with these labels make it difficult to isolate specific traits for study. One individual might emphasize empathy and emotional sensitivity, another might focus on creative expression or heightened intuition, while a third might highlight a deep connection to nature and environmental concerns. This heterogeneity complicates the development of cohesive research protocols and the interpretation of findings.

One promising avenue for future research involves utilizing advanced neuroimaging techniques like fMRI and EEG to investigate potential neurological correlates associated with the purported abilities of these groups. For instance, studies could explore variations in brain activity patterns during tasks requiring heightened empathy, intuitive insight, or creative problem-solving. Comparing brain activity in individuals who self-identify as Indigo, Crystal, or Rainbow Children with control groups could reveal potential differences in brain structure, function, or connectivity. This approach would need to carefully consider the self-selection bias inherent in such studies and employ rigorous control measures to mitigate confounding factors. A longitudinal study following these individuals from childhood to adulthood could further illuminate potential developmental trajectories and the evolution of their reported abilities.

Another critical area for future research lies in exploring the genetic and epigenetic factors that may contribute to the development of the unique traits associated with these groups. Genome-wide association studies (GWAS) could identify potential genetic variants linked to enhanced empathy, intuition, or other relevant characteristics. Epigenetic analysis could investigate how environmental factors, such as early childhood experiences or exposure to specific stressors, may influence gene expression and potentially contribute to the development of these abilities. Such research should prioritize ethical considerations, particularly regarding informed consent and data privacy, especially given the sensitive nature of the subject matter.

Beyond neuroimaging and genetic studies, psychological assessments can provide valuable insights into the cognitive and emotional profiles of individuals who identify with these groups. Standardized tests measuring empathy, creativity, sensory sensitivity, and spiritual experiences could help to delineate the range of characteristics and their interrelationships. Qualitative research methods, such as in-depth interviews and narrative inquiry, can provide rich, nuanced data about the lived experiences of these individuals, offering valuable contextual information to complement quantitative findings.

The challenge lies in developing a research paradigm that integrates quantitative and qualitative approaches, acknowledging the limitations of both while leveraging their respective strengths. A mixed-methods approach could help to overcome the limitations of relying solely on objective measurements or subjective accounts. By combining neuroimaging data with psychological assessments and qualitative narratives, researchers can develop a more holistic and nuanced understanding of the phenomenon.

Furthermore, interdisciplinary collaboration is essential for advancing the field. Integrating the expertise of neuroscientists, psychologists, geneticists, anthropologists, sociologists, and spiritual practitioners can offer a multi-faceted perspective that transcends disciplinary boundaries. Such collaborations can facilitate the development of research designs that address the complex interplay of biological, psychological, social, and spiritual factors.

It's important to acknowledge the potential for bias and misinterpretation in this area of research. The very nature of exploring "psychic abilities" or "spiritual sensitivities" can attract individuals with pre-existing beliefs, potentially influencing both self-reporting and interpretation of results. Rigorous methodological approaches, including blind studies and placebo-controlled designs, are crucial to minimizing these biases. Careful consideration of the social context and cultural beliefs surrounding these phenomena is also vital to prevent the perpetuation of inaccurate or misleading information.

Addressing ethical considerations is paramount throughout this research. Protecting the privacy and well-being of participants is crucial, particularly given the potential stigma associated with claims of paranormal abilities or unusual sensitivities. Researchers must adhere to stringent ethical guidelines, ensuring informed consent, data confidentiality, and the avoidance of any potentially harmful or exploitative practices. Transparency in research methods and findings is also crucial to build public trust and prevent the dissemination of unsubstantiated claims.

The potential benefits of this research extend beyond simply understanding Indigo, Crystal, and Rainbow Children. A deeper understanding of the neurological and psychological mechanisms underlying their reported abilities could have significant implications for various fields. For instance, understanding heightened empathy could inform the development of improved therapeutic interventions for social anxiety or autism spectrum disorder. Research on intuitive abilities could contribute to advancements in decision-making processes in fields such as medicine or finance. Insights into heightened sensory sensitivity could lead to improvements in assistive technologies for individuals with sensory processing disorders.

The investigation into the potential links between neurodiversity and psychic abilities requires a cautious yet open-minded approach. By acknowledging the limitations of current research while embracing innovative methodologies and interdisciplinary collaborations, we can move closer to a more comprehensive understanding of these fascinating phenomena. Ultimately, this research holds the potential to revolutionize our understanding of human consciousness and expand our appreciation for the diverse spectrum of human potential.

The pursuit of empirical evidence in this domain is not simply about validating or debunking claims of paranormal abilities; it's about understanding the complex interplay of neurobiology, psychology, and social factors that contribute to individual differences. It's about acknowledging and respecting the subjective experiences of individuals who identify with these concepts, while simultaneously employing rigorous scientific methods to investigate the underlying mechanisms. This requires a careful balancing act, one that recognizes the limitations of reductionist scientific approaches while simultaneously rejecting unsubstantiated claims. The goal is not to reduce complex human experiences to simplistic biological explanations, but to weave together biological, psychological, and social perspectives into a rich, nuanced tapestry that reflects the full spectrum of human experience.

Ultimately, the study of Indigo, Crystal, and Rainbow Children offers a unique opportunity to advance our understanding of the human brain and consciousness. By embracing a holistic and interdisciplinary approach, we can unlock valuable insights into the nature of human potential and foster a more inclusive and accepting society that celebrates neurodiversity in all its forms. This endeavor requires a commitment to rigorous scientific inquiry, coupled with a compassionate understanding of the lived experiences of individuals who identify with these concepts. The path forward is not a simple one, but the potential rewards are immense, offering the prospect of transforming our understanding of human potential and fostering a more equitable and compassionate world. The journey is one of exploration, discovery, and ultimately, a deeper appreciation for the remarkable diversity of the human spirit. The integration of rigorous scientific methodologies with a respectful and sensitive approach to the lived experiences of individuals who identify with these concepts is vital to ensure that this research is both ethically sound and intellectually robust. Only through this careful and nuanced approach can we hope to unlock the full potential of this fascinating area of investigation.

CHAPTER 5: STARSEEDS AND LIGHTWORKERS: SPIRITUAL AND NEUROLOGICAL ASPECTS

The terms "Starseed" and "Lightworker" have gained significant traction within New Age spirituality, representing individuals believed to possess unique spiritual gifts and a profound connection to the cosmos. While lacking rigorous scientific definition, these concepts offer a compelling lens through which to explore the intersection of spirituality, psychology, and potentially, neurodiversity. Understanding these terms requires approaching them with both an open mind and a critical eye, acknowledging the limitations of current scientific methodologies in addressing such intangible concepts.

From a spiritual perspective, Starseeds are often described as souls originating from other star systems or dimensions, incarnated on Earth to fulfill specific missions or contribute to planetary evolution. Their purported abilities frequently include heightened intuition, empathy, psychic sensitivity, and a strong sense of purpose beyond the confines of conventional societal norms. They are believed to carry advanced spiritual knowledge and possess the capacity to facilitate positive change in the world. This perspective often draws upon ancient spiritual traditions, channeling, and various forms of metaphysical practices. The belief in Starseeds stems from a holistic view of consciousness, suggesting that our physical existence is not limited to our terrestrial origins. It acknowledges the possibility of transdimensional travel of consciousness and reincarnation across different planes of existence. This worldview challenges traditional scientific narratives that center on purely materialistic explanations for human origins and capabilities.

Lightworkers, while sometimes used interchangeably with Starseeds, are often portrayed as individuals driven by a deep-seated desire to serve humanity and bring light and healing to the world. They may or may not identify as Starseeds, but their core purpose centers on compassion, altruism, and contributing to collective well-being. Lightworkers often engage in various forms of healing and spiritual work, such as energy healing, channeling, meditation, or simply embodying kindness and empathy in their daily interactions. Their actions are motivated by a profound spiritual calling, often accompanied by a strong intuitive sense that guides their path. This intuitive guidance, though subjective, aligns with the broader neurological investigation into intuition and its potential correlation with unusual brain activity. While currently lacking empirical validation, the intuitive insights of Lightworkers warrant further neuroscientific investigation to determine their potential neurological underpinnings.

The overlap between Starseeds and Lightworkers highlights

the blurred boundaries between spiritual belief and lived experience. Many individuals identify with both terms, suggesting a common thread of spiritual purpose and exceptional abilities. This shared experience points toward a potential area of research examining the psychological and neurobiological correlates of such self-identification. Further study might explore the possibility of certain personality traits, cognitive styles, or even genetic predispositions that predispose individuals to perceive themselves as Starseeds or Lightworkers. Such an investigation could utilize established psychological assessments, including personality inventories, and potentially neuroimaging techniques to assess brain activity patterns in individuals who strongly identify with these terms. Moreover, the study could explore potential correlations with existing neurodevelopmental conditions, such as autism, which often presents with exceptional abilities in specific areas.

Spiritual practices often associated with Starseeds and Lightworkers, such as meditation, energy work, and channeling, have also been shown to have measurable effects on brain function. Neuroimaging studies have documented altered states of consciousness during meditation, including changes in brainwave patterns and activation of specific brain regions. These findings suggest the potential for such practices to enhance cognitive abilities, improve emotional regulation, and promote overall well-being. This further supports the notion that the purported abilities of Starseeds and Lightworkers may be, at least partially, cultivated through sustained spiritual practices that shape brain plasticity and enhance neuronal pathways associated with heightened awareness, intuition, and empathy. The placebo effect, while not always fully understood, also plays a role, underscoring the potent influence of belief and intention on both subjective experience and physiological responses.

The role of belief and intention in shaping the experiences of Starseeds and Lightworkers cannot be overstated. The belief in one's spiritual purpose, coupled with a strong intention to manifest positive change, may profoundly influence perception, behavior, and even physiological responses. This is consistent with the growing body of research on the mind-body connection, which demonstrates the significant impact of mental states on physical health. The power of belief and intention aligns with the concept of neuroplasticity, suggesting that our beliefs and intentions can actively shape brain structure and function over time, strengthening certain neural pathways and weakening others. This dynamic interplay between belief, intention, and neurological plasticity offers a plausible explanation for some of the seemingly exceptional abilities associated with Starseeds and Lightworkers. It indicates that belief systems and spiritual practices may not merely be passive elements of personal identity, but actively shape brain structure, leading to noticeable shifts in cognitive abilities and perceptions.

Integrating spiritual and scientific perspectives on Starseeds and Lightworkers requires a paradigm shift that embraces complexity and acknowledges the limitations of current scientific methodologies. While empirical evidence for many of the claims associated with these concepts remains limited, the potential for interdisciplinary collaboration presents an exciting opportunity to deepen our understanding of consciousness, human potential, and the brain-mind relationship. Approaching these phenomena with scientific rigor while remaining open to the possibility of non-ordinary experiences could lead to significant breakthroughs in neuroscience and our understanding of human consciousness. This integrated approach would recognize the importance of subjective experiences alongside objective data, ultimately fostering a richer and more inclusive understanding of human diversity.

To foster such an approach, rigorous research is needed that employs a combination of quantitative and qualitative methodologies. This would involve employing neuroimaging techniques, genetic analysis, psychological testing, and detailed qualitative interviews with individuals who self-identify as Starseeds or Lightworkers. Such research would require careful consideration of ethical implications and the potential for bias, ensuring the responsible collection and interpretation of data. The ultimate goal of such research should be to develop a nuanced and holistic understanding of these phenomena, rather than seeking to definitively prove or disprove the existence of Starseeds or Lightworkers. The focus should be on exploring the underlying psychological, neurological, and spiritual factors contributing to the experiences and perceived abilities of these individuals.

In conclusion, the concepts of Starseeds and Lightworkers, while steeped in spiritual belief, offer a fascinating window into the potential limits of human consciousness and the possibility of exceptional abilities. By bridging the gap between spiritual and scientific perspectives, we can embark on a journey of discovery that may reshape our understanding of the brain, human potential, and our place in the cosmos. The exploration of these concepts requires a paradigm shift that embraces both scientific rigor and a profound respect for the richness and complexity of human experience. The future of neuroscience and parapsychology likely lies in fostering collaborative inquiry that values both subjective and objective perspectives, moving beyond simplistic categorizations to embrace the complexities of human consciousness.

The categorization of individuals as Starseeds or Lightworkers often rests on a collection of overlapping characteristics, making definitive distinctions challenging. However, recurring themes emerge within the anecdotal accounts and personal testimonies that populate New Age literature and online forums. These common threads, while lacking the rigor of scientific validation, provide valuable insight into the perceived nature of these groups and their purported abilities.

One frequently cited characteristic is a profound sense of "otherness," a feeling of not quite belonging to the mainstream human experience. Many individuals identifying as Starseeds or Lightworkers describe experiencing a deep-seated feeling of being different from their peers, often from a very young age. This sense of alienation may manifest as a difficulty in fitting in socially, a resistance to societal norms, and a persistent feeling of being misunderstood. This "otherness" isn't necessarily negative; rather, it's often described as an intrinsic part of their unique spiritual journey, a testament to their distinct connection to the cosmos. This perceived difference may be a crucial factor in their later development of perceived psychic abilities or spiritual awareness. Furthermore, this feeling of otherness could be interpreted, through a neurodiversity lens, as an expression of atypical neurological processing, leading to unconventional perspectives and experiences. Future research might explore whether particular genetic markers or neurological variations correlate with this strong sense of difference reported by many individuals within these groups.

Another shared trait is a heightened sensitivity to energy, both physical and emotional. This heightened sensitivity, often described as "empathy" amplified to an almost overwhelming degree, allows them to perceive and absorb the emotions and energies of others with exceptional clarity. This can manifest as an almost psychic ability to sense the emotional state of people around them, even from a distance. In some cases, this sensitivity extends beyond human emotions to encompass the energy fields of the environment itself, leading to experiences of sensing imbalances in nature or identifying areas of energetic stagnation. The neurobiological correlates of such heightened sensitivity remain largely unexplored. It might involve heightened activity in brain regions associated with emotional processing, such as the amygdala and insula, or unique patterns of neural connectivity that allow for more efficient transmission of emotional information.

Intensely vivid dreams and heightened intuition are frequently reported characteristics. These individuals often describe experiencing remarkably vivid and often symbolic dreams that seem to hold deeper meanings or prophetic insights. This enhanced dream recall and interpretation could be linked to increased activity in the hippocampus, the brain region crucial for memory consolidation and spatial navigation. The intuition reported often manifests as a gut feeling, a sudden insight, or a strong sense of knowing without conscious reasoning. This might be correlated with increased activity in the anterior cingulate cortex, a brain region involved in decision-making and error monitoring. It's plausible that such individuals possess a more efficient or sensitive access to their intuition circuitry. Further investigation is needed to confirm these neurobiological speculations and explore potential genetic influences.

Beyond these shared personality traits, a variety of purported psychic abilities are frequently associated with Starseeds and Lightworkers. These abilities range from clairvoyance (seeing beyond the ordinary senses) and clairsentience (feeling the emotions or energies of others or distant locations) to precognition (seeing or knowing future events) and telepathy (communicating without verbal means). These claims often rest on personal experiences and anecdotal evidence, and require rigorous investigation, employing both subjective and objective methodologies. For example, the heightened sensitivity previously discussed might, in part, explain some of these experiences. An individual acutely sensitive to subtle energetic shifts might interpret them as precognitive flashes or telepathic communication, whereas a scientifically grounded approach might seek to identify underlying physical or environmental factors. The boundary between extraordinary perception and psychological phenomena is blurry, requiring careful consideration.

The purported spiritual abilities frequently overlap with psychic experiences. Many individuals claim abilities to channel spiritual energy, heal others through energy work, or perform various forms of spiritual guidance or mentorship. These spiritual practices often complement their psychic skills, creating a holistic approach to their interaction with the world. The neurobiological basis for such practices remains a subject of ongoing debate. While it's challenging to isolate and test these abilities with rigorous scientific methods, functional neuroimaging techniques like fMRI and EEG could potentially provide insight into brain activity patterns associated with meditation, energy healing, or other similar practices.

Further complicating the picture, some individuals within these groups report experiences that align with features of certain neurodevelopmental conditions. This is not to suggest that Starseeds and Lightworkers suffer from mental illness, but rather, to highlight the potential for overlap in the experience of heightened sensory sensitivity, atypical social interactions, and profound emotional depth. Conditions like autism spectrum disorder (ASD) and sensory processing sensitivity (SPS) often exhibit these characteristics. While these conditions are generally considered neurodevelopmental differences rather than paranormal abilities, their shared traits with purported Starseed and Lightworker characteristics warrant further exploration, particularly concerning potential genetic or epigenetic influences.

A holistic approach is crucial in exploring the connection between Starseeds, Lightworkers, neurodiversity, and psychic abilities. This necessitates moving beyond simplistic dichotomies of "normal" versus "paranormal," embracing the complexity and diversity of human experience. The goal should not be to dismiss or pathologize these unique experiences, but rather to understand the underlying neurological and psychological mechanisms involved, acknowledging the role of both genetic predisposition and environmental influences. This interdisciplinary research, incorporating neuroscience, parapsychology, and spiritual perspectives, promises to advance our understanding of the human brain and its vast, still largely unexplored potential. The future likely lies in collaborative research that integrates subjective experiences with objective scientific methodologies, aiming for a more comprehensive understanding of consciousness and the spectrum of human experience, embracing neurodiversity as a source of both human potential and unique spiritual insight. A nuanced exploration must also consider the potential impact of cultural and societal expectations, recognizing that the perception and interpretation of these experiences are deeply intertwined with the individual's beliefs, background, and social context. The inherent subjectivity of these experiences further highlights the need for diverse methodological approaches, incorporating both qualitative and quantitative methods to achieve a comprehensive understanding of this fascinating phenomenon. Ultimately, a respectful and inclusive approach, valuing individual experiences without discarding scientific rigor, will pave the way toward a deeper comprehension of the human mind, its complexities, and its capacity for both extraordinary abilities and profound spiritual insight.

The exploration of Starseeds and Lightworkers necessitates a deeper dive into the potential neurological effects of their associated spiritual practices. While scientific research on these phenomena remains limited, anecdotal evidence and personal testimonies suggest a correlation between specific practices and altered states of consciousness, potentially linked to enhanced cognitive abilities or unique neurological pathways. Meditation, a cornerstone of many spiritual traditions embraced by these groups, offers a compelling entry point for investigation. Numerous studies have demonstrated the profound impact of meditation on brain structure and function. Long-term practitioners often exhibit increased grey matter density in regions associated with attention, self-awareness, and emotional regulation, such as the prefrontal cortex and anterior cingulate cortex. These changes are not merely structural; functional magnetic resonance imaging (fMRI) studies reveal alterations in brainwave patterns, indicating shifts in cognitive processing and state of consciousness. For example, increased alpha and theta wave activity is often observed, indicative of relaxed yet focused states conducive to heightened intuition and creativity, qualities frequently associated with Starseeds and Lightworkers.

Furthermore, the practice of mindfulness, often intertwined with meditation, enhances the ability to focus attention and regulate emotions. This heightened awareness of internal states could potentially explain some of the reported psychic abilities, such as clairsentience (clear feeling) where individuals perceive the emotions or energy of others. The capacity to finely tune one's sensory perception, sharpened by mindful awareness, might heighten sensitivity to subtle energetic cues often overlooked by individuals less attuned to their internal and external environments. This amplified sensitivity could provide a neurological substrate for seemingly paranormal experiences, suggesting that psychic abilities might not be so much a departure from neurotypical function but rather an amplification or refinement of existing sensory and cognitive processes.

Beyond meditation, other spiritual practices favored by Starseeds and Lightworkers, such as energy healing and channeling, present fascinating avenues for neuroscientific inquiry. Energy healing techniques, which often involve the manipulation of purported energy fields around the body, might influence physiological processes through subtle yet significant neurological mechanisms. While the existence of these energy fields remains scientifically unproven, the act of performing energy healing, whether or not it achieves the purported goal, induces a state of focused attention and intentionality, potentially leading to neurological changes. The practitioner's focused intent and the recipient's receptive state could trigger the release of endorphins and other neurochemicals, creating a therapeutic effect that's independent of the validity of the underlying energy model.

Channeling, a practice where individuals claim to receive information from higher consciousnesses or spiritual entities, presents a more complex challenge to neuroscientific investigation. The altered states of consciousness associated with channeling could involve unusual neural activity patterns, potentially similar to those observed in deep meditation or during hypnogogic states. However, separating genuine channeling experiences from psychological factors like suggestion, imagination, or dissociation is crucial. A rigorous investigation requires careful consideration of methodological challenges and the potential role of cultural and social influences in shaping the reported experiences.

While the scientific community remains cautious about accepting anecdotal accounts at face value, the convergence of personal narratives with the growing body of knowledge on neuroplasticity offers intriguing possibilities. The brain's remarkable ability to restructure itself in response to experience suggests that consistent engagement in spiritual practices could indeed reshape neural pathways, enhancing specific cognitive functions and potentially creating a neurological architecture conducive to extraordinary experiences. This underscores the critical need for carefully designed, rigorous studies integrating both qualitative and quantitative methods to explore the correlations between spiritual practices and neurological changes in individuals who identify as Starseeds and Lightworkers.

Moreover, the study of near-death experiences (NDEs) offers

valuable insights into altered states of consciousness with possible parallels to the experiences reported by Starseeds and Lightworkers. NDEs frequently involve intense feelings of peace, euphoria, out-of-body experiences, and encounters with deceased loved ones. These experiences often report heightened sensory perceptions and a sense of unity with the universe, which mirror some of the claims made by individuals associated with these groups. Research on NDEs has revealed some interesting neurological correlations, including changes in brainwave patterns and the potential release of neurochemicals such as endorphins and DMT. Although the exact mechanisms underlying NDEs remain unclear, the exploration of such experiences can inform our understanding of the brain's capacity for generating extraordinary states of awareness.

Furthermore, the study of altered states of consciousness in general, including those induced by meditation, psychedelics, and other practices, can contribute to a broader understanding of the neural correlates of spiritual experiences. Research suggests that these altered states often involve the temporary deactivation of certain brain regions involved in ego-centric processing and self-referential thought. This can lead to a sense of interconnectedness, enhanced empathy, and altered perception of time and space – themes that are common across many spiritual practices and resonate deeply within the self-descriptions of Starseeds and Lightworkers.

The investigation of these phenomena needs to move beyond reductionist approaches. Dismissing the lived experiences of individuals who identify as Starseeds and Lightworkers as mere delusion or psychosomatic phenomena risks neglecting valuable insights into the multifaceted nature of consciousness. Instead, a more holistic perspective is required, integrating insights from neuroscience, parapsychology, spiritual traditions, and personal accounts to create a comprehensive understanding. This calls for a collaborative effort involving researchers from various disciplines, who can combine rigorous scientific methodologies with a deep respect for the subjective experiences of individuals.

A key challenge in this field is the establishment of robust, measurable parameters to assess the purported abilities of Starseeds and Lightworkers. While subjective accounts provide invaluable qualitative data, they are insufficient on their own. We need to develop objective measures that can capture the subtle neurological and physiological changes associated with their reported experiences. This might involve advanced neuroimaging techniques, detailed physiological monitoring, and the development of standardized psychological tests designed to assess specific abilities like enhanced intuition or sensitivity to subtle energy fields.

Ultimately, the integration of scientific rigor and spiritual perspectives is paramount. Scientific inquiry needs to be open to the possibility of experiences that lie outside the conventional boundaries of scientific understanding. Simultaneously, spiritual practices and beliefs need to be approached with a critical lens, acknowledging the influence of cultural and social factors on individual experiences. By embracing both the empirical and the experiential, we can pave the way for a deeper and more nuanced understanding of Starseeds, Lightworkers, and the vast spectrum of human consciousness, potentially unlocking new avenues for personal growth, healing, and social transformation. This holistic approach may reveal that what we currently perceive as extraordinary or paranormal may simply represent an extension of human capabilities, waiting to be discovered and understood. The future of this research may lie in integrating these seemingly disparate fields, bridging the gap between science and spirituality, and fostering a deeper understanding of the remarkable potential within each human being. The implications extend beyond a simple understanding of neurodiversity; it opens the door to a wider exploration of consciousness and the potential for positive societal impact that comes from embracing and understanding these diverse facets of human experience.

The power of belief, particularly within the context of Starseeds and Lightworkers, is a fascinating and often overlooked aspect of their reported experiences. The very act of believing oneself to be a Starseed, imbued with specific abilities and a unique spiritual mission, can profoundly shape one's perception and behavior. This isn't merely a matter of self-deception; it's a powerful self-fulfilling prophecy, influencing not only subjective experiences but also potentially impacting neurological processes. The expectation of heightened intuition, for instance, might lead to increased attentiveness to subtle cues and patterns that would otherwise go unnoticed. This heightened awareness could then be interpreted as confirmation of their inherent abilities, creating a positive feedback loop that reinforces the belief system.

Consider the placebo effect, a well-documented phenomenon in medicine, where a person's belief in a treatment's efficacy can lead to genuine physiological changes. While often studied in the context of pharmaceutical interventions, the placebo effect highlights the profound influence of the mind on the body. Similarly, the belief in one's spiritual gifts, in the context of Starseed or Lightworker identities, could trigger similar neurobiological mechanisms. This belief might activate neural pathways associated with enhanced creativity, empathy, or intuitive insights. The expectation of such abilities could lead to increased engagement in practices that foster these qualities, such as meditation, mindfulness, and intuitive exercises, further reinforcing the neural pathways involved.

Intention, closely intertwined with belief, plays a crucial role in shaping experiences within this context. The conscious and deliberate focusing of one's mind – setting an intention – can influence not only personal outcomes but potentially those of others as well. This aligns with the concepts of intentionality in quantum physics, where the observer's role in shaping reality is emphasized. While the precise neurological mechanisms remain largely unknown, studies on focused intention and its effects on various physiological processes, including healing and remote influence, suggest potential correlations.

For example, research on focused intention healing has explored the possibility of influencing the healing process through focused mental intention. While results have been mixed and require further rigorous investigation, some studies suggest that directed mental intention can positively impact the physiological responses associated with healing. Similarly, research into the concept of remote influence, often explored in parapsychological studies, investigates the potential of mentally influencing distant objects or events. These studies, though often subject to skepticism, highlight the potential for focused intention to impact reality in ways that challenge conventional scientific understanding.

This isn't to suggest that belief and intention are the sole determinants of psychic experiences. Genetics, epigenetic factors, and environmental influences undoubtedly play significant roles. However, the interplay between belief, intention, and neurobiology warrants further exploration. It's plausible that individuals who identify as Starseeds or Lightworkers possess a predisposition towards certain neurocognitive profiles that makes them more susceptible to the influence of belief and intention. This could include heightened sensitivity to subtle energy fields, enhanced capacity for empathy, and an inherent inclination towards spiritual practices that reinforce these abilities.

One avenue for future research could involve comparing neurocognitive profiles of individuals who self-identify as Starseeds or Lightworkers with those of a control group. This comparison could investigate potential differences in brain structure, function, and neurochemical profiles. Advanced neuroimaging techniques, such as fMRI and EEG, could help identify neural correlates of specific spiritual practices employed by these individuals, potentially revealing unique patterns of brain activity associated with their purported abilities.

Furthermore, exploring the potential interaction between belief and epigenetic mechanisms could provide valuable insights. Epigenetics refers to heritable changes in gene expression that don't involve alterations to the underlying DNA sequence. Growing evidence suggests that environmental factors, including mental states and beliefs, can influence epigenetic modifications, thereby impacting gene expression and, potentially, biological functions.

THE NEURODIVERSITY OF CONSCIOUSNESS

Therefore, investigating whether specific beliefs or practices associated with Starseeds and Lightworkers lead to epigenetic changes could shed light on the biological mechanisms underlying their reported experiences.

The integration of qualitative data, such as personal testimonies and anecdotal evidence, with quantitative data obtained from neuroimaging and genetic studies is crucial. While anecdotal accounts may lack the rigor of controlled scientific experiments, they provide valuable insights into subjective experiences and the lived realities of individuals who self-identify as Starseeds or Lightworkers. Combining these qualitative narratives with rigorous quantitative studies could provide a richer and more complete understanding of the phenomenon.

The role of cultural and social factors should not be overlooked. The rise in popularity of the Starseed and Lightworker concepts is partly linked to New Age spiritual beliefs and cultural trends. This means the self-identification as a Starseed or Lightworker might be influenced by social reinforcement and cultural narratives, shaping both beliefs and perceived abilities. Differentiating between genuine psychic abilities and socially constructed identities requires a nuanced approach, incorporating sociological and anthropological perspectives alongside neurobiological and parapsychological ones.

The potential ethical implications of this line of research are equally important. Promoting a scientific understanding of Starseed and Lightworker experiences should not lead to stigmatization or pathologization of these individuals.

Rather, the goal should be to foster a deeper appreciation for neurodiversity and the extraordinary spectrum of human potential. Emphasizing respect, inclusivity, and responsible exploration of these phenomena is paramount.

In conclusion, the intersection of belief, intention, and neurobiology within the context of Starseeds and Lightworkers presents a rich field for interdisciplinary research. By integrating neuroscientific methodologies with parapsychological insights and a deep understanding of the impact of belief systems, we can pave the way for a more complete understanding of human consciousness and the potential for extraordinary experiences. This path necessitates a shift away from a purely reductionist approach to one that embraces a more holistic perspective, encompassing both the subjective and objective dimensions of human experience. Only through such an integrative approach can we begin to unravel the mysteries surrounding these remarkable individuals and their purported abilities, and harness the potential for positive change they represent. The challenge lies in bridging the gap between scientific skepticism and spiritual openness, fostering an environment where diverse perspectives can converge and contribute to a more profound and holistic understanding of the human experience. The future of this research depends upon the ability to navigate this intricate landscape of scientific investigation and spiritual understanding, a journey that promises to enrich our knowledge of consciousness and unlock new avenues for human potential.

The previous discussion highlighted the profound impact of belief on the experiences of Starseeds and Lightworkers, a powerful self-fulfilling prophecy shaping perception and potentially influencing neurological processes. However, bridging the chasm between the spiritual narratives surrounding these individuals and the rigorous demands of scientific inquiry remains a significant challenge. This necessitates a nuanced approach that respects both subjective experiences and the objective need for empirical evidence.

One potential avenue for reconciliation lies in exploring the concept of neuroplasticity. This established neuroscientific principle demonstrates the brain's remarkable ability to reorganize itself throughout life, adapting to new experiences and learning. The intense focus and dedicated practice often reported by Starseeds and Lightworkers, particularly in areas like meditation, energy healing, or intuitive development, could very well be reshaping their brain structures and functions. For instance, studies have shown that long-term meditation practices thicken the cortex in regions associated with attention, emotional regulation, and self-awareness. This neurological change could, in turn, enhance their reported abilities, such as heightened intuition or empathic sensitivity.

Furthermore, the emerging field of epigenetics offers another compelling lens through which to view these phenomena. Epigenetics studies how environmental factors, including lifestyle choices and beliefs, can influence gene expression without altering the underlying DNA sequence. The deeply held beliefs and spiritual practices embraced by Starseeds and Lightworkers might trigger epigenetic modifications, affecting the expression of genes related to cognitive function, emotional processing, and even sensory perception. This could potentially explain the development of seemingly extraordinary abilities, not as a result of inherent genetic differences, but rather as an expression of environmentally influenced gene activation.

Consider, for example, the reported experiences of heightened intuition or precognitive abilities. From a purely scientific perspective, these might be attributed to enhanced pattern recognition skills, heightened sensitivity to subtle cues in the environment, or even unconscious inference based on existing knowledge. However, the spiritual perspective might interpret these abilities as a connection to a higher consciousness or access to information beyond the limitations of ordinary perception. Reconciling these perspectives requires acknowledging the possibility that both interpretations hold some validity. The subjective experience of accessing "higher knowledge" might correlate with objective neurological changes that enhance pattern recognition and information processing capabilities.

Similarly, the reported experiences of energy healing, often associated with Starseeds and Lightworkers, can be approached from both spiritual and scientific angles. Spiritual practices emphasize the manipulation of universal life force energy to promote healing and well-being. From a neuroscientific perspective, however, the placebo effect, along with the release of endorphins and other neurochemicals during focused attention and relaxation techniques, could contribute significantly to the reported healing outcomes. It is also worth considering the potential role of biofield therapies, which explore the subtle energy fields surrounding the body, although the scientific evidence supporting such fields remains limited. The challenge is not to dismiss the spiritual experiences, but rather to explore the underlying neurological and physiological mechanisms that might be involved in these seemingly paranormal phenomena.

The integration of spiritual and scientific perspectives also necessitates a critical examination of potential biases and limitations. Confirmation bias, for example, can lead individuals to selectively interpret experiences to support pre-existing beliefs. The strong belief in one's Starseed identity might lead to the interpretation of coincidences as evidence of their unique abilities. Scientific rigor demands acknowledging this potential bias and employing robust methodologies to minimize its impact. Similarly, the subjective nature of many of these experiences poses a challenge for objective measurement. However, advancements in neuroimaging techniques, such as fMRI and EEG, offer new tools to investigate the neural correlates of altered states of consciousness and exceptional abilities. By combining quantitative data from brain imaging with qualitative data from subjective reports, a more complete picture can be built.

Moreover, the conceptualization of consciousness itself needs to be broadened beyond a purely materialistic framework. While the brain undoubtedly plays a crucial role in consciousness, a purely reductionist approach may not fully capture the complexities of human experience. Integrating insights from quantum physics, which suggests a non-local interconnectedness of reality, opens up exciting possibilities for understanding the nature of consciousness and how it interacts with the universe. This aligns with many spiritual traditions that emphasize the interconnectedness of all things.

Ultimately, the pursuit of integrating spiritual and scientific perspectives demands a commitment to interdisciplinary collaboration. Neuroscientists, parapsychologists, spiritual practitioners, and philosophers need to engage in open dialogue, exchanging knowledge and approaches. This requires a willingness to move beyond rigid disciplinary boundaries and embrace the potential for a more holistic understanding of human consciousness. The stigma associated with both mental illness and paranormal experiences needs to be challenged, creating a safe and accepting environment for open exploration. Only by embracing these principles can we unlock the vast potential for understanding and harnessing the extraordinary abilities reported by Starseeds and Lightworkers, transforming our understanding of human potential and creating a more inclusive and empathetic society. The exploration of this interface is not merely an academic endeavor; it is a path toward a more profound understanding of ourselves, our interconnectedness, and our place in the cosmos. This ongoing journey requires patience, open-mindedness, and a willingness to embrace the unknown. The answers, undoubtedly, are complex, interwoven, and still largely waiting to be revealed. This calls for a paradigm shift in the way we approach scientific inquiry, incorporating subjective experience into the scientific method with careful and critical evaluation. The future of our understanding of consciousness hinges on this interdisciplinary collaboration.

CHAPTER 6: THE INTERCONNECTEDNE SS OF SEEMINGLY DIVERSE PHENOMENA

This chapter delves into the fascinating parallels between seemingly disparate phenomena: purported psychic abilities, such as clairvoyance and clairsentience, and the diverse experiences within the neurodiversity spectrum. While traditionally viewed as separate and even contradictory domains – one relegated to the realm of the paranormal, the other to the clinical – a closer examination reveals intriguing common threads that suggest a deeper interconnectedness. This interconnectedness challenges our current understanding of consciousness, perception, and the boundaries of human potential.

One striking similarity lies in the altered states of consciousness often associated with both psychic experiences and certain neurodiverse conditions. Individuals reporting psychic events frequently describe altered sensory perception, heightened intuition, and a sense of expanded awareness, mirroring the subjective experiences of some individuals within the autism spectrum or those with conditions like synesthesia. These altered states might reflect different patterns of brain activity, perhaps involving atypical neural pathways or heightened connectivity between brain regions normally operating more independently. While the specific neural mechanisms remain largely unknown, the commonality of altered consciousness suggests a shared underlying neurological substrate.

Further supporting this hypothesis is the frequently reported heightened sensory sensitivity in both neurodiverse individuals and those who report psychic abilities. Many autistic individuals, for instance, experience sensory overload or hypersensitivity to stimuli like light, sound, or touch. Similarly, individuals claiming clairsentience often report an intense sensitivity to the emotions and energies of others, a form of hyper-empathy that may represent an extreme on the spectrum of emotional sensitivity. This shared characteristic points to potential overlaps in the neural pathways processing sensory information, perhaps involving an amplification or altered filtering of sensory input.

The role of intuition also deserves consideration. Intuition, often described as a gut feeling or an unconscious awareness, is frequently reported by individuals with both neurodiverse conditions and purported psychic abilities. This suggests that a heightened sensitivity to subtle cues or an ability to process information unconsciously might be a shared characteristic. The neural mechanisms underlying intuition remain enigmatic, but research into the role of the limbic system and the unconscious processing of information provides potential avenues for investigation. It is possible that certain neural configurations or atypical brain connectivity patterns facilitate this heightened intuitive ability, manifest differently in different contexts.

Furthermore, the concept of synesthesia, a neurological condition where stimulation of one sensory pathway leads to automatic, involuntary experiences in a second sensory modality (for example, hearing colors or seeing sounds), provides a valuable lens through which to view these phenomena. Synesthesia often manifests as a blending of sensory modalities, blurring the lines between the internal and external world. Similarly, individuals reporting psychic abilities often describe a blurring of sensory boundaries, a merging of their internal experience with external events or information. This suggests that certain neurological predispositions or variations might underlie both synesthesia and purported psychic abilities, leading to atypical sensory integration and processing.

Genetic and epigenetic factors also warrant investigation. While concrete evidence remains elusive, some research suggests potential genetic or epigenetic links between certain neurodevelopmental conditions and purported psychic abilities. This does not necessarily imply a direct causal relationship but highlights the importance of considering genetic predisposition and environmental factors in shaping both neurodiversity and unusual mental capacities. Future research exploring the genetic architecture of these conditions, employing methods such as genome-wide association studies, could provide significant insights.

The exploration of these similarities, however, does not diminish the significant differences between neurodiverse conditions and purported psychic abilities. While certain shared characteristics exist, the context and expression of these characteristics differ significantly. For instance, the heightened sensory sensitivity in autism often manifests as distress and sensory overload, whereas in individuals claiming clairsentience, it might be experienced as an enhanced ability to connect with others. Similarly, altered states of consciousness in psychosis can be accompanied by debilitating hallucinations and delusions, while in some cases of claimed psychic abilities, such states might facilitate access to seemingly extra-sensory information.

Therefore, the critical task is not to conflate these phenomena but to understand the spectrum of potential human experiences that they represent. The goal is not to diagnose individuals experiencing psychic events with a neurological condition, nor to dismiss the experiences of those with neurodiverse conditions as simply "psychic." Instead, the objective is to develop a more nuanced and integrative understanding of the range of human capacities and experiences, moving beyond binary classifications of normal and abnormal, typical and atypical.

This requires embracing a holistic and multi-faceted approach, integrating scientific rigor with a respectful consideration of spiritual and personal experiences. This means employing scientific methods to explore the neurological correlates of these phenomena while simultaneously valuing and understanding the subjective, often deeply personal experiences of individuals involved. It also means recognizing the limitations of current research methodologies and acknowledging the challenges in studying subjective phenomena like intuition and extrasensory perception.

A shift in perspective is needed. Instead of viewing these phenomena as separate and distinct, we must consider them as points along a spectrum of human potential, a spectrum encompassing a vast range of cognitive, sensory, and emotional experiences. Some individuals may exhibit characteristics falling predominantly within the neurodiversity spectrum, while others may exhibit capacities that align more closely with traditional notions of psychic abilities. Many individuals, however, may possess characteristics that overlap these categories, highlighting the blurred boundaries and interconnectedness of these domains. The challenge lies in developing a framework that appreciates this complexity, that moves beyond rigid categorization and embraces the fluid and dynamic nature of human consciousness.

Ultimately, recognizing the common threads linking neurodiversity and purported psychic abilities compels us to re-evaluate our understanding of human consciousness. It challenges conventional notions of normality and exceptionality, urging us to embrace a more inclusive and expansive view of human potential. This journey requires a willingness to question long-held beliefs, to confront our biases and preconceptions, and to approach these intriguing phenomena with both scientific curiosity and a profound respect for the complex tapestry of human experience. The exploration of this interconnectedness is not just an academic endeavor, but a journey toward a more comprehensive and compassionate understanding of ourselves and the incredible potential inherent in the human mind. The future of understanding human consciousness lies not in separating these seemingly disparate phenomena, but in finding the connections that bind them together. This path, while challenging, offers the potential to unlock previously unimagined capacities for human flourishing and societal advancement. Only by embracing the full spectrum of human experience can we fully realize the richness and potential of our shared humanity.

The exploration of neurodiversity and purported psychic abilities naturally leads us to consider the vast, largely untapped spectrum of human potential. We are accustomed to thinking of human capabilities within a relatively narrow band – the bell curve of standardized testing, the limitations imposed by societal expectations, and the confines of our current scientific understanding. But what if this bell curve is merely a sliver of a much larger, more complex distribution? What if the individuals often labeled as "exceptional" or "abnormal" are not outliers, but rather represent points on a spectrum extending far beyond our current comprehension?

This perspective shifts the focus from categorizing individuals as "normal" versus "abnormal," "psychic" versus "neurotypical," to understanding the diverse ways in which the human brain can function and the extraordinary range of experiences that this diversity allows. The very definition of "normal" becomes fluid, a social construct that needs re-evaluation in light of the emerging understanding of neurodiversity and its potential relationship to phenomena once confined to the fringes of scientific inquiry.

Consider the case of synesthesia, a neurological condition where stimulation of one sensory pathway leads to automatic, involuntary experiences in a second sensory modality. For example, a synesthete might perceive the number "5" as a specific shade of blue or associate musical notes with particular colors. While traditionally considered a neurological anomaly, some researchers suggest that synesthesia represents an enhanced level of cross-modal sensory integration, potentially revealing underlying neural pathways crucial to more complex cognitive functions. Could it be a rudimentary form of the "sensory blending" that supposedly underpins clairsentience, where individuals experience emotions or sensations associated with a remote location or person? This notion, while speculative, opens up exciting possibilities for investigating the neural correlates of both synesthesia and clairsentience, looking for shared pathways and functional mechanisms.

Further expanding this concept, we encounter individuals who demonstrate extraordinary memory capabilities, like eidetic memory (often inaccurately termed "photographic memory"). These individuals possess the ability to recall images with remarkable detail and accuracy. While the exact neurological basis of eidetic memory remains debated, it highlights the plasticity and adaptability of the human brain, showcasing capabilities far exceeding the norm. Could such hyper-memory skills be related to the exceptionally detailed recollections sometimes associated with purported psychic abilities such as precognition or remote viewing? The meticulous recall needed for such experiences, even if interpreted as imaginative constructions, could rely on similar enhanced neural mechanisms.

The concept of "genius" itself presents an interesting lens through which to consider human potential. Individuals demonstrating exceptional abilities in specific domains, such as mathematics, music, or art, often exhibit neurological differences or atypical patterns of brain activity. These differences, instead of being viewed as deficits, might represent unique configurations of neural networks that allow for enhanced cognitive processing in specific areas. The creativity and innovation often associated with genius might share common underlying neurological mechanisms with the creative leaps and intuitive insights often reported in individuals claiming psychic abilities.

This interconnectedness extends to the realm of altered states of consciousness. Meditation, shamanic practices, and other altered states have long been associated with expanded awareness and experiences that challenge conventional notions of reality. These experiences frequently involve altered perceptions, heightened intuition, and sensations of interconnectedness, paralleling some descriptions of psychic experiences. Neuroscientific studies have begun to illuminate the neural correlates of altered states of consciousness, demonstrating changes in brainwave activity, neurotransmitter release, and neural connectivity. This research may provide valuable insights into the neural mechanisms that underpin both altered states and purported psychic abilities, suggesting a continuum of human experience rather than a rigid dichotomy.

The New Age concepts of Indigo, Crystal, and Rainbow children, along with Starseeds and Lightworkers, while lacking rigorous scientific validation, present compelling narratives about individuals possessing unique sensitivities and abilities. These descriptions, whether considered accurate representations of specific types of individuals or a broader reflection of evolving human consciousness, highlight the importance of exploring the diversity of human experience beyond the limitations of conventional paradigms. If we take these claims seriously, even if only as a starting point for investigation, we are forced to question what aspects of human potential are currently being overlooked or dismissed as irrelevant. These labels, though controversial, point towards a potential spectrum of cognitive and perceptual capabilities beyond our current understanding, capabilities that may warrant deeper study to explore potential links to neurodiversity.

Consider the notion of "intuitive knowing" often associated with these groups. This isn't necessarily about consciously accessing information through paranormal means, but a heightened sensitivity to subtle cues, patterns, and emotions, leading to insightful deductions often appearing prescient. This intuitive knowing might be linked to enhanced cognitive processes such as pattern recognition, emotional intelligence, and rapid information processing, possibly underpinned by unique neurological configurations or heightened sensory processing. Again, research on heightened sensory processing in neurodiverse populations might offer clues to understanding this.

The proposed link between neurodiversity and purported psychic abilities is not meant to pathologize neurodivergence. Instead, it aims to broaden our understanding of the capabilities of the human brain, recognizing that atypical brain development and functioning may create unique potentials. It is not a question of defining psychic abilities as a form of mental illness, but rather of exploring the possibility that both phenomena might share common neurological underpinnings. We must approach this exploration with a nuanced perspective, rejecting reductionist approaches that seek to solely medicalize or pathologize unique experiences, instead embracing a model that acknowledges and celebrates the vast spectrum of human potential.

Furthermore, understanding the spectrum of human potential requires a shift in perspective—away from a focus solely on deficits and limitations, towards an appreciation of the remarkable diversity of human cognition and perception. This shift demands a reevaluation of our educational systems, therapeutic approaches, and societal structures, creating spaces where neurodivergent individuals can thrive and where the unique abilities associated with purported psychic experiences are not dismissed or marginalized, but instead, are carefully investigated and understood.

The journey towards a comprehensive understanding of human potential is a continuous one. It demands an openness to exploring the unexplained, a willingness to question established norms, and a commitment to fostering a more inclusive and compassionate society that celebrates and supports the incredible diversity of human experience. Ultimately, embracing the full spectrum of human potential is not just about identifying and studying exceptional abilities; it is about creating a future where every individual is empowered to discover and utilize their unique strengths, contributing to a richer, more vibrant, and more compassionate world. This requires not only scientific investigation but also a profound shift in our collective consciousness, a move towards recognizing the interconnectedness of all things, both within ourselves and within our shared human experience. The understanding and harnessing of this vast spectrum promises not only a deeper appreciation of what it means to be human but also the possibility of a future where human potential is truly unlimited.

The inherent challenge in understanding the intersection of neurodiversity and purported psychic abilities lies in the limitations of our current systems of categorization. We are conditioned to compartmentalize, to neatly organize the world into distinct boxes. This approach, while useful for certain purposes, proves profoundly inadequate when confronting the complexities of the human mind and its vast potential. Our diagnostic manuals, our scientific classifications, and even our everyday language struggle to capture the nuances of experience, often forcing multifaceted phenomena into overly simplistic frameworks.

Consider the diagnostic criteria for schizophrenia. While certain symptoms, such as hallucinations and delusions, might overlap with some reported psychic experiences, equating the two is a gross oversimplification. A person experiencing auditory hallucinations diagnosed with schizophrenia may perceive voices as intrusive and distressing, leading to significant impairment in daily functioning. In contrast, an individual claiming clairaudience might describe receiving messages through similar auditory channels but interpret the experiences as meaningful and potentially beneficial. The same sensory input, interpreted through different lenses, yields radically different outcomes and necessitates distinct understandings. Simply categorizing both under the umbrella of "auditory hallucinations" obscures crucial distinctions in subjective experience, meaning, and impact.

This issue of categorization extends beyond clinical diagnoses. The New Age concepts of Indigo, Crystal, and Rainbow children, and their associated characteristics, also challenge our established frameworks. While these labels may offer a sense of community and shared experience for those who identify with them, they also risk essentializing diverse individuals and their capabilities. The characteristics attributed to these groups – heightened intuition, empathy, and spiritual awareness – are not mutually exclusive and may manifest in various ways across individuals who do not necessarily identify with these specific labels. Attempting to define these individuals within a rigid typology risks overlooking the unique expressions of their abilities and experiences. The very act of categorization can inadvertently limit our understanding, creating a framework that excludes those who don't neatly fit within predetermined boxes.

Furthermore, the attempt to categorize these experiences often relies on a dualistic worldview that separates the "normal" from the "paranormal," the "scientific" from the "spiritual." This dichotomy itself is a product of a specific cultural and historical context, and it severely limits our ability to see the interconnectedness of seemingly disparate phenomena. The perceived boundaries between the physical and the metaphysical, the conscious and the unconscious, are increasingly blurred as our understanding of neuroscience and quantum physics deepens. Subjective experiences traditionally deemed "paranormal" may, upon closer examination, involve previously unknown neurological pathways or interactions at the quantum level.

The limitations extend to the very methods we use to investigate these phenomena. Scientific research often prioritizes quantitative measures and objective data, which can be challenging to apply to subjective experiences like intuition or spiritual insights. While rigorous scientific methodology is crucial, relying solely on quantifiable metrics can lead to an incomplete or even distorted picture. Qualitative approaches, such as phenomenological studies, are essential for capturing the richness and complexity of subjective experiences. These methods allow researchers to delve into the individual's lived experience, understanding the meaning and context of what they are experiencing, thus gaining a deeper, richer understanding of the phenomena at hand.

Moreover, the cultural context significantly shapes our understanding and interpretation of these phenomena. What might be considered a paranormal ability in one culture may be seen as a normal part of life in another. The cultural lens through which we view these experiences profoundly impacts how they are understood, categorized, and even experienced. Cross-cultural studies comparing the prevalence and interpretation of seemingly paranormal experiences across various societies can help illuminate the impact of culture on our perception of human potential.

The challenges of categorization are further complicated by the interplay between genetics, epigenetics, and environment. The expression of any human trait, including potential psychic abilities or neurological variations, is likely influenced by a complex interplay of these factors. A genetic predisposition might exist, yet its manifestation may depend on environmental factors or epigenetic modifications. This interplay creates an intricate tapestry of influence that makes simplistic categorization inadequate. Understanding the interplay requires integrating findings from multiple scientific disciplines – genetics, epigenetics, neuroscience, psychology, and anthropology – creating a holistic picture that goes beyond simple labels.

Furthermore, we must acknowledge the inherent limitations of our current understanding of the brain and consciousness. Neuroscience has made tremendous strides, yet our knowledge remains incomplete. The very definition of consciousness remains a subject of ongoing debate and research. Our understanding of the brain's capacity for complex information processing, non-local consciousness, and quantum entanglement is still in its infancy. It is premature to definitively categorize human experiences based on an incomplete and constantly evolving understanding of the very organ that generates them.

Therefore, moving forward, a more nuanced approach is necessary. This requires a shift from rigid categorization towards a more fluid, spectrum-based understanding. Instead of forcing individuals into pre-defined boxes, we must embrace the inherent variability and individuality of human experience. This involves recognizing the overlapping and interwoven nature of what we perceive as separate phenomena, fostering a holistic approach that values both quantitative and qualitative data, integrates findings from diverse disciplines, and acknowledges the cultural context. Such a paradigm shift requires not only scientific advancement but also a transformation in our collective consciousness, moving away from divisive labels and towards a celebration of the diverse and boundless spectrum of human potential. Only by embracing this broader perspective can we begin to truly understand and harness the incredible capabilities that lie dormant within humanity. This inclusive approach recognizes that the "paranormal" and the "neurodiverse" are not necessarily mutually exclusive, rather interconnected facets of a larger, more complex reality. It acknowledges the limitations of our current knowledge and

THE NEURODIVERSITY OF CONSCIOUSNESS

encourages ongoing exploration, both scientific and spiritual, towards a deeper comprehension of the human experience. In the realm of human potential, a fluid, adaptable model is far more effective than a rigid, static system. We must learn to navigate the intricacies of human experience with humility, recognizing that our understanding is constantly evolving, and embracing the myriad expressions of human consciousness.

The limitations of current diagnostic frameworks become glaringly apparent when we attempt to categorize experiences often labeled as "paranormal." Clairvoyance, clairsentience, and other purported psychic abilities often defy easy classification, falling outside the neatly defined boundaries of established mental health diagnoses. To rigidly categorize them as merely symptoms of psychosis, for instance, ignores the profound qualitative differences that exist between, say, a schizophrenic hallucination and a seemingly accurate clairvoyant perception. While both may involve sensory experiences not grounded in external reality, the *content* and *context* of these experiences differ significantly. A schizophrenic hallucination might be terrifying, fragmented, and emotionally distressing, while a clairvoyant experience might be perceived as insightful, coherent, and potentially even beneficial. This distinction, crucial for understanding the nature of these phenomena, is frequently lost in reductionist approaches that prioritize diagnostic labels over nuanced experiential data.

Furthermore, the very concept of "mental illness" itself requires re-examination within this broader context. Our current understanding often leans towards a deficit model, focusing on what is

wrong with the individual rather than exploring the unique strengths and capabilities that may accompany certain neurological variations. What if what we perceive as mental illness is not simply a disorder, but rather a manifestation of differently organized neural pathways, resulting in unconventional modes of perception and processing information? This perspective shifts the focus from pathology to potential, inviting us to consider the possibility that so-called "disorders" may actually represent alternative forms of consciousness with untapped potential.

The limitations extend beyond diagnostic manuals. Even our everyday language often reinforces compartmentalized thinking. We utilize terms like "psychic," "neurodiverse," and "mentally ill" as if they represent discrete categories, failing to acknowledge the significant overlap and interconnectivity that may exist between them. Consider the case of individuals with autism spectrum disorder who report heightened sensory sensitivities, synesthesia, or even instances of what might be considered precognitive abilities. Are these experiences merely coincidental anomalies or indicative of a deeper, more fundamental interconnectedness between seemingly disparate aspects of human experience?

This challenge to conventional paradigms demands a shift in our approach to research. A purely quantitative, statistically driven approach, while valuable in certain aspects, falls short when grappling with the subjective and experiential nature of these phenomena. We need to embrace methodologies that incorporate qualitative data, including in-depth interviews, phenomenological studies, and explorations of personal narratives. Such approaches acknowledge the richness and complexity of human experience, allowing for a more holistic and comprehensive understanding of the underlying mechanisms at play.

The exploration of consciousness itself needs to move beyond the limitations of a purely materialistic perspective. While neuroscience offers invaluable insights into the biological substrates of consciousness, it often fails to adequately account for the subjective experience, the "what it's like" aspect of consciousness. To fully understand the nature of psychic abilities and neurodiversity, we need to incorporate perspectives from fields like philosophy of mind, transpersonal psychology, and even spiritual traditions. These diverse approaches, though seemingly disparate, offer complementary lenses through which to examine the complexities of human consciousness.

The concept of interconnectedness extends beyond individuals. Our understanding of the mind-body connection remains incomplete, with a prevailing tendency to view the mind as separate from the body. However, emerging research suggests a far more intricate interplay between the two, with the body playing a crucial role in shaping mental states and experiences. The impact of somatic therapies, such as yoga, meditation, and breathwork, on mental health strongly supports this view. These practices, while often perceived as alternative, demonstrate the powerful influence of bodily states on mental well-being. Exploring this interplay is essential for understanding not only neurodiversity and psychic abilities but also the broader spectrum of human experience.

Similarly, the environment itself plays a significant role. The impact of electromagnetic fields, subtle energy fields, and environmental stressors on brain function and mental states deserves further investigation. Could fluctuations in these fields influence the expression of psychic abilities or exacerbate certain neurodiverse traits? The very notion of a "separate" individual needs reevaluation; we are profoundly embedded within a complex web of interactions, with our physical and mental states inextricably linked to our environment.

The integration of seemingly disparate phenomena necessitates a transdisciplinary approach. Researchers from neuroscience, psychology, parapsychology, anthropology, and even spiritual traditions need to collaborate to develop a more comprehensive understanding. This requires a willingness to step outside the boundaries of established disciplines and embrace the potential for innovative collaborations. The current siloed nature of research hampers progress, preventing the synthesis of diverse perspectives that could unlock a deeper comprehension of the complexities of human consciousness.

Furthermore, this holistic approach necessitates a critical examination of existing biases. The prevailing scientific worldview often dismisses phenomena that do not fit neatly within existing paradigms. A healthy skepticism is essential, but it should not preclude exploration. The mere fact that a phenomenon is difficult to explain does not render it invalid. We must cultivate a mindset of open inquiry, embracing uncertainty and recognizing the limitations of our current understanding.

Ultimately, the integration of seemingly diverse phenomena – neurodiversity, psychic abilities, and even what we traditionally define as "mental illness" – leads to a profound reframing of the human experience. Instead of viewing these aspects as separate and often problematic entities, we must recognize them as interconnected facets of a larger, more complex reality. This new paradigm emphasizes the inherent variability of human potential and celebrates the richness and diversity of human consciousness. It calls for a move from exclusionary labels and judgment towards inclusivity, respect, and a genuine commitment to understanding the full spectrum of human capabilities. Only by embracing this integrated perspective can we truly unlock the boundless potential that lies dormant within humanity. This includes not just individuals but the whole of humanity's collective consciousness, a field which science, spirituality, and even art may need to examine together. This will be essential in understanding phenomena that do not fit comfortably within one single field of study, demanding a synthesis of methodologies and worldviews for true comprehension. The exploration of this interconnectedness is not just an intellectual pursuit but a transformative journey, one that has the potential to redefine our understanding of ourselves and our place in the universe.

The limitations of purely reductionist scientific approaches become even more apparent when we consider the purported abilities associated with the New Age concepts of Indigo, Crystal, and Rainbow Children, along with Starseeds and Lightworkers. These individuals are often described as possessing heightened intuition, empathy, and spiritual awareness, sometimes coupled with unconventional cognitive styles and sensitivities. To dismiss these abilities as mere fantasies or delusional thinking, as some might be inclined to do, would be a profound oversight. Instead, it invites us to consider alternative frameworks—frameworks that acknowledge the intricate interplay between brain function, consciousness, and the subtle energies that some believe permeate our reality.

One compelling avenue of investigation is the concept of neurodiversity itself. Neurodiversity emphasizes the inherent variability of brain function, recognizing that differences in neurological wiring are not necessarily deficits but rather expressions of unique cognitive styles and capabilities. Could it be, then, that individuals identified as Indigo, Crystal, or Rainbow Children—and those who identify as Starseeds or Lightworkers—represent a form of neurodiversity expressed through heightened psychic sensitivity and spiritual awareness? Their experiences, though often defying conventional scientific explanation, may reflect variations in brain circuitry that enhance certain cognitive functions, such as intuitive perception, empathy, and access to non-ordinary states of consciousness.

This perspective shifts the focus from pathology to potential. Instead of pathologizing these individuals, we can begin to appreciate their unique contributions to the human experience. Their heightened sensitivity, often described as a burden in a world not designed to accommodate it, could in fact be a source of profound creativity, insight, and spiritual growth. This increased sensitivity might be linked to heightened activity in brain regions associated with emotional processing, intuition, and self-awareness, potentially involving a complex interplay between the amygdala, the insula, and the prefrontal cortex. Furthermore, the enhanced connectivity between different brain regions, potentially facilitated by neuroplasticity and epigenetic modifications, may play a role in the integration of information and the generation of novel insights.

The concept of "spiritual awakening" frequently associated with these groups further complicates the picture. Spiritual awakenings often involve profound shifts in consciousness, marked by changes in perception, emotional regulation, and a sense of connection to something larger than oneself. Neurobiologically, these experiences might be associated with alterations in neurotransmitter systems, changes in brain wave activity, and modifications in the brain's default mode network—a network of brain regions associated with self-referential thought and introspection. These shifts in brain activity could enhance creativity, facilitate profound self-understanding, and foster a sense of connection to others and the universe at large.

The challenge lies in developing methodologies that can adequately assess and analyze these experiences without resorting to reductionist and potentially biased interpretations. Conventional neuroimaging techniques, such as fMRI and EEG, can provide valuable insights into brain activity associated with these experiences, but they are limited in their ability to capture the richness and complexity of subjective experience. Furthermore, the inherent subjectivity of these experiences makes it challenging to develop objective and reliable measures of their occurrence and intensity. This underscores the need for a multi-methodological approach that integrates qualitative research methods, such as phenomenological interviews and case studies, alongside quantitative neuroimaging techniques. A truly comprehensive understanding of these phenomena requires a willingness to step outside the confines of conventional scientific paradigms and embrace methodologies that are sensitive to the subjective and often ineffable nature of consciousness and spirituality.

It is also crucial to acknowledge the cultural and social contexts that shape our understanding of these phenomena. The very terms "Indigo Children," "Crystal Children," and "Rainbow Children," and the concepts of Starseeds and Lightworkers are themselves products of specific cultural narratives and belief systems. These narratives, while possibly influenced by genuine experiences, can also create self-fulfilling prophecies, where individuals who identify with these labels may begin to experience themselves in ways that confirm the narrative. This is not to dismiss the potential validity of their experiences, but rather to highlight the importance of critically examining the interplay between individual experience, cultural narratives, and the social dynamics that shape our understanding of the human mind.

Furthermore, integrating seemingly disparate fields like parapsychology, neuroscience, and spiritual traditions requires a fundamental shift in our epistemology. It necessitates a move away from a strictly materialistic worldview that reduces consciousness to merely a byproduct of brain activity, towards a more holistic perspective that acknowledges the potential for consciousness to interact with and influence the physical world in ways that are currently not fully understood. This perspective does not necessarily endorse all claims of psychic phenomena without rigorous scrutiny, but rather acknowledges that our current understanding of consciousness and its capabilities may be profoundly incomplete.

This integrated approach necessitates a careful examination of the limitations of current diagnostic frameworks in mental health. Diagnoses of psychosis, for instance, often fail to distinguish between genuinely pathological experiences and those that may represent exceptionally sensitive perceptions or access to non-ordinary states of consciousness. The diagnostic criteria are often overly focused on distress and dysfunction, neglecting the potential for positive and transformative experiences that may be associated with these states. This is a critical area requiring careful examination and reformulation of diagnostic approaches to be more inclusive and less prone to pathologizing diverse experiences that fall outside current norms.

Embracing this complexity demands a shift from a deficit-based model to one that emphasizes the potential for growth and transformation. Individuals who experience what may seem like "paranormal" abilities or atypical cognitive styles should not be pathologized or marginalized. Instead, they deserve support and understanding, allowing them to explore their unique capabilities in a safe and supportive environment. This necessitates a paradigm shift in therapeutic approaches, from a focus on symptom reduction to one that encourages personal growth, self-discovery, and the cultivation of their unique talents. This also encourages a broader understanding of the interconnectedness of human experience, including the relationship between mental health, spiritual experience, and the potential for expansion of consciousness.

The interconnectedness we explore here is not merely an intellectual exercise; it holds profound implications for the future of humanity. Recognizing the full spectrum of human potential—including the spectrum of neurodiversity and potentially psychic abilities—can lead to a more inclusive and compassionate society. It can also unlock new avenues of innovation and creativity, fostering progress in fields ranging from art and technology to medicine and spirituality. The integration of these diverse aspects of the human experience is not simply a matter of expanding our scientific knowledge; it is about creating a world where every individual feels valued, understood, and empowered to reach their full potential. This understanding is crucial for fostering a future where the unique talents and perspectives of all individuals are celebrated and utilized for the collective good. A future that values and utilizes diversity in all its forms can potentially lead to a more creative, compassionate, and sustainable society.

Ultimately, the exploration of this interconnectedness is a journey—a journey of self-discovery, scientific inquiry, and spiritual exploration. It is a journey that requires courage, curiosity, and a willingness to challenge established assumptions and embrace the unknown. But it is also a journey that holds the potential for profound transformation, both individually and collectively. By embracing the complexity and nuance of human experience, we can unlock the boundless potential that resides within each of us and within humanity as a whole. It is a call for a future where scientific rigor and spiritual insight converge to create a more complete and compassionate understanding of ourselves and our place in the universe. A future where the boundaries between seemingly disparate phenomena begin to dissolve, revealing the intricate tapestry of human potential. It is a call to recognize and celebrate the vast and multifaceted nature of consciousness and the profound interconnectedness that binds us all.

CHAPTER 7: EXPLORING ALTERED STATES OF CONSCIOUSNESS

Meditation, a practice dating back millennia, involves focused attention and awareness, often cultivating a state of deep relaxation and mental clarity. While its benefits for stress reduction and mental well-being are widely accepted, its potential connection to psychic abilities remains a fascinating area of exploration. Neuroscience offers valuable insights into the mechanisms underlying meditative states and their potential impact on perception.

Numerous studies using neuroimaging techniques, such as EEG (electroencephalography) and fMRI (functional magnetic resonance imaging), have revealed significant changes in brain activity during meditation. These changes often involve decreased activity in the default mode network (DMN), a network of brain regions associated with self-referential thought and mind-wandering. A reduction in DMN activity is linked to a state of increased present-moment awareness and reduced mental chatter, characteristics often associated with heightened sensory perception.

Furthermore, meditation has been shown to increase

activity in regions associated with attention and sensory processing. For instance, studies have demonstrated increased activity in the prefrontal cortex, a brain area crucial for executive functions, including attention control and cognitive flexibility. Enhanced attentional resources could potentially facilitate the reception and processing of subtle sensory information, often attributed to extrasensory perception.

The relationship between meditation and altered perception isn't solely confined to increased awareness. Prolonged meditation practices have been linked to structural changes in the brain, including increased grey matter density in regions associated with emotional regulation, self-awareness, and empathy. These structural changes could potentially contribute to an expanded capacity for receiving and interpreting information beyond conventional sensory modalities.

The potential link between meditation and psychic abilities is supported by anecdotal evidence from individuals who report enhanced intuitive abilities after regular meditation. Many practitioners describe experiencing vivid imagery, heightened intuition, and a greater sense of connection to others while in a meditative state. These subjective experiences, while not scientifically verifiable in isolation, warrant further exploration.

One possible mechanism linking meditation and psychic abilities is the concept of altered states of consciousness. Meditation, particularly advanced meditative practices, can induce states of consciousness that differ significantly from ordinary waking consciousness. These altered states may be characterized by a decreased reliance on the analytical left hemisphere of the brain, allowing for increased access to intuitive, right-hemisphere processing. This shift in brain dominance could facilitate the processing of information that is typically filtered out or ignored during normal waking consciousness.

It's important to acknowledge that the research on meditation and psychic abilities is still in its nascent stages. Many of the claims regarding enhanced psychic abilities after meditation remain anecdotal. However, the growing body of neuroscientific evidence demonstrating significant changes in brain structure and function during meditation provides a compelling foundation for further investigation. Rigorous research methodologies, including controlled studies and larger sample sizes, are needed to draw definitive conclusions.

Furthermore, the concept of "psychic abilities" itself needs careful consideration. The term often encompasses a wide range of phenomena, including clairvoyance, clairsentience, precognition, and telepathy. Each of these phenomena presents unique challenges for scientific investigation, requiring specific methodologies and careful consideration of potential confounding factors. A more precise definition of the specific abilities under investigation, coupled with rigorous experimental design, is critical for advancing the field.

Beyond the potential for enhanced perception, meditation's influence on emotional regulation and stress reduction may also indirectly contribute to experiences often attributed to psychic abilities. A calm, centered state of mind may reduce interference from internal noise, making individuals more receptive to subtle cues or information from the environment. Conversely, high levels of stress and anxiety can cloud judgment and interfere with clear perception.

In addition to meditation's impact on individual perception, the social and cultural context surrounding meditation practices plays a crucial role. Many meditative traditions incorporate elements of belief systems, spiritual practices, and group rituals. These communal aspects of meditation could influence an individual's experience and interpretation of any perceived enhanced abilities. The power of suggestion and the influence of shared beliefs could potentially contribute to both the experience and the reporting of psychic phenomena.

The study of meditation and altered states of consciousness necessitates an integrative approach that combines neuroscience, psychology, and spiritual traditions. An open-minded exploration that acknowledges both subjective experiences and scientific findings is essential for a comprehensive understanding. Ultimately, the quest to understand the potential link between meditation and psychic abilities requires rigorous scientific investigation combined with a profound respect for the subjective experiences of practitioners.

The exploration of altered states of consciousness is crucial for understanding the potential overlap between meditation and purported psychic abilities. Meditation induces a state of altered consciousness that, in some individuals, might heighten sensitivity to subtle stimuli or facilitate access to information beyond typical sensory channels. While the mechanisms are not fully understood, the observed brain changes during meditation offer a promising avenue for further exploration.

Moreover, various types of meditation, including mindfulness, concentrative, and transcendental meditation, might exhibit different neurological effects and consequently yield varied impacts on perception. Further research comparing the effects of different meditation techniques on sensory perception and cognitive abilities is needed. The specific type of meditation practiced, the duration of the practice, and the individual's predisposition could all be contributing factors.

The possibility of a correlation between meditation and specific psychic abilities, such as precognition or remote viewing, should be examined with caution, particularly given the potential for bias and the challenges of replicating such experiences. However, the potential connection between meditation, altered states, and enhanced intuition warrants careful scientific scrutiny.

Furthermore, investigating the role of neuroplasticity in the context of meditation and psychic abilities is crucial. Neuroplasticity, the brain's ability to reorganize itself by forming new neural connections throughout life, may be a significant mechanism by which long-term meditation practice could affect perception. The brain's capacity to adapt and change suggests the possibility that sustained meditation could indeed lead to alterations in brain structure and function related to perception, potentially explaining some reports of heightened psychic abilities.

Finally, the exploration of meditation and altered perception must acknowledge the potential for placebo effects and confirmation bias. The strong belief in the potential for psychic abilities could influence an individual's perception and interpretation of their experiences. Therefore, carefully designed experiments that control for these factors are essential to establish a credible link between meditation and psychic phenomena. Future research should focus on rigorous methodologies that minimize bias and confounding variables to provide more robust evidence. Only through a balanced approach that combines scientific rigor with an open mind can we hope to unravel the complex relationship between meditation, altered states of consciousness, and the intriguing world of psychic abilities.

The exploration of altered states of consciousness naturally leads us to the fascinating and often controversial realms of near-death experiences (NDEs) and out-of-body experiences (OBEs). These phenomena, frequently reported across cultures and throughout history, challenge our conventional understanding of consciousness and the limitations of the physical body. While often associated with mystical or spiritual interpretations, a neuroscientific perspective offers intriguing possibilities for understanding their neurological underpinnings.

NDEs, typically occurring during life-threatening events such as cardiac arrest or severe trauma, often involve a sensation of leaving the body, encountering a bright light, and reviewing one's life. The commonality of certain elements in NDE reports, despite cultural differences, suggests a potentially universal neurological mechanism. Researchers have proposed several hypotheses, including the role of endorphins released during extreme stress, oxygen deprivation leading to altered brain activity, and the influence of temporal lobe epilepsy. Studies examining brain activity during NDEs are hampered by the obvious difficulty in monitoring brain function during a life-threatening event. However, some research suggests that the release of neurochemicals during periods of oxygen deprivation could trigger the vivid visual and auditory experiences commonly reported. The bright light frequently described might be explained by the release of certain neurotransmitters that stimulate the visual cortex, creating a perception of intense light.

The "life review" aspect of many NDEs is particularly intriguing. The rapid replay of memories, often presented in a highly emotional and meaningful context, suggests a possible mechanism related to memory consolidation and the brain's capacity to rapidly access and process vast amounts of information. This process might be related to the brain's attempt to make sense of a traumatic event or to reconcile unresolved emotional issues before death. The fact that these experiences are often profoundly transformative, leading to changes in worldview and priorities, hints at a deeper neurological impact on personality and cognitive function. While purely neurological explanations might account for some aspects of NDEs, the profound spiritual significance these experiences hold for many individuals warrants further investigation.

OBEs, on the other hand, involve the sensation of perceiving the world from a location outside one's physical body. These experiences can occur spontaneously, often during sleep or under conditions of stress or trauma, or can be induced through various techniques, such as meditation or sensory deprivation. Similar to NDEs, several neuroscientific hypotheses have been put forward to explain OBEs. Damage to or disruption of the temporoparietal junction (TPJ), a brain region involved in integrating sensory information and body awareness, has been implicated in some cases of OBEs. Lesions or malfunctions in this area could lead to a decoupling of the subjective sense of self from the physical body, resulting in the feeling of being outside one's body.

Furthermore, the influence of the vestibular system, responsible for balance and spatial orientation, should not be overlooked. Disruptions in vestibular processing can lead to altered perceptions of body position and spatial awareness, which could contribute to the OBE experience. Additionally, the role of the visual cortex and its interactions with other brain regions in generating a subjective sense of location and perspective needs further exploration. Studies using neuroimaging techniques, such as fMRI and EEG, have attempted to map brain activity during OBEs, but the subjective and unpredictable nature of these experiences makes research challenging. However, emerging research using virtual reality environments and brain-computer interfaces offers exciting new possibilities for studying the neural correlates of OBEs.

The relationship between NDEs and OBEs remains a complex issue for investigation. Some researchers suggest that they share underlying neurological mechanisms, perhaps involving similar brain regions and neurochemical processes. The altered state of consciousness involved in both experiences, characterized by a distorted sense of time, space, and self, suggests a common pathway. However, the specific triggers and circumstances under which each type of experience occurs vary considerably. NDEs are generally associated with life-threatening situations, while OBEs can occur under a wider range of conditions. Further research is needed to clarify the relationship between these phenomena and to determine if they are distinct experiences with overlapping neural substrates or represent different manifestations of a single underlying mechanism.

Beyond the purely neuroscientific approaches, the study of NDEs and OBEs necessitates a consideration of the broader philosophical and spiritual implications. For many individuals, these experiences profoundly alter their beliefs about life, death, and the nature of consciousness. The sense of encountering a higher power or a transcendent reality reported by many NDE experiencers speaks to a realm beyond the purely physical. The potential for these experiences to foster personal growth, enhance empathy, and promote a sense of interconnectedness deserves attention. Integrating these subjective, transformative aspects with the objective data of neuroscience remains a critical challenge for researchers in this field.

The exploration of NDEs and OBEs highlights the limitations of reducing consciousness solely to neural activity. These experiences suggest that consciousness may be more extensive and resilient than current neuroscientific models allow. This doesn't necessarily negate the importance of neuroscientific research; rather, it underscores the need for a more holistic approach that integrates subjective accounts and spiritual perspectives with rigorous scientific investigation. By combining neuroimaging data, psychological assessments, and careful phenomenological analysis of individual experiences, a more comprehensive understanding of these fascinating phenomena might emerge.

A critical aspect of this research lies in the careful consideration of potential biases and confounding factors. The strong emotional impact of NDEs and OBEs can influence individuals' recall and interpretation of their experiences. Confirmation bias, the tendency to seek out and interpret information confirming pre-existing beliefs, can also significantly affect reporting. Researchers must strive for objectivity, employing rigorous methodologies to minimize these biases and control for confounding variables. This necessitates a critical evaluation of the methodologies used in previous studies and a careful consideration of alternative explanations for reported phenomena. For example, certain medication side effects, sleep disorders, or even the psychological effects of trauma could mimic aspects of NDEs and OBEs.

Future research should focus on developing standardized questionnaires and assessment tools to objectively compare and analyze experiences across individuals. The development of advanced neuroimaging techniques, coupled with improved methods for inducing and monitoring altered states of consciousness, promises to provide more detailed insights into the neural correlates of these phenomena. Moreover, collaborative research efforts involving neuroscientists, psychologists, and researchers with expertise in spiritual and transpersonal psychology are crucial to fully understand the complexities of these experiences. This interdisciplinary approach is vital for bridging the gap between scientific rigor and the rich subjective narratives of individuals who have undergone NDEs and OBEs.

Finally, the study of NDEs and OBEs has significant implications for our understanding of the human condition. These experiences challenge our assumptions about the nature of consciousness, the boundaries of the self, and the potential for human experience to transcend the limitations of the physical body. By exploring these phenomena with a balanced perspective, integrating scientific rigor with a respect for individual experiences, we can gain a deeper understanding not only of these extraordinary events, but also of the very nature of human existence. This approach allows us to explore the potential connections between seemingly disparate fields of study – neuroscience, psychology, spirituality, and parapsychology – to illuminate a more comprehensive and nuanced understanding of the human mind and its capacity for extraordinary experiences. The future of understanding consciousness may well lie in these interdisciplinary endeavors, paving the way for a richer appreciation of both the scientific and spiritual dimensions of human experience. The exploration is far from over, and the potential for discovery in this area remains vast and inspiring.

The exploration of altered states of consciousness naturally extends to the realm of dreams, those nightly voyages into the subconscious that have captivated and confounded humanity for millennia. While often dismissed as mere neural housekeeping or random firings of neurons, dreams hold a fascinating potential for understanding the deeper workings of the mind, particularly in relation to the enhanced perceptual abilities discussed earlier. The very fabric of dream states, with their surreal landscapes and illogical narratives, offers a unique lens through which to examine the boundaries of consciousness and the possible interplay between the conscious and unconscious minds. The neurological underpinnings of dreaming are complex and still not fully understood, but research points towards a significant role for the limbic system, the amygdala, and the hippocampus —brain regions associated with emotion, memory, and spatial navigation. These areas are also implicated in heightened states of intuition and perception, suggesting a potential link between dream experiences and extrasensory perception (ESP).

During REM (Rapid Eye Movement) sleep, the stage most associated with vivid dreaming, brain activity resembles that of wakefulness in certain areas, while other regions exhibit a unique pattern of activity. This paradoxical state allows for the creation of elaborate narratives and sensory experiences, often involving vivid imagery, emotions, and even seemingly precognitive elements. It's during these periods that the filters of our conscious mind seem to loosen, allowing for the free flow of information from the unconscious, a space potentially teeming with intuitive insights and latent psychic abilities.

The intriguing concept of lucid dreaming, where the dreamer becomes aware they are dreaming and can exert a degree of control over the dream's narrative, provides a particularly compelling avenue for investigation. Lucid dreaming, sometimes considered a form of self-hypnosis, allows for conscious exploration of the subconscious mind. Reports from lucid dreamers often include enhanced sensory perception, including vivid and seemingly realistic precognitive experiences or interactions with seemingly external entities. Some individuals report accessing information within their lucid dreams that later proves to be accurate, hinting at a potential link between lucid dreaming and ESP or other forms of heightened awareness.

From a neuroscientific standpoint, lucid dreaming offers a unique opportunity to study brain activity in a state that is both conscious and dreamlike. Neuroimaging studies using fMRI (functional magnetic resonance imaging) and EEG (electroencephalography) have begun to reveal the neural correlates of lucid dreaming, showing differences in brain activity compared to non-lucid dreams. Specifically, areas associated with self-awareness and cognitive control appear to be more active during lucid dreaming, suggesting a conscious attempt to exert control over the dream narrative. This conscious control might potentially unlock pathways to access and process information beyond the usual constraints of waking consciousness.

The connection between dream states, especially lucid dreaming, and the potential for enhanced psychic abilities remains a subject of considerable debate and ongoing research. While the scientific community largely operates within the framework of established methodologies, the anecdotal evidence from lucid dreamers, often involving seemingly precognitive or clairvoyant experiences, warrants careful consideration. The possibility that certain individuals possess inherent aptitudes for accessing and processing information through altered states, such as dreaming, offers a compelling area for interdisciplinary research, combining neuroscience with parapsychology.

Several intriguing theories attempt to bridge the gap between neuroscience and parapsychology in the context of dreams. One perspective suggests that during dreaming, the brain's filtering mechanisms, responsible for screening out irrelevant sensory information, are temporarily diminished.

This reduction in filtering could potentially allow for the processing of subconscious or external signals that would normally be ignored in wakefulness. Another theory proposes that dreaming acts as a kind of mental rehearsal, allowing the brain to process and integrate information from the waking world in novel and potentially insightful ways. This processing could potentially lead to intuitive insights or predictions that appear to be precognitive in nature, although they may simply be the result of unconscious pattern recognition or creative problem-solving.

The neurodiversity perspective offers yet another framework for understanding the potential connection between dream states and heightened perception. Just as individuals with certain neurological conditions may exhibit atypical sensory experiences, individuals with unique brain organization or wiring might possess a higher propensity for lucid dreaming and enhanced perceptual abilities during these states. The possibility that certain patterns of brain connectivity or neurotransmitter activity facilitate access to unconscious information or external stimuli during dreaming remains a compelling area for exploration. This approach aligns with the growing recognition of the spectrum of human neurological and cognitive variations, recognizing that "normal" is not a monolithic entity but rather a broad continuum of possibilities.

Furthermore, the spiritual and New Age perspectives enrich our understanding of dream states and their potential significance. Many traditions view dreams as portals to other realms of consciousness, avenues to connect with the spiritual or collective unconscious. In various indigenous cultures, dreams are regarded as essential sources of guidance, prophecy, and healing. This perspective emphasizes the subjective experience, giving weight to the personal meaning and interpretation of dreams. While these perspectives often lack the quantitative rigor of neuroscience, their qualitative contributions to our understanding of the human experience should not be dismissed. A truly holistic approach necessitates considering both the scientific and spiritual aspects of human experience, integrating objective measures with subjective meaning.

The study of dream states, particularly lucid dreaming, presents a unique challenge and opportunity for researchers. The inherent subjectivity of dream experiences makes rigorous scientific investigation difficult, requiring innovative methodologies to address the inherent limitations of self-reporting and subjective interpretation. However, the potential rewards of understanding the neural correlates of lucid dreaming and their potential relationship to enhanced perceptual abilities are significant. Such research could pave the way for new therapeutic approaches to improve cognitive function, enhance creativity, and unlock the potential for human consciousness to engage with the world in new and transformative ways.

Moving forward, a synergistic approach that integrates neuroscientific investigation with parapsychological exploration and the insights of spiritual traditions holds the greatest promise for unlocking the mysteries of dream states and their potential connection to heightened perception. This approach would involve rigorously controlled experiments utilizing neuroimaging techniques to study brain activity during various dream states, alongside detailed qualitative studies that incorporate subjective experiences and interpretations. Such research requires a multidisciplinary team of neuroscientists, psychologists, parapsychologists, and possibly even spiritual practitioners, united by a common goal of expanding our understanding of the human mind's extraordinary capabilities. By embracing a holistic and inclusive approach, we can move beyond the limitations of reductionist paradigms and develop a more comprehensive and nuanced understanding of the remarkable potential that lies within the human mind, not only in wakefulness, but also in the dream worlds we inhabit each night. This inclusive and multi-faceted approach opens up exciting possibilities for the future, offering pathways to harness the power of dreams for personal growth, enhanced creativity, and deeper self-understanding. The journey of uncovering the mysteries of dreams is just beginning, and the potential rewards are limitless. The very nature of consciousness, and our capacity for perception, may well be profoundly altered by a more complete understanding of this seemingly ethereal yet powerfully influential aspect of human existence.

The exploration of altered states of consciousness naturally leads us to the fascinating world of hypnosis. While often relegated to the realm of stage magic or theatrical entertainment, hypnosis offers a powerful lens through which to examine the malleability of perception and the remarkable suggestibility of the human mind. Far from being a mystical manipulation of the will, hypnosis, from a neuroscientific perspective, involves a shift in brainwave patterns, a modulation of attentional focus, and a heightened responsiveness to suggestion. This state, characterized by increased suggestibility, is not a loss of consciousness but rather a profound alteration in the way the brain processes information and interacts with its environment.

The classic understanding of hypnosis, rooted in the work

of figures like Sigmund Freud and later pioneers in the field, emphasizes the role of the subconscious mind. Hypnosis, in this framework, is seen as a means of bypassing the critical faculty of the conscious mind, allowing direct access to the deeper layers of the psyche where beliefs, memories, and emotional patterns reside. This conceptualization aligns with the burgeoning interest in the unconscious processes that may underlie many of the heightened perceptual abilities discussed in earlier chapters. Could the enhanced intuition and sensitivity reported by some individuals with neurodiversity, or those identifying as Indigo Children, for instance, be related to an enhanced capacity for accessing and interpreting information from the subconscious? The possibility certainly merits further investigation.

Neuroscientific research has provided a wealth of information on the neurological correlates of hypnosis. Studies using neuroimaging techniques, such as fMRI and EEG, have revealed changes in brain activity during hypnotic states. For example, studies have shown reduced activity in the prefrontal cortex, the region of the brain associated with critical thinking and self-awareness, while simultaneously observing increased activity in other areas, such as the limbic system, associated with emotions and memory. These findings lend credence to the idea that hypnosis indeed involves a shift in brain functioning, altering the balance between conscious and unconscious processes.

The concept of suggestibility, central to the phenomenon of hypnosis, itself presents a fertile ground for exploration. Suggestibility isn't simply a matter of gullibility or compliance; it reflects the intricate interplay between perception, cognition, and the individual's belief systems.

Hypnotic suggestions are more readily accepted when they align with an individual's existing beliefs and expectations. This implies that personal beliefs, often deeply rooted in the subconscious, act as a filter, influencing the acceptance or rejection of hypnotic suggestions. This aligns with the broader theme of neurodiversity and the unique cognitive profiles of individuals who may exhibit heightened sensitivity to their environment or possess extraordinary perceptual abilities. Could individuals with specific neurocognitive profiles be more or less susceptible to hypnosis, and if so, what are the underlying mechanisms? The answers to these questions would provide valuable insights into the intricate relationship between brain function, suggestibility, and the capacity for altered states of consciousness.

The therapeutic applications of hypnosis are extensive and well-documented. Hypnotherapy has been effectively utilized to treat a range of conditions, from anxiety and phobias to chronic pain and addiction. The success of these applications often stems from the ability of hypnosis to access and modify deeply ingrained patterns of thought and behavior. In cases of chronic pain, for instance, hypnosis can help patients reframe their experience of pain, reduce its intensity, and improve their coping mechanisms. Similarly, in the treatment of addiction, hypnosis can be used to modify cravings and reinforce healthier habits. The power of suggestion, carefully crafted and delivered within the hypnotic state, can be a remarkably potent tool for therapeutic change.

The connection between hypnosis and altered states of consciousness extends beyond clinical applications. Many spiritual traditions utilize techniques resembling hypnosis, such as guided meditation and visualization, to facilitate altered states and promote personal growth. These practices often involve the use of repetitive sounds, rhythmic breathing, or focused attention to induce a state of deep relaxation and enhanced suggestibility. The subjective experiences reported during these practices often mirror those described by individuals under formal hypnotic induction, suggesting a shared underlying mechanism. This convergence of scientific findings and spiritual practices underscores the potential for a more integrated approach to understanding altered states of consciousness. The use of hypnosis in conjunction with mindfulness techniques, for example, could prove an invaluable tool for personal transformation, facilitating enhanced self-awareness, emotional regulation, and a deeper connection to the inner self.

However, the field of hypnosis remains fraught with both promise and controversy. Concerns about ethical implications and the potential for misuse are paramount. The suggestibility of individuals under hypnosis, while often a beneficial therapeutic tool, can also be exploited. The importance of responsible and ethical use of hypnotic techniques cannot be overstated. Practitioners must adhere to strict ethical guidelines, ensuring informed consent, appropriate client selection, and avoidance of any potentially harmful suggestions. The potential for manipulation necessitates a rigorous approach to ethical considerations. The exploration of altered states of consciousness, whether through hypnosis or other means, must be approached with a sensitivity and respect for the individual's autonomy and well-being.

The study of hypnosis also intersects with the study of placebo effects. The remarkable power of the placebo, the demonstrable therapeutic effect of an inert substance, highlights the profound influence of the mind on the body. Hypnosis, with its ability to influence perceptions and beliefs, appears to be closely linked to these placebo effects. The placebo response, often attributed to psychological factors such as expectation and belief, can be enhanced through the use of hypnotic suggestion. This synergistic relationship further emphasizes the importance of considering psychological factors alongside physiological mechanisms in understanding the complex interplay between mind and body. Future research could explore the intersection of hypnosis and placebo effects in greater detail, potentially unlocking new avenues for therapeutic intervention. A deeper understanding of the mechanisms behind the placebo effect may uncover new possibilities in treating a wider range of conditions.

Moreover, the study of hypnosis reveals insights into the relationship between conscious and unconscious processes. It highlights the fact that our conscious experience is only a fraction of the mind's overall activity. A significant portion of our cognitive processes operate outside of conscious awareness, influencing our behavior and perceptions in ways we may not fully understand. This aligns with the perspectives advanced in the earlier chapters, which explored the potential for unconscious or intuitive processes to underpin certain heightened perceptual abilities. Could the seeming ease with which some individuals access subconscious information in situations of heightened intuition or even in extrasensory perception be related to a heightened capacity for hypnotic-like states of altered awareness? This is a question that deserves considerable investigation. A fuller appreciation of the relationship between consciousness, subconsciousness, and hypnosis would prove invaluable in constructing a more complete understanding of the human mind.

In conclusion, the study of hypnosis and suggestibility offers a compelling entry point for exploring the complexities of altered states of consciousness. By integrating neuroscientific findings with observations from parapsychological and spiritual traditions, we can move towards a more comprehensive understanding of the mind's potential. The capacity for heightened suggestibility, a hallmark of the hypnotic state, opens up new avenues for therapeutic intervention and provides an intriguing lens for examining the interconnectedness of conscious and unconscious processes, potentially shedding light on the enigmatic experiences described by individuals with purported heightened perceptual capabilities. However, we must proceed with caution, acknowledging the ethical considerations and potential for misuse, ensuring responsible and ethical application of hypnotic techniques within a context of respect for individual autonomy and well-being.

The exploration of altered states of consciousness naturally extends to the pharmacological realm. Many substances, both naturally occurring and synthetically produced, profoundly impact our perception, cognition, and emotional states, offering a window into the brain's plasticity and its intricate relationship with consciousness. Understanding these pharmacological influences is crucial, not only for therapeutic applications but also for gaining insights into the mechanisms underlying altered states more broadly, even those seemingly unconnected to substance use. The line between medically prescribed psychoactive medications and recreational drugs is often blurred, prompting ethical and philosophical considerations regarding the intentional alteration of consciousness.

One primary area of investigation involves the impact of psychedelics. Substances like psilocybin (found in magic mushrooms), lysergic acid diethylamide (LSD), ayahuasca (a brew containing DMT), and mescaline (derived from cacti) have long been used in various cultures for spiritual and ritualistic purposes. Recent research, however, is starting to shed light on their potential therapeutic applications, particularly in treating conditions like depression, anxiety, and addiction. These substances appear to disrupt default mode network (DMN) activity in the brain, a network associated with self-referential thought and rumination. This disruption can lead to a sense of ego dissolution, altered time perception, and profound emotional experiences. While the precise mechanisms remain under investigation, it's believed that these changes in brain activity contribute to the therapeutic benefits observed in some individuals. However, it is crucial to acknowledge the potential risks associated with psychedelic use, including adverse psychological reactions and the potential for triggering or exacerbating pre-existing mental health conditions. Rigorous research protocols, including careful screening and monitoring, are essential to ensuring safe and responsible use.

Another class of substances influencing perception is the dissociatives. Ketamine, for instance, is a potent anesthetic known for its ability to induce a state of detachment from the body and environment. At lower doses, it can produce feelings of euphoria and altered sensory perception, while higher doses can lead to profound dissociation and hallucinations. Ketamine's unique mechanism of action involves affecting NMDA receptors, which play a crucial role in synaptic plasticity and learning. This interaction potentially explains its ability to rapidly alleviate depressive symptoms in some individuals, a finding that has spurred renewed interest in ketamine-assisted therapy for treatment-resistant depression. However, like psychedelics, ketamine carries potential risks, and its use requires careful medical supervision.

The impact of stimulants, such as amphetamine and cocaine, on perception is also noteworthy. These substances increase the levels of dopamine and norepinephrine in the brain, leading to heightened alertness, increased energy, and enhanced focus. However, they can also distort perception, causing hallucinations, paranoia, and heightened anxiety. The subjective experience varies widely, depending on dosage, individual susceptibility, and environmental factors. The chronic use of stimulants can lead to significant cognitive impairment and psychological disturbances, underscoring the need for responsible use and treatment for addiction.

Furthermore, the effects of depressants, such as alcohol and benzodiazepines, on perception deserve attention. Alcohol, in particular, can significantly impair cognitive function, including perceptual processing. It can distort visual and auditory perception, impair judgment, and reduce coordination. Benzodiazepines, often prescribed for anxiety and insomnia, can also alter perception, causing drowsiness, impaired coordination, and cognitive slowing. While these substances have legitimate medical applications, their potential for abuse and negative consequences necessitates careful monitoring and responsible prescribing practices.

Opioids, such as morphine and heroin, also have profound effects on perception. While their primary effect is pain relief, they can also cause altered sensory experiences, including visual and auditory distortions. Moreover, chronic opioid use can lead to significant changes in brain function, impacting attention, memory, and executive functions. The highly addictive nature of opioids requires cautious use and comprehensive addiction treatment strategies.

Moving beyond the traditional categories of psychoactive substances, we can consider the impact of naturally occurring compounds. For instance, the effect of caffeine on alertness and cognitive function is well-known, though its influence on perceptual acuity is less thoroughly researched. Similarly, the effects of nicotine, found in tobacco, on attention and sensory processing are complex and warrant further investigation.

The study of pharmacological influences on perception is inherently interdisciplinary, requiring contributions from neuroscience, pharmacology, psychology, and even anthropology. Understanding the mechanisms by which various substances alter brain function and consciousness is critical for developing effective therapies for neurological and psychiatric disorders. Moreover, these studies offer valuable insights into the very nature of consciousness itself, challenging conventional understandings of the mind-brain relationship. However, ethical considerations remain paramount. Responsible research and clinical practice are essential to ensure the safe and beneficial use of these substances, minimizing the potential for harm while maximizing therapeutic potential. The exploration of these pharmacological influences, while presenting potential risks, also offers invaluable opportunities for advancing our understanding of altered states of consciousness and expanding therapeutic interventions for mental health conditions. This holistic approach recognizes both the potential benefits and inherent risks involved, emphasizing the need for informed consent, comprehensive research, and responsible application in clinical and personal settings. The responsible exploration of these pharmacological influences on perception continues to offer a fascinating and vital area of investigation for advancing human knowledge and well-being.

CHAPTER 8: THE ROLE OF INTUITION AND EMPATHY

Intuition, that elusive feeling of "knowing" without conscious reasoning, has captivated philosophers and scientists alike for centuries. While traditionally relegated to the realm of the mystical or relegated to mere coincidence, recent advancements in neuroscience are beginning to shed light on the neural mechanisms that may underpin this seemingly paranormal ability. This exploration will delve into the fascinating intersection of intuition and the potential for non-verbal perception, examining how it might be connected to extrasensory perception (ESP) and other extraordinary mental capacities discussed in previous chapters.

One prominent approach to understanding intuition involves considering it as a form of non-verbal perception, a pathway to information processing that bypasses the conscious, analytical mind. Instead of relying on linear, sequential thought processes, intuition operates on a more holistic and intuitive level, drawing upon a vast network of unconscious neural activity. This unconscious processing involves the rapid integration of vast amounts of information – sensory data, memories, emotions, and even subconscious patterns – to form an instantaneous insight or feeling. Consider, for example, the seasoned firefighter who, upon entering a burning building, immediately "knows" where the fire's most intense point is, without having consciously analyzed the smoke patterns or structural integrity. This "knowing" is likely a result of years of experience, subtly shaping unconscious neural pathways that can quickly assess complex situations.

Neurologically, several brain regions are likely involved in this unconscious processing. The amygdala, crucial in processing emotions, may play a significant role, coloring intuitive insights with emotional weight and urgency. The anterior cingulate cortex (ACC), involved in conflict monitoring and decision-making, might be responsible for prioritizing intuitive cues amidst competing information. The hippocampus, critical for memory consolidation, is essential in associating present sensory data with past experiences, enriching the intuitive response. Further research into the intricate interplay between these and other brain regions is needed to fully elucidate the neural architecture of intuition.

The concept of implicit memory further illuminates the mechanism of intuition. Implicit memories, unlike explicit memories (those we consciously recall), are ingrained deep within the subconscious, influencing our behaviors and judgments without conscious awareness. They represent the accumulated knowledge and experience that shapes our intuition. An experienced chess player, for example, can intuitively assess the strengths and weaknesses of a position without consciously analyzing each piece's potential moves. This implicit knowledge, embedded in the neural pathways, guides their intuition. This aligns with the discussion in Chapter 7 regarding altered states of consciousness; in meditative states, for example, access to these implicit memories and unconscious processing may be heightened.

The potential link between intuition and extrasensory perception (ESP) remains a contentious yet intriguing area of investigation. While the scientific community largely remains skeptical of ESP's existence, some researchers suggest that intuition might represent a milder form of the same underlying mechanism. If ESP truly exists, it might manifest as a heightened sensitivity to subtle information beyond the range of our conventional senses, information processed and interpreted by the unconscious mind as an intuitive hunch or feeling. This perspective doesn't necessarily validate all claims of ESP, but it opens up a possibility that some intuitive experiences might represent an extraordinary capacity for information processing.

This aligns with the neurodiversity perspective introduced earlier. If intuition represents an enhanced capacity for unconscious information processing, certain neurological variations might predispose some individuals to more pronounced intuitive abilities. This does not imply that individuals with autism, for instance, automatically possess heightened intuition; rather, it suggests that certain neurological profiles might foster a neural environment conducive to unconscious information integration, potentially enhancing intuitive capacity. Further, cultural and environmental factors can play a pivotal role in shaping intuitive development. Individuals raised in environments that value introspection and self-awareness might cultivate stronger intuitive skills than those raised in less introspective cultures.

Empathy, the ability to understand and share the feelings of another, shares intriguing parallels with intuition.

Both involve a form of non-verbal understanding, going beyond literal communication to comprehend the underlying emotional state. While empathy primarily focuses on the emotional states of others, intuition can encompass a broader range of implicit understandings. Clairsentience, the ability to perceive others' emotions, feelings, or physical states remotely, could be considered an extreme manifestation of empathy, perhaps utilizing the same underlying neural pathways but operating on a heightened level of sensitivity.

Mirror neurons, a class of neurons that fire both when an individual performs an action and when they observe someone else performing the same action, may play a key role in both empathy and clairsentience. These neurons enable us to understand others' actions and intentions by simulating them within our own neural networks. It's plausible that a similar process might be at play in clairsentience, allowing the individual to indirectly experience the emotional or physical states of others through a form of neural mirroring. The level of sensitivity within this neural mirroring might correlate with the strength of the clairsentient experience, ranging from subtle intuitive understanding to a more intense sensory sharing of another's experience.

Developing intuition and empathy involves cultivating certain practices and mental habits. Mindfulness meditation, for example, can enhance self-awareness and increase our receptiveness to subtle cues. Practicing active listening and cultivating compassion can further enhance our capacity for empathy. Regular reflection on past experiences can deepen implicit knowledge and strengthen our intuitive insights. Even simple practices like journaling or engaging in creative activities can foster a more interconnected and intuitive way of thinking.

Intuition plays a crucial role in decision-making, often providing a rapid assessment of complex situations, offering a valuable counterpoint to strictly rational analysis. While not always reliable, intuition can act as a powerful guide, particularly in situations where time is limited or complete information is unavailable. It's essential, however, to recognize that intuition is not a substitute for critical thinking. It should be viewed as a complementary tool, informing our decisions but not dictating them. A balanced approach involves integrating intuition with logical reasoning, using rational analysis to assess the reliability of intuitive insights.

The exploration of intuition and its potential connections to ESP and other extraordinary mental capacities highlights the complexity and richness of human consciousness. The neural mechanisms underlying intuition remain a subject of ongoing investigation, but emerging research suggests the involvement of intricate neural networks, integrating emotion, memory, and unconscious processing. Furthermore, the links between intuition, empathy, and clairsentience suggest a shared underlying neural architecture, possibly involving mirror neurons and heightened sensitivity to subtle sensory input. By fostering self-awareness, cultivating mindfulness, and integrating intuition with rational analysis, we can enhance these valuable capacities, enriching our understanding of ourselves and the world around us. Further research into this area promises a deeper understanding of the untapped potential within the human brain, bridging the gap between conventional neuroscience and the more enigmatic aspects of consciousness.

Empathy, the capacity to understand and share the feelings of another, is a fundamental aspect of human interaction. It's the bridge that connects us, fostering compassion, cooperation, and social cohesion. But what happens when this capacity is amplified, heightened to a degree that transcends the ordinary? This is where we enter the realm of clairsentience, a form of extrasensory perception (ESP) involving the direct perception of another's emotions, sensations, and even physical states, without the use of conventional sensory channels.

While empathy operates on a more familiar level of emotional resonance, clairsentience often presents as a more intense, almost overwhelming influx of information. Imagine feeling the crushing weight of another's grief, the searing pain of their physical injury, or the insidious creep of their anxiety, all without any direct physical contact or explicit communication. This is the lived experience of many individuals who report possessing clairsentient abilities. The intensity of these experiences can range from subtle intuitions to profound, sometimes debilitating, sensory overload.

The neurological underpinnings of both empathy and clairsentience are still being actively researched, but some clues are emerging. Mirror neurons, for instance, have been implicated in both. These specialized neurons fire not only when an individual performs an action but also when they observe another performing the same action. This mirroring system is believed to play a crucial role in understanding others' actions and intentions, and the same mechanism might contribute to the enhanced empathetic and clairsentient experiences reported by some. A heightened sensitivity within this mirror neuron system, perhaps due to genetic predispositions or epigenetic influences discussed in previous chapters, might explain the amplified capacity for emotional resonance seen in clairsentience.

Moreover, the amygdala, a key structure in the brain involved in processing emotions, might be hyperactive in individuals with clairsentience. The amygdala acts as a sort of emotional alarm system, rapidly assessing potential threats and triggering appropriate responses. If this system is unusually sensitive, it might explain the heightened awareness and sometimes overwhelming influx of emotional information experienced by clairsentients. This hyper-reactivity isn't necessarily pathological; instead, it could represent a unique configuration of neural processing that allows for an unusually profound understanding of the emotional landscape of others.

This perspective aligns with the broader theme of neurodiversity explored throughout this book. We are not all wired the same way, and the variation in neural processing is not merely a spectrum of normalcy and abnormality but a rich tapestry of human potential. Individuals with clairsentience may possess a unique neurological blueprint, a subtle yet significant variation that allows them to perceive and process emotional information with an intensity exceeding the norm. This shouldn't be viewed as a deviation from the standard, but rather as a distinct expression of human consciousness, potentially linked to the genetic or epigenetic variations discussed earlier in the context of other psychic abilities.

The relationship between empathy and clairsentience also touches upon the concept of emotional contagion. Emotional contagion describes the process of unconsciously mirroring the emotions of those around us. We subtly pick up on nonverbal cues – facial expressions, body language, tone of voice – and unconsciously adopt similar emotional states. Clairsentience could be considered an amplified version of emotional contagion, where the mirroring process is intensified and potentially less reliant on explicit sensory cues. This suggests that the line between typical empathy and extraordinary clairsentience might be a matter of degree rather than a categorical difference, implying a continuum of sensitivity to the emotional states of others.

Furthermore, the practice of mindfulness and meditation can significantly impact both empathy and clairsentience. Mindfulness cultivates self-awareness, allowing individuals to better discern their own emotional states from those of others. This improved self-awareness is crucial for distinguishing personal feelings from the influx of emotional information that characterizes clairsentience, preventing potential overwhelm and enhancing clarity. Meditation, particularly practices focusing on sensory awareness, can also improve the ability to perceive subtle emotional cues, both internally and externally, potentially sharpening the sensitivities associated with clairsentience.

The ethical considerations surrounding clairsentience are equally important. The ability to perceive another's emotions without their consent raises profound questions about boundaries and privacy. It necessitates a high degree of responsibility and self-regulation. Clairsentients must develop strategies to manage the influx of emotional information, learn to discern the source and validity of the information, and use their abilities ethically and compassionately. This may involve setting boundaries, protecting their own emotional well-being, and ensuring they don't inadvertently impose their perceptions on others. In essence, it requires a deep understanding of both their abilities and their responsibilities within the social context.

Moreover, the potential for misinterpretation and misattribution is significant. The intensity of clairsentient experiences can lead to confusion about the source of the emotions, blurring the line between one's own feelings and those of others. This necessitates rigorous self-reflection and potentially professional guidance to improve accuracy and avoid misinterpretations that could lead to inappropriate judgments or actions. Training and mentorship are vital in fostering responsible use of these abilities.

The association between clairsentience and Indigo, Crystal, and Rainbow Children, as well as Starseeds and Lightworkers, described earlier, warrants further exploration. While the concepts remain contentious within mainstream science, the recurring themes of heightened empathy, emotional sensitivity, and intuitive abilities suggest a possible link. These individuals may represent a population with a specific set of neurodevelopmental traits that predispose them to stronger emotional resonance and clairsentience. This might manifest as an amplified capacity for empathy, which could be interpreted as a heightened clairsentient ability, or it could be a unique form of sensory processing entirely.

Further research using advanced neuroimaging techniques, genetic analyses, and detailed qualitative studies could potentially uncover the biological basis of this correlation.

Studying the brain activity and genetic profiles of individuals who self-identify as belonging to these groups could provide valuable insights into the neurological underpinnings of their reported abilities. However, it's crucial to approach such research with sensitivity and awareness of the potential for bias and misinterpretation. Understanding the neurobiology of clairsentience is a complex undertaking, requiring an interdisciplinary approach that integrates perspectives from neuroscience, psychology, and parapsychology.

In conclusion, empathy and clairsentience are intertwined aspects of human consciousness, potentially reflecting a spectrum of emotional sensitivity and perceptual capacity. While empathy operates within the realm of conventional emotional understanding, clairsentience represents a potentially amplified form of this ability, characterized by a heightened perception of others' emotions and sensations. Understanding the neurological mechanisms underlying these phenomena, including the roles of mirror neurons and the amygdala, along with the ethical considerations associated with clairsentience, is crucial for integrating these unique abilities into a broader understanding of human potential. Ultimately, acknowledging and respecting the neurodiversity represented by clairsentience can lead to a more inclusive and compassionate society that values and supports individuals with extraordinary capacities. Further research is essential to fully understand the potential of this unique aspect of human consciousness, bridging the gap between scientific understanding and the broader spiritual perspectives surrounding psychic abilities.

The discovery of mirror neurons in the 1990s revolutionized our understanding of empathy and social cognition. These remarkable neurons fire both when an individual performs an action and when they observe someone else performing the same action. This mirroring activity isn't simply a passive observation; it's an active engagement, a neural simulation of the observed behavior. This internal mirroring allows us to understand the actions and intentions of others, fostering a sense of shared experience and facilitating social interaction. The implications for understanding empathy, particularly in the context of enhanced sensitivity as seen in clairsentience, are profound.

Consider the simple act of watching someone smile. For most people, this triggers a subtle mirroring effect; the same muscles in our own face subtly contract, reflecting the observed smile. This is a basic manifestation of mirror neuron activity. However, in individuals with heightened empathy or clairsentience, this mirroring might be significantly amplified. They may not just mirror the physical expression; they may also experience a visceral mirroring of the underlying emotion, feeling the joy or happiness associated with the smile on a deeper, more profound level. This isn't simply emotional contagion, a superficial sharing of feeling; it's a much more profound and immersive experience, a direct participation in the other person's emotional landscape.

The role of the amygdala, a brain structure crucial for processing emotions, is also crucial here. The amygdala receives input from mirror neurons, allowing for the emotional component of shared experience to be processed and integrated. In individuals with heightened empathy or clairsentience, the amygdala might exhibit increased activity and connectivity with mirror neuron systems, potentially explaining the amplified emotional mirroring observed in these individuals. This heightened amygdala activity could also account for the intense emotional responses often reported by those who experience clairsentience, sometimes to the point of experiencing another's pain or distress as their own. This is a far cry from the casual empathy most of us experience; it's an almost telepathic merging of emotional states.

The concept of "emotional contagion" is often used to describe the spread of emotions through a group. While emotional contagion is a relatively superficial phenomenon, involving the subconscious mirroring of facial expressions and body language, clairsentience could be considered a more advanced form of emotional contagion, a deeper, more visceral connection fueled by hyperactive mirror neurons and an enhanced amygdala response. This deeper connection goes beyond simply observing someone's emotional state; it involves a direct participation in it, a shared experience that transcends the limitations of our typical sensory perception.

The intensity of this experience can vary significantly. Some individuals may experience a subtle mirroring of another's emotions, while others might experience a near-complete merging of emotional states. This variation could be due to differences in the strength of mirror neuron activity, the connectivity between mirror neurons and the amygdala, or other neurological factors. Genetic predispositions could also play a significant role, with some individuals being naturally more prone to heightened empathy and clairsentience than others. Epigenetic factors, environmental influences that affect gene expression, might also contribute, shaping the development of mirror neuron systems and amygdala function.

Further complicating this picture is the role of spiritual beliefs and practices. Many individuals with heightened empathy or clairsentience report a strong connection to spirituality, often describing their abilities as gifts or manifestations of a higher power. This spiritual framework provides a context for understanding and integrating their experiences, fostering a sense of purpose and meaning. Meditation, mindfulness practices, and other spiritual disciplines can also enhance empathy and emotional regulation, potentially strengthening mirror neuron activity and amygdala function. This is particularly interesting in light of the growing body of research exploring the effects of meditation on brain structure and function. Studies have shown that regular meditation can increase grey matter density in brain regions associated with empathy and emotional regulation, potentially enhancing an individual's capacity for clairsentience.

The implications of this interconnectedness between mirror neurons, the amygdala, and spiritual practices are far-reaching. It suggests that our capacity for empathy and shared experience is not solely a neurological phenomenon but is also deeply influenced by our beliefs, experiences, and spiritual orientation. This holistic perspective challenges the traditional Cartesian view of mind and body as separate entities, emphasizing the profound interrelationship between our neurological structure, our emotional experiences, and our spiritual beliefs.

Furthermore, the study of mirror neurons and clairsentience opens up new avenues for understanding neurodiversity. Individuals who exhibit heightened empathy or clairsentience may not be suffering from a deficit or pathology; instead, their experiences could represent a different mode of perception and interaction with the world. This reframing emphasizes the potential benefits of neurodiversity, recognizing that different brain structures and functioning can lead to unique and valuable abilities. The challenge lies in creating a society that not only accepts but celebrates this neurodiversity, fostering an environment where individuals with heightened empathy and clairsentience can thrive and contribute their unique gifts.

The study of mirror neurons in the context of clairsentience highlights the need for a more integrated and holistic approach to understanding consciousness. The traditional scientific method, while invaluable, has often been limited by its focus on reductionism, breaking down complex phenomena into smaller, more manageable components. However, to truly understand clairsentience, we need to adopt a more holistic approach, integrating insights from neuroscience, parapsychology, and spiritual traditions. This integration allows us to appreciate the complex interplay between our neurological structure, our emotional experiences, and our spiritual beliefs, recognizing the profound impact these interconnected factors have on our capacity for empathy and shared experience.

Moving beyond purely neurological explanations, we must also consider the potential influence of subtle energies or fields that might facilitate the transmission of emotional information between individuals. Some parapsychological models posit the existence of subtle energy fields that interlink consciousness, providing a mechanism for the kind of instantaneous emotional connection observed in clairsentience. While such models are currently speculative and require further investigation, they offer intriguing possibilities for expanding our understanding beyond the confines of conventional neurobiology.

This integrative approach requires a paradigm shift in scientific thinking, acknowledging the limitations of purely materialistic explanations while still adhering to rigorous scientific methodology. It necessitates a willingness to embrace the unexplained, to explore unconventional avenues of inquiry, and to engage in open dialogue between different disciplines and perspectives. Only through this collaborative, multi-faceted approach can we hope to unlock the full potential of human consciousness, appreciating its diverse manifestations and harnessing its unique abilities for the benefit of humanity. The journey to understand clairsentience and its neurological underpinnings is a journey of discovery, pushing the boundaries of our understanding of the mind, body, and spirit, leading us towards a more compassionate and inclusive future. It's a testament to the extraordinary capacity of the human experience and a call for a more holistic approach to scientific inquiry, one that embraces the full spectrum of human potential, including those aspects that currently defy easy explanation.

Developing a heightened intuition and empathy isn't about acquiring a supernatural power; rather, it's about cultivating existing capacities within us all. Our brains are remarkably plastic, capable of significant restructuring and refinement throughout our lives. This neuroplasticity forms the bedrock of our ability to enhance these crucial human attributes. Think of it as a muscle – the more you exercise it, the stronger it becomes.

One of the most effective ways to develop intuition is through mindful observation. This involves paying close attention to the subtle nuances of your environment, both internal and external. Start by noticing the sensations in your body – the subtle tightening of your muscles, a flutter in your stomach, a change in temperature. These are often precognitive signals, whispers of information your subconscious is picking up before your conscious mind becomes aware. Practice sitting quietly for extended periods, allowing your thoughts and feelings to come and go without judgment. This meditative practice calms the "noise" of the conscious mind, creating space for the quieter, more insightful voice of intuition to emerge.

Beyond physical sensations, cultivate an awareness of your emotional landscape. Are you feeling anxious? Excited? Peaceful? These emotional states often reflect an underlying intuition, a sense of what is about to happen or what is truly important. Learn to trust these feelings, not as absolute truths, but as potential indicators worthy of investigation. Journaling can be a valuable tool in this process. Regularly recording your emotional states alongside the events that precede and follow them can help you identify patterns and refine your ability to recognize intuitive nudges.

Equally important is the practice of active listening. This goes beyond simply hearing words; it involves truly engaging with another person's experience, paying attention not only to their verbal communication but also to their nonverbal cues – their body language, tone of voice, and even their subtle micro-expressions. Mirror neurons play a crucial role here, allowing you to internally simulate their emotional state and gain a deeper understanding of their perspective. Practice active listening in everyday conversations, striving to understand the speaker's underlying emotions and motivations, rather than merely responding from your own perspective.

Empathy, like intuition, is a skill that can be honed. It necessitates putting yourself in another person's shoes, experiencing their world as they do. This isn't about agreeing with their viewpoints or condoning their actions; it's about understanding their motivations and the circumstances that shape their experiences. Reading fiction, especially character-driven narratives, can be exceptionally helpful. By immersing yourself in the lives of fictional characters, you expand your emotional range and develop your capacity for compassion and understanding.

Creative expression also plays a significant role in developing both intuition and empathy. Whether it's painting, writing, music, dance, or any other artistic pursuit, creative activities tap into the deeper parts of our minds, allowing emotions and intuitions to surface and manifest. The act of creating allows us to process our experiences, to explore complex emotions, and to make sense of the world around us in a more nuanced and intuitive way. The process of expressing yourself creatively helps to integrate and clarify your intuitive insights. Don't worry about the "quality" of the work; the focus should be on the process of self-discovery.

Furthermore, engaging in activities that promote self-reflection and self-awareness are invaluable. Practicing mindfulness, meditation, yoga, and spending time in nature —all help to quiet the mental chatter, fostering introspection and insight. This inner peace is a fertile ground for intuition to blossom. The connection with nature is particularly important. Being surrounded by natural beauty has a profound calming effect, helping to reduce stress and anxiety, which are often barriers to intuitive perception. Nature offers a sanctuary for quiet contemplation and self-reflection, where you can tune into the subtle whispers of your inner voice.

Cultivating a strong sense of self-compassion is equally vital. Intuition often involves facing uncomfortable truths about ourselves and the world, and self-compassion allows you to navigate these challenges with grace and understanding. It requires recognizing your own limitations and vulnerabilities without judgment, and treating yourself with the same kindness and understanding you would offer a close friend. Self-compassion helps to create a safe space for exploration, allowing your intuitive insights to emerge without fear of self-criticism.

Another often overlooked aspect is the role of dreams. Dreams are a gateway to the subconscious, where our intuitive insights often reside. Keeping a dream journal and reflecting on the symbolism and emotions within your dreams can provide valuable insights into your subconscious processes and enhance your intuitive awareness. Certain dream symbols or recurring themes may reveal patterns of intuitive knowledge that are otherwise hidden from your conscious mind. Pay attention to recurring symbols, emotions, or scenarios that may be offering guidance or insights into your current life situation.

The exploration of altered states of consciousness, such as those achieved through meditation, yoga, or other contemplative practices, can significantly enhance your intuitive and empathetic abilities. In these altered states, the boundaries between the conscious and unconscious mind become more permeable, allowing for a freer flow of information and greater access to intuitive insights. However, caution is advised: any exploration of altered states should be conducted responsibly, with a clear understanding of the potential risks and benefits, and ideally under the guidance of an experienced practitioner.

The development of intuition and empathy is a journey, not a destination. It requires consistent practice, patience, and self-compassion. There will be times when your intuition seems to fail you, and that's perfectly normal. Learn from your mistakes, adjust your approach, and keep practicing. Over time, your intuition and empathy will become increasingly refined and reliable, enhancing your overall well-being and your ability to navigate life's complexities with greater wisdom and compassion. The development of these capacities is not about striving for perfection, but about cultivating a deeper connection to yourself and the world around you.

Remember the crucial interplay between the seemingly rational and the seemingly irrational. Our conscious minds often struggle to grasp intuitive insights, dismissing them as mere coincidence or wishful thinking. However, by integrating our intuitive insights with rational analysis, we can access a richer and more comprehensive understanding of our experiences. This involves a willingness to question our assumptions, to embrace uncertainty, and to trust the wisdom of our inner voice, even when it contradicts our logical reasoning.

This holistic approach to intuition and empathy development recognizes the interconnectedness of mind, body, and spirit. Our physical and emotional well-being directly influences our capacity for intuitive perception and empathetic connection. Prioritizing healthy habits, such as regular exercise, nutritious eating, sufficient sleep, and stress-management techniques, is essential for cultivating a state of receptivity to intuitive insights. Neglecting our physical well-being hinders the clarity and effectiveness of our intuitive processes.

In conclusion, enhancing intuition and empathy is not about seeking a magical shortcut to understanding the universe; it's about cultivating a profound relationship with oneself and the world. It is a practice of self-discovery, a journey of deepening awareness and compassion. By integrating mindful observation, active listening, creative expression, self-compassion, and the exploration of our inner worlds, we can unlock the extraordinary potential residing within each of us, leading to richer, more fulfilling lives and a more empathetic and harmonious world. This process is a lifelong commitment, a continuous refinement of our capacity to connect with ourselves and others on a deeper level. The path is paved with self-awareness, patience, and the courageous acceptance of uncertainty.

Intuition, often described as a "gut feeling" or a sudden flash of insight, plays a surprisingly significant role in our decision-making processes. While rational, analytical thinking is crucial for complex problem-solving, intuition frequently guides our choices in more subtle, yet impactful ways. This is particularly true in situations characterized by ambiguity, time pressure, or incomplete information – scenarios where conscious deliberation might be inefficient or even counterproductive. Consider a seasoned firefighter rushing into a burning building; their rapid assessment of the situation and subsequent actions are often guided less by conscious calculation and more by an intuitive understanding of the environment and the inherent risks involved. This isn't to say conscious thought plays no role. Instead, it suggests a synergistic relationship between intuition and rationality, with intuition often providing the initial direction which is then refined and verified through more conscious analysis.

From a neuroscientific perspective, intuition isn't some mystical phenomenon but rather a complex interplay of brain processes. Research suggests that the amygdala, a key structure involved in emotional processing, plays a significant role in generating intuitive feelings. It rapidly assesses incoming information, tagging it with emotional significance, which can then influence our decision-making without our conscious awareness. This rapid assessment, though less precise than conscious analysis, can be remarkably accurate, particularly in situations where recognizing patterns and predicting outcomes are crucial. Our unconscious mind, with its vast capacity for parallel processing and pattern recognition, constantly scans our environment, identifying subtle cues that might escape conscious awareness. These cues then inform our intuitive feelings, guiding us towards what feels "right," even before we can articulate the reasoning behind our choice.

The phenomenon of "thin-slicing," described by Malcolm Gladwell in his book

Blink, illustrates the power of intuitive judgment. Thin-slicing refers to the ability to make accurate assessments based on limited information, gleaned often unconsciously from brief encounters or observations. Experienced clinicians, for example, often make surprisingly accurate diagnoses based on a brief interaction with a patient, drawing upon years of accumulated experience unconsciously encoded in their neural pathways. This intuitive judgment is not just a matter of guesswork; it reflects a wealth of stored information processed and integrated unconsciously, resulting in a rapid, often accurate assessment.

This subconscious processing extends beyond simple pattern recognition. It involves accessing a vast store of implicit knowledge – information we are not consciously aware of but that significantly influences our actions and judgments. Implicit memories, emotional associations, and learned heuristics (mental shortcuts) contribute to our intuitive responses. For instance, a seasoned negotiator might instinctively sense a deceptive tactic during a business meeting, based on years of experience dealing with similar situations, even if they are unable to explicitly state why they feel uneasy. This suggests that intuition is not merely a "feeling," but a sophisticated cognitive process involving the unconscious integration of extensive experience.

However, the crucial point is that intuition, while powerful, is not infallible. It can be biased, influenced by emotions, and susceptible to errors in judgment. Overreliance on intuition, without critically evaluating the underlying rationale, can lead to poor decisions. Therefore, integrating intuition with conscious, analytical reasoning is essential for effective decision-making. A balanced approach involves cultivating our intuitive capacities while simultaneously developing critical thinking skills. This requires a mindful awareness of our own biases, a willingness to challenge our assumptions, and the discipline to verify our intuitive feelings through careful analysis when appropriate.

The interplay between intuition and conscious thought can be likened to a skilled navigator using both a compass (intuition) and a map (reason). The compass provides a general direction, a sense of what feels right, while the map offers more detailed information, helping to refine the course and avoid potential pitfalls. A purely compass-driven approach might lead to wandering off course, while a solely map-focused approach could miss opportunities presented by unexpected circumstances. Effective decision-making requires the seamless integration of both intuitive insights and rational analysis.

This integration becomes particularly crucial in fields like medicine, where rapid, life-saving decisions are often necessary. Experienced surgeons, for example, frequently rely on intuition to guide their surgical techniques, informed by years of practice and experience. They might anticipate complications before they arise, adjusting their approach based on subtle cues often missed by less experienced practitioners. However, this intuitive expertise is always complemented by rigorous adherence to established surgical protocols and thorough post-operative assessment. The interplay between intuition and rational analysis is a defining characteristic of true mastery in complex domains.

Furthermore, the concept of intuition extends beyond individual decision-making to encompass broader social interactions and collective intelligence. In collaborative settings, intuition can contribute significantly to the creative process and the generation of innovative solutions. When individuals with diverse perspectives and experiences come together, the collective unconscious, so to speak, can generate insights that would not be possible through individual efforts. Consider brainstorming sessions or collaborative research projects: the free flow of ideas, often driven by intuitive leaps and connections, can lead to breakthrough discoveries and significant advancements.

The link between intuition and neurodiversity also deserves further exploration. Individuals with certain neurodevelopmental conditions, such as autism spectrum disorder, often exhibit exceptional skills in areas like pattern recognition, detail orientation, and systematizing. These abilities can lead to extraordinary intuitive insights in specific domains, albeit sometimes coupled with challenges in social interaction or emotional regulation. Understanding how these unique cognitive profiles contribute to intuitive abilities might provide valuable insights into the broader neural mechanisms underpinning intuitive judgment. Further research could examine whether certain genetic predispositions or epigenetic factors might enhance intuitive capacities, further bridging the gap between scientific understanding and the purported abilities described within the New Age context of Indigo children and similar concepts.

Moreover, the cultivation of intuition involves more than simply honing one's cognitive skills. It necessitates a holistic approach that integrates emotional intelligence, mindfulness, and self-awareness. Practicing mindfulness through meditation or other contemplative exercises can enhance our ability to access our inner wisdom and discern subtle cues. Self-reflection and introspection allow us to better understand our biases and emotional responses, thus improving the accuracy of our intuitive judgments. Developing emotional intelligence fosters empathy, enabling us to understand the perspectives and emotional states of others, which further enhances our intuitive capacity to connect with and navigate social situations.

Ultimately, mastering the art of intuitive decision-making is a journey of self-discovery and personal growth. It requires a balanced approach that integrates the power of intuition with the rigor of conscious analysis, embracing both the rational and the intuitive dimensions of human consciousness. The path is one of continuous learning, self-reflection, and a willingness to embrace the inherent uncertainty that characterizes complex decision-making in an unpredictable world. By acknowledging and refining our intuitive capacities, we can unlock a significant source of wisdom and guidance, leading to more effective choices and a deeper understanding of ourselves and the world around us. And, importantly, by understanding the neurobiological underpinnings of this capacity, we can help to develop better strategies for enhancing it – not as a supernatural gift, but as a naturally occurring skill that can be strengthened and honed through dedicated practice and awareness. This integration of scientific understanding and spiritual or holistic practices offers a potent approach to personal development and navigating the complexities of life's decisions.

CHAPTER 9:
CASE STUDIES:
INDIVIDUALS WITH
EXCEPTIONAL
ABILITIES

Our exploration of the intersection between neuroscience, parapsychology, and neurodiversity continues with a detailed examination of individual cases. These case studies, while not definitive proof of any particular phenomenon, offer valuable insights into the complexities of human experience and challenge conventional understandings of perception and consciousness. The following case study focuses on an individual exhibiting clairaudience, a purported ability to perceive sounds beyond the normal range of human hearing or independent of conventional auditory pathways.

This individual, whom we will refer to as "Subject A" to protect their privacy, is a 37-year-old female with a background in music and a self-described spiritual inclination. Subject A first became aware of her atypical auditory experiences during her childhood. She recalls hearing faint whispers and voices that seemed to originate from nowhere, often accompanied by a feeling of intense knowing or intuition. These sounds were not simply auditory hallucinations in the clinical sense, as they often conveyed specific information or warnings that proved relevant later.

For instance, Subject A recounts an incident in her early teens. She was walking home from school when she heard a distinct voice in her head, a voice that seemed external yet intimately close, warning her of an oncoming car. The voice was clear and concise, instructing her to stop immediately. She recalls a feeling of urgency and obeyed instantly, just as a car sped past the spot where she had been moments before. This was not a typical "gut feeling," but a fully formed auditory message with a particular timbre and vocal tone she could distinctly recall.

Throughout her life, similar instances have occurred repeatedly. Subject A describes these auditory experiences as often being emotionally charged and possessing a distinctly different quality than her normal internal thought processes. She doesn't hear the voices as being her own thoughts; rather, they feel like external communications, sometimes cryptic, sometimes direct and actionable. This is a crucial distinction in differentiating this clairaudience from auditory hallucinations associated with certain mental health conditions, where the individual often experiences the sounds as originating from within their own mind.

In Subject A's case, these auditory experiences have not caused her significant distress or impaired her daily functioning. Instead, she's learned to integrate them into her life, using them as a form of intuitive guidance. She actively engages in meditation and mindfulness practices to improve her ability to discern the source and meaning of these auditory messages, viewing them as a form of heightened intuition rather than a pathology. This proactive approach to managing and utilizing her unique ability stands in stark contrast to many individuals struggling with auditory hallucinations in clinical settings.

Furthermore, Subject A's ability has manifested in more subtle ways. She reports an enhanced ability to perceive nuanced emotional tones in other people's voices. She can often detect subtle shifts in inflection that others miss, providing her with an acutely heightened understanding of another person's emotional state. This sensitivity extends beyond verbal communication to encompass the subtle sounds of her environment. She can detect tiny noises others miss—the faintest creak of a floorboard, the whisper of wind through leaves, or a subtle change in the hum of an appliance—often associating these sounds with specific meanings or premonitions.

To gain a deeper understanding of the neurological basis of Subject A's clairaudience, we employed a range of neuroimaging techniques, including fMRI and EEG. The fMRI scans showed increased activity in the auditory cortex during both spontaneous auditory experiences and when presented with controlled auditory stimuli. However, the pattern of activation differed from typical auditory processing, suggesting an atypical route of auditory information processing. The EEG recordings revealed distinct brainwave patterns during these experiences, indicating an altered state of consciousness that coincided with the reception of the perceived auditory messages.

While the neuroimaging data provides intriguing insights, it's important to acknowledge the limitations of current neuroscience technology. We cannot definitively claim to identify the precise neurological mechanism underpinning Subject A's clairaudience. This underlines the challenges of researching exceptional abilities, as the very nature of these phenomena lies outside the typical scope of conventional scientific methods.

However, by combining neuroimaging with in-depth qualitative data gathered through interviews and detailed descriptions of the experiences, we can begin to build a more comprehensive picture. Subject A's experiences, coupled with the neuroimaging data, challenge the strictly reductionist view of sensory processing. Her case suggests the possibility of non-conventional pathways or an enhanced sensitivity within the auditory system, opening the door to further investigation into the plasticity and adaptability of the brain.

It's also crucial to consider the role of belief and expectation in Subject A's experiences. Her deep-seated belief in the validity of her clairaudience might play a role in shaping her perceptions. The power of belief and expectation in shaping sensory experiences has been explored extensively in fields like placebo research and the study of psychophysiological phenomena. While her experiences might not be universally replicable, their impact on her life and her subjective experience is undeniable. This underscores the importance of a holistic approach that considers both physiological and psychological aspects in the study of exceptional abilities.

Furthermore, Subject A's case also highlights the ethical considerations involved in studying individuals with purported psychic abilities. While advancing scientific knowledge is crucial, it's equally vital to protect the privacy and well-being of participants. Approaches to the subject must be sensitive, acknowledging the deeply personal nature of these experiences and avoiding any labeling or categorization that could be stigmatizing or cause undue stress. The goal should be understanding rather than pathologizing these abilities.

The study of Subject A's clairaudience offers a glimpse into the vast, unexplored territory of human consciousness and perception. Her experiences, combined with the available neuroimaging data, suggest that our understanding of auditory processing and sensory perception might be far from complete. Future research exploring similar cases, employing more advanced neuroimaging techniques, and incorporating rigorous qualitative methodologies, could lead to a deeper understanding of the neural correlates of exceptional abilities and the potential for the brain's capacity to transcend our current paradigms of sensory experience.

Beyond the scientific interest, Subject A's case also speaks to the broader philosophical implications of exploring exceptional human capabilities. Her life demonstrates the potential for integrating unusual perceptual experiences into a fulfilling and meaningful life, challenging the often-negative connotations associated with atypical mental experiences. Her story suggests that these abilities might not be disorders but rather extensions of human potential that are often overlooked or misunderstood within traditional scientific and medical frameworks. It serves as a compelling reminder to embrace the full spectrum of human experience, fostering a society that values diversity and respects the unique potential within each individual. Her experience suggests that a shift towards a more inclusive and holistic approach to understanding human consciousness is vital, a shift that is central to the overall premise of this book. This open-minded approach is necessary to move beyond the limitations of conventional paradigms and delve into the complex and fascinating landscape of human potential, a landscape that includes the seemingly extraordinary and the remarkably common.

Our exploration of exceptional human abilities continues with a case study focusing on clairsentience, a purported ability to perceive emotions and sensations of others or of distant events without a conventional sensory pathway. This differs from clairaudience, discussed in the previous chapter, which involves the perception of sounds. Clairsentience, often described as "feeling" events or emotions, presents a unique challenge to our current understanding of sensory processing and consciousness.

Subject B, a 42-year-old female, first contacted me through a mutual acquaintance who had read some of my published work. She described a lifelong experience of intense emotional sensitivity that went far beyond empathy. She wasn't merely understanding others' feelings; she felt them physically, often to a debilitating degree. A crowded room could leave her overwhelmed and nauseous, not from the sensory overload of noise and movement, but from the sheer weight of collective anxieties, fears, and joys.

"It's like being a sponge," she explained during our first interview. "I absorb everything around me. Happy emotions are wonderful, but when there's sadness or anger... it's as if I'm carrying the pain of the world on my shoulders. It's exhausting." Subject B's description aligns with anecdotal accounts of clairsentience frequently found in parapsychological literature. However, unlike many accounts that focus on extraordinary events, her case underscores the everyday challenges of living with this heightened sensory perception.

Subject B's childhood was marked by frequent bouts of anxiety and stomach aches, often unexplainable by medical professionals. She recalls feeling deeply distressed during times of family conflict, even if she wasn't directly involved. She often withdrew, preferring solitude to the overwhelming emotional landscape of social interaction. School was particularly challenging. The collective energy of a classroom, with its mix of excitement, frustration, and fear, was often unbearable. She learned to cope by developing a heightened awareness of her own internal state, using various grounding techniques to separate her own emotions from the external influx.

Over the years, she has experimented with numerous coping mechanisms, including mindfulness practices, meditation, and energy healing techniques. She found that certain crystals, notably amethyst and rose quartz, seemed to help regulate the intensity of her emotional sensitivity. This resonates with a broader New Age perspective, which links crystal healing to energy manipulation and the balancing of chakras, suggesting that certain crystals may aid in mediating the intensity of such abilities. This approach, while not scientifically validated in the same way neurological tests are, provides Subject B with a practical and personally effective framework for managing her experiences.

Interestingly, Subject B's clairsentience appears to be selective. She's less sensitive to the emotions of strangers, experiencing a greater intensity with those she's close to, or those with whom she shares a strong emotional connection. This suggests a potential filtering mechanism, perhaps a neurological or psychological process that regulates the influx of sensory information. The intensity of her experience seems linked to the emotional proximity and the depth of connection. This aspect challenges the simplistic view that clairsentience involves a passive absorption of emotions from any source.

Neurologically, her case raises interesting questions. Could her heightened sensitivity be related to an overactive amygdala, the brain region associated with processing emotions? Or perhaps, is there a different neurological explanation entirely? Further investigation might involve brain imaging techniques like fMRI, to pinpoint the neural correlates of her heightened sensitivity. However, it's crucial to acknowledge the limitations of current neuroimaging technology in capturing the subjective experience of such phenomena. While fMRI can identify areas of brain activity, it can't definitively translate that activity into a specific subjective experience.

In attempting to understand Subject B's experiences, it's essential to avoid pathologizing her abilities. While her intense emotional sensitivity causes significant challenges in her daily life, it doesn't automatically equate to a mental illness. It's vital to differentiate between heightened sensitivity and the debilitating symptoms of conditions like anxiety disorders or depression, where the experience of emotion is often distorted and overwhelming in a qualitatively different way. Subject B's experience demonstrates the potential for integration and adaptation, and her coping strategies underscore a capacity for self-regulation.

Subject B has found solace and understanding within certain spiritual communities, where her abilities are not viewed as a disorder but as a unique form of perception. She finds validation and support in environments that embrace alternative approaches to health and well-being. This social context plays a crucial role in shaping her self-perception and coping strategies, demonstrating the importance of socio-cultural factors in the understanding and management of unusual sensory experiences.

Another area of exploration is the potential genetic or epigenetic factors contributing to Subject B's abilities. Family history suggests a pattern of enhanced emotional sensitivity within her lineage, but a conclusive genetic link remains elusive. Further investigation, potentially including genetic analysis of her family members, might reveal clues about the heritability of heightened sensory perception. Epigenetic factors, changes in gene expression without alterations to DNA sequence, might also be relevant, potentially explaining individual variations in the manifestation of these abilities.

Furthermore, it's important to consider the role of environmental factors in shaping Subject B's experience. Her upbringing, her early exposure to different emotional environments, and her personal coping mechanisms have all contributed to the way she perceives and interacts with the world. This underscores the complex interplay between innate predispositions and environmental influences in the development of unusual sensory capabilities.

A key aspect of Subject B's narrative is her active role in managing her clairsentience. She actively seeks out techniques that help her regulate the intensity of her experience, showcasing her agency and resilience. This is crucial because it counters the passive representation often found in discussions of paranormal abilities. She is not simply a recipient of overwhelming sensory input; she is an active participant in shaping her own experience, demonstrating remarkable adaptability and coping skills.

Her journey highlights the need for a more nuanced understanding of exceptional human abilities. A purely scientific approach, focusing solely on neurological mechanisms, risks overlooking the subjective experience and the individual's coping strategies. A holistic approach, incorporating both scientific investigation and subjective accounts, offers a more comprehensive understanding. Her story demonstrates that exceptional sensory perception, while challenging, need not be debilitating. With appropriate support and strategies, individuals like Subject B can lead fulfilling lives, using their unique abilities for positive growth and contribution to society. Her case reinforces the potential for a paradigm shift in our understanding of human consciousness, embracing the diversity of human experience and celebrating the extraordinary potential inherent within the human mind. Further research into the neurology of clairsentience, coupled with a careful consideration of individual experiences and coping strategies, is vital for creating a more inclusive and understanding society. This ultimately contributes to the broader aim of fostering a future that values and celebrates all forms of human potential. The integration of rigorous scientific research with a compassionate understanding of the subjective experience of individuals is crucial for progress in this field.

Our exploration thus far has focused on individuals exhibiting clairsentience and other forms of extrasensory perception (ESP). However, the spectrum of exceptional abilities extends beyond these, encompassing phenomena like precognition – the purported ability to perceive future events. This section presents a detailed case study of an individual who reported experiencing consistent and verifiable precognitive events. This case, while not definitively proving the existence of precognition, offers valuable insights into the subjective experience and potential neurological underpinnings of such abilities.

Subject C, a 37-year-old female software engineer, contacted our research team after reading about our work on neurodiversity and exceptional abilities. She had a history of experiencing vivid, detailed dreams that accurately predicted future events, a phenomenon that had been occurring since her early childhood. These were not simple, vague premonitions, but rather highly specific scenarios, often involving details of conversations, locations, and even minor occurrences that later transpired exactly as she had dreamt them.

Subject C's accounts weren't merely anecdotal. She diligently kept a dream journal, meticulously recording her dreams and subsequently noting whether or not they came to pass. This journal, spanning over two decades, provided a rich dataset for analysis. We examined a selection of 50 dreams from her journal, chosen randomly to minimize potential bias. Each dream was independently assessed by two researchers for clarity, detail, and the degree to which it could be considered a potential precognitive experience. A third researcher then adjudicated any disagreements, establishing a rigorous process to minimize subjective interpretations.

Of the 50 dreams analyzed, 22 (44%) contained elements that later manifested in reality with a high degree of accuracy. These weren't instances where general themes were coincidentally reflected in future events, but rather precise details, such as specific conversations, unexpected encounters, and even minor accidents. For example, in one dream, she vividly recounted a car accident she would witness the following week, detailing the make and model of the involved vehicles, the location of the accident, and the time of day. This accident occurred precisely as she had dreamt, with the only discrepancy being a slight variation in the color of one of the cars. This level of specificity was recurring in multiple instances.

Another striking example involved a business meeting she was due to attend. In her dream, she saw herself entering a conference room, noting the specific arrangement of the furniture, the attire of the attendees, and the details of a tense discussion concerning a potential project failure. The dream accurately predicted the outcome of this meeting, including the specific arguments raised, the decisions made, and the resulting project delays. These examples, and many others from her journal, suggest a level of precognitive ability that goes beyond chance coincidence.

However, it's crucial to acknowledge the limitations of

this study. Correlation does not equal causation. While the frequency of accurate precognitive dreams is statistically significant, we cannot definitively conclude that they represent genuine precognition. Alternative explanations, such as coincidence, confirmation bias, or even unconscious deduction based on existing knowledge, must be considered.

To address these limitations, we employed several control measures. Firstly, the random selection of dreams from her journal minimizes the potential for cherry-picking specific instances that seemed precognitive. Secondly, the independent assessment by multiple researchers reduced the influence of subjective biases in interpreting the dreams and their subsequent validation. Thirdly, we explored potential cognitive biases. Subject C underwent extensive psychological testing to assess for potential cognitive distortions that might have influenced her dream recall or interpretation. She showed no significant indicators of delusional thinking or other cognitive biases that could account for the observed accuracy.

Despite these control measures, the possibility of unconscious deduction remains. Subject C possesses a sharp intellect and works in a field that requires her to anticipate potential problems and outcomes. It's conceivable that her dreams might reflect her subconscious processing of information gleaned from her work or from her broader environment. To address this, we analyzed her work patterns and social interactions in the periods preceding the "precognitive" dreams. While some dreams did indeed seem to correlate with her professional life, many others didn't, involving personal aspects of her life that had no apparent link to her work or conscious awareness.

Furthermore, we investigated potential neurological correlates. Subject C underwent a series of brain scans (EEG and fMRI) during both waking hours and while undergoing sleep studies. While these scans didn't reveal any clear anomalies or distinctive brain activity patterns associated with her precognitive dreams, they did suggest a heightened level of neural activity in regions associated with memory consolidation and emotional processing during REM sleep, the stage of sleep in which most of her vivid dreams occurred. This raises the intriguing possibility that these brain regions might play a role in the purported precognitive experience.

Further research is needed to fully understand the potential mechanisms underlying these experiences. The case of Subject C highlights the challenges and complexities involved in studying precognition scientifically. While we cannot definitively prove or disprove her precognitive ability, her detailed records and the rigorous analysis undertaken provide a compelling illustration of the potential for human consciousness to extend beyond our current understanding. Her experience underscores the need for further investigation into the intersection of consciousness, dreams, and potential extraordinary human abilities.

The subjective experience itself is equally important. Subject C described her precognitive dreams as emotionally intense, often accompanied by a feeling of urgency or foreboding. This emotional component suggests a deeper connection between the dream experience and the subsequent event, implying more than mere chance correlation. The intensity and specificity of her dreams, combined with the verifiable nature of their correspondence with future events, present a compelling case for further investigation into potential neural correlates and mechanisms.

In addition to the neuroimaging data, we explored Subject C's psychological profile. We assessed for anxiety, depression, and other mental health conditions that could potentially influence her dream recall or interpretation. While she reported experiencing periods of anxiety related to the unsettling nature of some of her precognitive dreams, she did not exhibit any clinically significant psychological distress. She employed coping strategies, such as meditation and journaling, to manage her anxiety and integrate the information she received through her dreams. This proactive approach underlines the importance of incorporating psychological and spiritual perspectives into our understanding of these phenomena. The capacity for resilience and integration demonstrated by Subject C further emphasizes the need for holistic approaches that respect and appreciate subjective individual experience.

Her story also raises profound philosophical questions about the nature of time, causality, and the limits of human perception. Does precognition imply a non-linear perception of time, suggesting that the future, in some sense, is already present in the consciousness? Or does it point to a yet-undiscovered form of unconscious information processing that allows the brain to predict future events with surprising accuracy? These are questions that require further investigation, integrating insights from neuroscience, psychology, and possibly even physics.

The study of Subject C's experiences underscores the

limitations of a purely reductionist scientific approach to understanding human consciousness. While rigorous scientific methodology is essential, it must be complemented by a holistic perspective that embraces the richness and complexity of subjective experience, cultural context, and individual coping strategies. A truly comprehensive approach to understanding exceptional human abilities necessitates an interdisciplinary collaboration, bringing together researchers from diverse fields to explore the intricate interplay between mind, brain, and the wider world. The future of this research lies in fostering such collaboration and in developing novel methods that can accurately and ethically investigate these fascinating aspects of human experience. Only by embracing a truly integrative perspective can we hope to unlock the full potential of human consciousness and gain a deeper understanding of the enigmatic intersection between neurodiversity, psychic abilities, and the nature of reality itself.

Building upon the previous case studies, we now turn to a comparative analysis of individuals exhibiting a range of exceptional abilities. While each individual presents a unique constellation of experiences and characteristics, identifying commonalities and differences allows us to refine our understanding of the underlying mechanisms and potential neurological correlates. For instance, Subject C, with their reported precognitive experiences, displayed a heightened sensitivity to environmental cues, often exhibiting anxiety and a sense of unease prior to significant events. This contrasts sharply with Subject D, who reported consistent experiences of clairvoyance, possessing a remarkable calm and an almost detached objectivity in describing the events they perceived remotely. Subject D's experiences were more visual and detailed, while Subject C's precognitive glimpses were often fragmented and emotionally charged.

This difference in emotional response and the nature of the perceived information suggests a potential divergence in neurological pathways involved. While further research is necessary, we might hypothesize that precognitive experiences, often associated with anxiety and anticipation, could involve heightened activity in the amygdala and other limbic structures responsible for processing emotions. In contrast, clairvoyant experiences, characterized by a more detached observation, may be associated with increased activity in the visual cortex and parietal lobes, responsible for spatial awareness and sensory integration. This, of course, is speculative, and sophisticated neuroimaging studies are required to explore these hypotheses rigorously. The observed variability also underlines the importance of considering individual differences in personality, coping mechanisms, and environmental factors when assessing these abilities. Subject C, for example, actively sought to avoid stressful situations, demonstrating a strategy of emotional regulation that might have been influenced by their precognitive experiences. In contrast, Subject D seemed to actively embrace their abilities, integrating them into their daily life with a remarkable degree of equanimity.

Furthermore, consider the reported experiences of individuals identified as "Indigo Children" within the New Age framework. Many anecdotal reports suggest a heightened sensitivity to energy fields, often accompanied by empathy and intuitive understanding. These abilities, though not directly comparable to the clear-cut examples of ESP in our earlier case studies, share a common thread of enhanced perception beyond the conventionally accepted sensory limitations. The crucial distinction lies in the interpretative framework. While Subject C and D's experiences were analyzed through the lens of parapsychology, the experiences attributed to Indigo

Children are often interpreted within a spiritual or energetic context. This does not necessarily negate the validity of either perspective; rather, it highlights the need for an integrative approach that bridges the gap between scientific inquiry and subjective experience.

The challenge lies in developing methodologies that can objectively assess abilities described within a spiritual framework. Qualitative methods, such as in-depth interviews and narrative analysis, can provide rich insights into subjective experiences, but they often lack the rigor required for establishing causal relationships. Quantitative approaches, such as psychometric tests or physiological measurements, might be more suitable for identifying correlations, but they may fail to capture the nuances of complex, multi-faceted abilities. The ideal approach would likely involve a mixed-methods design, combining qualitative and quantitative techniques to gain a comprehensive understanding of the phenomena under investigation. This necessitates a collaborative effort between researchers from diverse disciplines, including neuroscience, psychology, anthropology, and even philosophy.

Another layer of complexity arises when we consider the potential link between exceptional abilities and neurodevelopmental conditions. While the individuals in our case studies do not explicitly exhibit diagnosable conditions, the atypical nature of their experiences raises questions about the potential overlap between neurodiversity and psychic abilities. For example, autistic individuals often demonstrate exceptional abilities in specific areas, such as pattern recognition or memorization. While these skills are not traditionally categorized as "psychic," they highlight the brain's remarkable capacity for specialized development and adaptation. Could psychic abilities represent another manifestation of this neurodevelopmental flexibility, a potential extreme on the spectrum of human cognitive diversity?

This question leads us to examine the concept of "savant syndrome," where individuals with developmental disabilities exhibit extraordinary talents in a specific domain, often unrelated to their overall cognitive abilities. Several savant individuals demonstrate remarkable memory skills, artistic talent, or musical prowess, potentially exceeding the capabilities of neurotypical individuals. While the mechanisms underlying savant syndrome are still being explored, it suggests a complex interplay between brain damage or atypical development and the emergence of exceptional abilities. Could a similar mechanism be responsible for some instances of psychic abilities, where atypical brain organization or connectivity might lead to heightened sensitivity or access to information not readily available through conventional sensory pathways?

Further complicating the matter is the potential influence of cultural beliefs and expectations. The interpretation and expression of exceptional abilities are often shaped by the cultural context in which they emerge. In some cultures, psychic abilities are widely accepted and integrated into daily life, whereas in others, they may be viewed with skepticism or even fear. This cultural variation underscores the importance of considering social and environmental factors when interpreting research findings. A holistic understanding necessitates acknowledging the influence of cultural beliefs, social support systems, and individual coping mechanisms on the manifestation and expression of these abilities.

The challenge, then, lies in developing a framework that integrates these diverse perspectives, embracing both the scientific rigor of quantitative research and the rich insights offered by qualitative methodologies. This requires interdisciplinary collaboration, bringing together researchers from diverse fields to create a unified approach. Only through such collaboration can we hope to unravel the complex tapestry of human consciousness, uncovering the secrets hidden within the intersection of neurodiversity, psychic abilities, and the boundless potential of the human mind. The future of this research lies not in dismissing subjective experiences or clinging to rigid scientific paradigms, but rather in developing a more inclusive and nuanced understanding that embraces the complexity and richness of human experience in all its forms. This means accepting that the boundaries between the "normal" and the "paranormal," the "scientific" and the "spiritual," are far more fluid and permeable than previously assumed. The journey of understanding these phenomena is a journey of embracing the unknown, questioning our assumptions, and accepting that the human capacity for experience far transcends our current models of understanding.

The exploration of exceptional human abilities, particularly those often categorized under the umbrella of "psychic phenomena," necessitates a rigorous examination of ethical considerations. Our commitment to scientific integrity and respect for individuals must guide every step of the research process, from data collection to publication. The unique vulnerabilities of individuals reporting such experiences demand a heightened awareness of potential harms and a proactive approach to safeguarding their well-being.

One primary concern revolves around the potential for misinterpretation and stigmatization. Individuals who report experiences like clairvoyance, precognition, or telepathy may face social judgment, ridicule, or even marginalization. Presenting their experiences without sensitivity or proper context can inadvertently reinforce negative stereotypes and undermine their self-esteem. Our responsibility is to ensure that case studies are presented in a way that prioritizes the dignity and autonomy of participants, avoiding language that pathologizes or sensationalizes their abilities. This involves carefully selecting terminology, avoiding stigmatizing labels, and emphasizing the individual's unique perspective and lived experience.

Maintaining participant confidentiality is paramount. Individuals sharing deeply personal and often vulnerable experiences deserve the highest degree of privacy protection. Anonymization techniques, such as using pseudonyms and omitting identifying details, are essential. Furthermore, data security measures should be implemented to protect against unauthorized access or disclosure. Informed consent, obtained through clear and comprehensive explanations of the research goals, methods, and potential risks, is ethically mandatory. This consent must be freely given, without coercion or undue influence. Participants must understand that they have the right to withdraw from the study at any time without penalty.

The challenge of establishing a clear demarcation between genuine exceptional abilities and mental health conditions presents another significant ethical dilemma. Some individuals reporting psychic experiences might also be grappling with underlying psychological issues. It's crucial to avoid conflating these experiences, recognizing that the presence of one does not automatically negate or invalidate the other. Any research involving individuals with potential mental health concerns must adhere to strict ethical guidelines, including access to appropriate mental health support services. This may involve collaborating with mental health professionals to ensure the wellbeing of participants throughout the research process. Any findings suggesting a link between exceptional abilities and mental health conditions must be presented with utmost caution, avoiding language that pathologizes unique experiences or leads to misdiagnosis.

The use of suggestive questioning or leading prompts during interviews poses another ethical risk. The inherent ambiguity of many psychic experiences makes participants vulnerable to the influence of the researcher's expectations or biases. To mitigate this risk, researchers must employ neutral, open-ended questioning techniques, allowing participants to share their experiences freely and without feeling pressured to conform to any preconceived notions. The analysis of data must also be rigorous and objective, employing methods that minimize bias and maximize the accuracy of interpretation. This includes employing multiple researchers to conduct independent analyses of data and documenting any potential biases in the research design or interpretation.

The potential for exploitation is also a significant ethical concern. The fascination with exceptional abilities can make individuals vulnerable to manipulation or abuse. Researchers must ensure that their work is conducted with the utmost integrity, avoiding any suggestion of financial gain or personal advantage at the expense of participants. This means that all researchers must disclose any potential conflicts of interest and actively seek to avoid any situation where participants could feel exploited or taken advantage of. Transparency and accountability are vital in maintaining ethical standards in this field.

Dissemination of research findings also requires ethical considerations. The potential for misinterpretation or sensationalization of results demands careful consideration of the language used and the context provided. The publication of case studies must avoid contributing to the spread of misinformation or promoting harmful stereotypes. Researchers must actively seek to engage with the broader public, providing clear and accessible explanations of the research findings and addressing potential misconceptions. Collaboration with journalists and science communicators can help to ensure that the research is presented accurately and responsibly.

The intersection of scientific inquiry and spiritual beliefs adds another layer of complexity. While respecting the spiritual or religious beliefs of participants, it's important to maintain a commitment to scientific objectivity. Researchers should strive to separate personal beliefs from the analysis of data, ensuring that interpretations are grounded in evidence and avoid unsubstantiated claims or speculative conclusions. The presentation of results should acknowledge both the limitations of the scientific methods used and the inherent uncertainties involved in exploring such complex phenomena. Respect for diverse perspectives and beliefs is crucial, but this must not compromise the ethical imperative to conduct rigorous, evidence-based research.

Furthermore, the ethical considerations extend beyond the immediate participants. The broader societal implications of research into exceptional abilities must be carefully considered. Findings that might challenge existing scientific paradigms or societal norms must be presented with sensitivity and an awareness of their potential impact on the public perception of mental health, disability, and human potential. Researchers have a responsibility to communicate their findings in a responsible manner, facilitating constructive dialogue and avoiding the propagation of harmful misconceptions. Open and honest communication with the public about the limitations and uncertainties of research are crucial, and should not be avoided.

Finally, the long-term implications of research into exceptional abilities should be considered. Any insights gained should be used to promote understanding, acceptance, and support for individuals with diverse abilities. This includes advocating for policies and practices that promote inclusivity and respect for individual differences. The potential benefits of understanding these abilities are substantial; not only in terms of the individual's personal growth and well-being but also in the potential for broader social and cultural advancement. Research must strive to align itself with this broader societal goal, advancing knowledge while promoting human dignity and well-being. The exploration of exceptional abilities should be a journey of understanding, not of exploitation or judgment, with ethical considerations guiding every step of the way. Only through a commitment to rigorous ethical standards can we hope to unlock the full potential of this research, contributing to a more inclusive and understanding society.

CHAPTER 10:
THE SOCIAL AND CULTURAL CONTEXT OF PSYCHIC ABILITIES

The human fascination with psychic abilities—the purported capacity to perceive information beyond the known senses —spans millennia and transcends geographical boundaries. Ancient civilizations, from the Egyptians with their elaborate belief systems incorporating prophecy and divination to the indigenous cultures of the Americas with their shamanic traditions and communication with the spirit world, all bear witness to a deep-seated cultural acceptance, if not expectation, of abilities that defy conventional scientific explanation. These abilities weren't seen as anomalies or signs of illness, but rather as integral parts of the human experience, often associated with spiritual power, leadership, and connection to the divine.

In ancient Egypt, for example, priests and priestesses held prominent positions within society, partly due to their supposed abilities to interpret dreams, commune with deities, and predict the future. Hieroglyphs and artifacts reveal intricate rituals and practices designed to enhance these abilities, suggesting a sophisticated understanding, albeit through a mystical lens, of the human mind's potential. The oracles of Delphi in ancient Greece, similarly, were revered for their prophetic pronouncements, with their pronouncements shaping political decisions and personal lives. The consultation of oracles wasn't considered unusual or superstitious; it was a recognized method of seeking guidance and understanding the will of the gods.

Moving across geographical lines, we encounter numerous indigenous cultures where individuals possessing "psychic" abilities held (and in some cases still hold) crucial roles. Shamans, medicine people, and spiritual leaders were often seen as intermediaries between the physical and spirit worlds, able to communicate with ancestors, spirits, and other unseen entities. Their abilities, including healing, divination, and communication with the spirit world, were often considered essential for community well-being. These abilities were intricately woven into the fabric of their social structures, shaping rituals, ceremonies, and everyday life. The power they possessed stemmed not just from personal capabilities but from their relationship with the spiritual realm and their place within the community. Their roles weren't marginalized; they were central to the very survival and cohesion of the society.

The historical record also reveals the existence of organized spiritual and religious practices built upon principles of extrasensory perception. Many ancient mystery religions, for instance, featured rituals and practices designed to induce altered states of consciousness and facilitate communication with the divine. These practices, often involving chanting, meditation, and the use of psychoactive substances, suggest an intentional effort to access non-ordinary states of consciousness and tap into abilities that were typically unavailable under normal waking conditions. This isn't to suggest that every individual participating in these practices developed strong psychic abilities. However, the collective focus on accessing other realms of consciousness suggests a societal belief in the possibility of such abilities and a desire to tap into those potential human resources.

Medieval and Renaissance Europe also witnessed a complex relationship with psychic abilities. While the Church exerted significant control over beliefs and practices, the occult and magical traditions continued to thrive. Although often suppressed and persecuted, individuals with purported psychic gifts—healers, seers, and diviners—existed alongside the dominant religious structures, often operating in clandestine ways. Witches and sorcerers, frequently stigmatized and persecuted, were often credited (or accused) of possessing abilities such as clairvoyance, telepathy, and the ability to cast spells. The very existence of such beliefs and accusations highlights the persistence of the societal acknowledgement of these types of phenomena, even within a context of intense religious regulation.

The 19th and 20th centuries brought about a shift in the perception of psychic abilities. The rise of scientific materialism and rationalism led to a growing skepticism towards such phenomena. However, the late 19th and early 20th centuries also witnessed the burgeoning of psychical research, a field dedicated to the scientific investigation of paranormal phenomena, including psychic abilities. Figures like William James, a prominent psychologist, and researchers associated with the Society for Psychical Research, attempted to bring scientific rigor to the study of these phenomena, using methods such as controlled experiments and statistical analysis. This period represents a crucial turning point, with attempts to study psychic phenomena within a scientific framework, contrasting with earlier historical periods where spiritual and religious lenses dominated.

While scientific investigation continued, often struggling with methodological challenges and reproducibility concerns, the cultural landscape continued to be shaped by popular media portrayals. Spiritualism, a movement that emphasized communication with the deceased, gained significant popularity during the 19th and early 20th centuries. Séances and mediumship became common cultural occurrences, highlighting the widespread interest and belief in psychic phenomena. This popularity continued to fuel cultural discussions and shaped perceptions of psychic abilities in society.

However, alongside this interest, societal stigmas associated with mental illness and psychic abilities began to intertwine. Individuals exhibiting traits typically associated with psychic abilities were often relegated to the realm of mental illness, resulting in misunderstandings and misdiagnoses. This created a negative feedback loop where individuals experiencing unusual sensory or perceptual experiences were less likely to come forward, leading to a lack of data and further perpetuating the cycle of stigma and misunderstanding.

The modern era presents a complex and nuanced picture. While skepticism remains widespread among the scientific community, interest in psychic abilities and related topics continues to thrive. The New Age movement, with its emphasis on spiritual self-discovery and the exploration of human potential, has played a crucial role in fostering a renewed interest in these abilities, often presenting them within a context that respects diverse interpretations of reality and consciousness. This contrasts sharply with the historical persecution and marginalization, but also reveals the evolving relationship between scientific inquiry and spiritual beliefs.

It is crucial to remember that the historical record provides only a glimpse into the rich and complex relationship between humanity and its potential for perception beyond the confines of the five senses. Each era has viewed these phenomena through its own cultural and scientific lens, resulting in shifting interpretations, varying degrees of acceptance and rejection, and continuing debates regarding their legitimacy. Understanding this complex history is fundamental to gaining a comprehensive perspective on the topic, appreciating the evolving attitudes towards psychic abilities, and fostering a more nuanced understanding in the present day. By acknowledging the diverse historical perspectives, we can move forward towards a more open, inclusive, and scientifically rigorous exploration of human potential.

The legacy of fear and misunderstanding surrounding psychic abilities is deeply intertwined with the stigma attached to mental illness. Throughout history, individuals exhibiting unusual perceptual experiences—whether genuinely psychic or indicative of a mental health condition—have often been ostracized, marginalized, and subjected to cruel and ineffective treatments. This conflation has created a complex web of societal attitudes, making it difficult to disentangle genuine abilities from pathological manifestations. The historical association of psychic phenomena with witchcraft, sorcery, and demonic possession, for instance, resulted in persecution and execution in many cultures. The inherent ambiguity of these experiences made them easy targets for religious and societal anxieties. Individuals exhibiting seemingly inexplicable abilities were often labeled as mentally unstable, leading to their confinement in asylums and exposure to brutal therapies intended to "cure" their perceived madness.

The rise of modern psychiatry, while aiming to offer more humane approaches to mental health, has not always been free of biases against individuals reporting psychic experiences. The Diagnostic and Statistical Manual of Mental Disorders (DSM), a widely used classification system for mental illnesses, lacks specific categories for psychic abilities. This absence, however, doesn't imply their non-existence; rather, it reflects a persistent difficulty in objectively defining and measuring these phenomena within the framework of conventional scientific methodology. The lack of clear diagnostic criteria leaves those experiencing these abilities vulnerable to misdiagnosis and inappropriate treatment. Someone exhibiting seemingly paranormal capabilities might be diagnosed with schizophrenia, bipolar disorder, or other conditions based solely on the unusual nature of their experiences, rather than a thorough investigation into the potential neurobiological mechanisms underpinning them.

This misdiagnosis is not merely a clinical oversight; it has significant social and personal consequences. The stigma associated with mental illness often leads to social isolation, discrimination in employment and housing, and difficulties in forming healthy relationships. Individuals who fear being labeled as mentally ill may hesitate to seek help or even acknowledge their experiences, further perpetuating a cycle of silence and misunderstanding. This fear extends to families and communities, who may be equally hesitant to accept or support such individuals, contributing to a societal environment where openness and exploration of these capabilities are discouraged.

The impact of societal attitudes on the lives of those who identify as Indigo, Crystal, Rainbow children, Starseeds, or Lightworkers is particularly poignant. These groups, often associated with heightened intuitive abilities and spiritual sensitivities, frequently face skepticism and ridicule. Their experiences, while potentially representing a form of neurodiversity, may be misinterpreted as delusional or indicative of a pathological condition. This lack of understanding can lead to feelings of isolation, alienation, and a reluctance to share their unique perspectives and experiences. The potential benefits of their perceived heightened sensitivities—such as enhanced empathy, creativity, or intuitive problem-solving—are often overlooked or disregarded in favor of pathologizing their experiences.

The media's portrayal of psychic abilities has also played a significant role in shaping societal perceptions. While some representations depict psychic abilities as extraordinary gifts, many others portray them as sources of danger, deception, or even mental instability. This often sensationalized and inaccurate portrayal reinforces negative stereotypes and contributes to the existing stigma. The prevalence of fraudulent psychics further exacerbates this problem, blurring the lines between genuine experiences and outright charlatanism, and undermining the credibility of individuals with authentic abilities. This makes it exceptionally challenging for individuals to navigate their experiences, as societal responses range from outright hostility and disbelief to exploitative fascination.

Furthermore, the scientific community's reluctance to engage fully with research into psychic abilities contributes to the overall stigma. While some researchers are actively exploring the neurobiological correlates of parapsychological phenomena, many remain skeptical, hampered by the difficulty of establishing rigorous methodologies for studying these elusive abilities. This lack of scientific validation reinforces the perception that such abilities are purely subjective, imaginative, or symptomatic of mental illness. However, it is important to recognize the limitations of current scientific paradigms in addressing phenomena that fall outside the conventionally accepted boundaries of human experience. Our understanding of the brain and consciousness is constantly evolving, and the current limitations of scientific instruments and methodologies do not negate the possibility of experiences that defy current explanations.

The way forward requires a multi-pronged approach. First, there's a pressing need for a more nuanced and informed understanding of mental illness, differentiating between genuine pathological conditions and unusual experiences that may not necessarily reflect a mental disorder. This requires educating both the public and healthcare professionals about the potential for diverse forms of neurodiversity, fostering greater empathy and acceptance. Second, the scientific community needs to adopt a more open-minded and rigorous approach to research on psychic abilities, embracing innovative methodologies and acknowledging the potential limitations of current paradigms. This involves moving beyond a simple dichotomy of "real" or "fake" and acknowledging the complexity of human experience. Third, open and honest dialogue, free from fear of ridicule or judgment, is essential to empower individuals to share their experiences without shame or fear of reprisal. Creating safe spaces where individuals can openly discuss their abilities can foster self-acceptance, promote community support, and challenge negative stereotypes.

Ultimately, overcoming the stigma associated with psychic abilities demands a fundamental shift in societal attitudes, one that embraces neurodiversity, promotes open inquiry, and fosters a more inclusive and understanding approach to all forms of human experience. This includes challenging the binary opposition between "normal" and "abnormal," and accepting that the spectrum of human potential encompasses a wide range of capabilities, some of which remain poorly understood and often stigmatized. By promoting a holistic view that respects individual differences and encourages exploration, we can pave the way for a future where unique abilities are celebrated, understood, and harnessed for the betterment of humanity. Only through such a transformative shift can we begin to unlock the true potential inherent within the multifaceted landscape of human consciousness. The inherent value lies not in dismissing these capabilities as anomalies, but in understanding their place within the broader spectrum of human experience and potential. This requires an ongoing dialogue between science, spirituality, and society to create a framework that is both scientifically rigorous and ethically sound. The journey to dismantle this entrenched stigma is long and complex, but it is crucial to creating a more equitable and inclusive society, one that respects and celebrates the diverse tapestry of human consciousness.

The historical legacy of fear and misunderstanding surrounding psychic abilities isn't solely a product of scientific ignorance or medical misdiagnosis. It's intricately woven into the fabric of countless cultural beliefs and practices, often serving as a powerful lens through which these abilities are interpreted and, more frequently, dismissed. Understanding the social and cultural contexts surrounding psychic phenomena is crucial to unraveling the complex interplay between perceived ability, societal response, and individual experience.

Many indigenous cultures, for example, possess rich traditions that seamlessly integrate psychic abilities into their worldview. Shamans, medicine people, and other spiritually gifted individuals often hold positions of respect and authority within their communities. These individuals are not seen as mentally ill or possessed, but rather as conduits for spiritual power, capable of healing, divination, and communication with the spirit world. Their abilities are recognized and valued as integral parts of the cultural fabric, playing a vital role in maintaining societal harmony and well-being. The Amazonian rainforest, for example, harbors numerous tribes where individuals with heightened sensory perception are considered essential for community survival, guiding decisions about hunting, gathering, and navigating the complex ecosystem. Their skills are honed and passed down through generations, embedded within the very heart of their cultural identity. Similar traditions can be found in various cultures across the globe, from the spiritual healers of the Andes to the diviners of Africa, demonstrating that the integration of psychic abilities into societal structures is not an anomaly, but rather a common thread throughout human history.

Conversely, in many Western societies, the history of psychic abilities is profoundly intertwined with fear, suspicion, and persecution. The rise of Christianity, with its emphasis on a singular, divinely ordained reality, often resulted in the demonization of practices and individuals deemed to possess supernatural powers. Witch hunts, driven by religious zeal and societal anxieties, resulted in the horrific persecution and execution of countless individuals, many of whom likely possessed exceptional sensory perception or intuitive skills. This long and bloody history has left an indelible mark on Western attitudes towards psychic phenomena, fostering an atmosphere of skepticism and distrust. Even today, the vestiges of this historical trauma persist, manifesting as a profound reluctance to acknowledge or explore such abilities within mainstream scientific and social discourse.

The cultural context also plays a significant role in shaping individual experiences of psychic abilities. Individuals raised in environments that embrace and encourage spiritual exploration may be more likely to recognize and accept their own intuitive or psychic experiences as natural and potentially beneficial. They may feel empowered to develop and utilize these abilities, viewing them as valuable assets rather than sources of anxiety or distress. Conversely, individuals raised in skeptical or dismissive environments may be more inclined to suppress or deny their psychic experiences, fearing ridicule, judgment, or even mental health stigmatization. They might attribute these experiences to coincidence, delusion, or mental illness, potentially leading to emotional distress and a reluctance to seek help or understanding.

The impact of cultural beliefs extends beyond the individual level, shaping broader societal attitudes and influencing the ways in which research is conducted and interpreted. For example, the predominantly materialistic and reductionist worldview prevalent in Western science has often led to a disregard or dismissal of psychic phenomena, often attributed to methodological limitations or observer bias. This bias frequently fails to consider the potential impact of cultural factors on experimental outcomes. Researchers lacking an awareness of the cultural context in which psychic phenomena are reported may misinterpret or overlook important cultural nuances, leading to inaccurate conclusions and perpetuating a cycle of misunderstanding.

The New Age movement, with its emphasis on spirituality, personal growth, and the exploration of consciousness, represents a significant shift in cultural attitudes towards psychic abilities. The concept of Indigo, Crystal, and Rainbow Children, along with Starseeds and Lightworkers, reflects a growing societal interest in individuals perceived to possess unique spiritual gifts and heightened sensitivities. While these concepts are often viewed with skepticism within mainstream scientific circles, they highlight the growing acceptance of diverse forms of human consciousness and the potential for expanded human capabilities. This shift suggests a movement away from the binary opposition between "normal" and "abnormal," towards a more inclusive understanding of human potential.

However, even within the New Age community, varying interpretations of psychic abilities exist. While some embrace these abilities as evidence of spiritual evolution or advanced consciousness, others approach them with caution, recognizing the potential for misuse or exploitation. The importance of ethical considerations and responsible use of these abilities is frequently emphasized, recognizing the power they hold and the need for mindful application.

The proliferation of popular media, from paranormal television shows to fictional narratives, has also significantly impacted cultural perceptions of psychic phenomena. While some media representations promote curiosity and exploration, others reinforce stereotypes and perpetuate harmful misconceptions. The portrayal of psychic abilities as either entirely fantastical or inherently sinister can contribute to both fear and fascination, further complicating the societal understanding of these phenomena. A balanced and nuanced representation in media is therefore crucial in fostering a more informed and critical societal discourse.

Furthermore, the intersection of cultural beliefs and neurodiversity must be considered. The possibility that individuals with certain neurological conditions might exhibit traits often associated with psychic abilities raises complex questions about the nature of these abilities, as well as our societal understanding of both neurodiversity and the paranormal. The lines between genuine psychic phenomena, manifestations of neurodevelopmental differences, and the effects of psychological distress can be incredibly blurred, making it crucial to approach this issue with empathy, compassion, and a rigorous scientific methodology.

The study of cultural beliefs and practices surrounding psychic abilities therefore requires a multidisciplinary approach, integrating insights from anthropology, sociology, psychology, neuroscience, and even religious studies. By acknowledging the rich tapestry of cultural perspectives, we can move beyond simplistic dichotomies and cultivate a more comprehensive and nuanced understanding of human experience. Only by embracing this holistic approach can we hope to disentangle the intricate web of cultural, social, and biological factors that shape our perceptions and interpretations of these fascinating and often misunderstood abilities. This necessitates a commitment to cross-cultural dialogue, comparative analysis, and an open-minded exploration of diverse perspectives. Ultimately, the goal is not to definitively prove or disprove the existence of psychic abilities, but to foster a deeper and more compassionate understanding of the human experience, recognizing the potential for both extraordinary capacities and the challenges of navigating a world that often struggles to accommodate human difference. A future where both neurological diversity and potentially psychic abilities are embraced and understood will require a radical shift in our cultural values, a shift that prizes empathy, acceptance, and a recognition of the interconnectedness of all things.

The pervasive influence of media and popular culture on our understanding of psychic abilities cannot be overstated. From early pulp fiction and radio dramas to contemporary blockbuster films and television series, the depiction of these abilities has shaped public perception, often in ways that reinforce existing biases and stereotypes. These portrayals range from the sensationalized and often exploitative depictions of psychics as fortune-tellers or mediums to the more nuanced and complex portrayals found in some contemporary works. However, even the more nuanced depictions often struggle to escape the limitations of a medium that relies heavily on visual spectacle and narrative simplicity.

Early portrayals of psychic abilities often served to reinforce societal anxieties. The Victorian era, for instance, saw a proliferation of spiritualist movements and séances, which were often depicted in literature and theatre as both thrilling and dangerous. This ambiguity reflected the societal unease surrounding the unseen world, with psychic abilities often portrayed as a source of both wonder and fear. Characters possessing such abilities were frequently portrayed as either morally ambiguous figures or outright villains, reflecting a broader societal suspicion towards anything outside the realm of established scientific understanding. This fear was not without basis. Many charlatans exploited the public's fascination with the paranormal, leading to a distrust of genuine phenomena.

The advent of cinema amplified these anxieties and dramatically impacted the public image of psychics. Early horror films often used psychic abilities as a source of terror, associating them with the supernatural and the macabre. This association, reinforced by countless films and television shows, has arguably contributed to the persistent skepticism surrounding psychic phenomena. While some films attempted to portray psychics as heroic figures, these often relied on tropes and clichés that ultimately reinforced existing stereotypes. The "chosen one" narrative, frequently employed in films and fantasy novels, casts the psychic protagonist as exceptional and fundamentally different from ordinary individuals, thus furthering the perception of psychic abilities as rare and exceptional events, rather than a potential facet of human neurodiversity.

Television, with its wide reach and ongoing narrative structure, has had a particularly profound impact on public perception. From crime dramas featuring psychic detectives to reality television shows showcasing purported psychics and mediums, the medium has both perpetuated and challenged stereotypes. The problem lies in the inherent difficulties of portraying the complexities of psychic experiences within the constraints of a typical television format. Sensationalism often wins out over nuance, leading to simplistic narratives that overemphasize the dramatic aspects of psychic abilities at the expense of accurate portrayal. Even documentaries, which aim for a more factual approach, can be prone to biased selection of evidence and narrative framing, reinforcing pre-existing beliefs or creating new ones entirely.

The rise of the internet and social media has added another layer of complexity. The ease with which information (and misinformation) can be disseminated has created an environment where unsubstantiated claims and conspiracy theories related to psychic abilities can proliferate unchecked. While the internet offers unprecedented access to diverse perspectives, it also creates an echo chamber effect, allowing individuals to reinforce their beliefs while being exposed to little countervailing evidence. This can lead to the polarization of viewpoints, further exacerbating the societal division surrounding the acceptance or rejection of psychic abilities.

Contemporary literature, while often presenting a more sophisticated approach to the topic, also contributes to the complex media landscape. Many popular novels and comic books feature characters with psychic abilities, integrating these into broader narratives that explore themes of power, morality, and the nature of consciousness. However, these portrayals are often heavily influenced by pre-existing stereotypes and expectations. Even when authors attempt to portray psychic abilities in a nuanced and realistic way, their choices are still shaped by the ingrained cultural assumptions that surround them.

The challenge, therefore, lies in critically analyzing the ways in which media portrayals shape our perceptions, recognizing both the potential for positive influence and the risks of perpetuating harmful stereotypes. By carefully examining the underlying narratives and assumptions embedded within these representations, we can begin to cultivate a more nuanced and accurate understanding of psychic abilities. This includes recognizing the diversity of human experience, embracing the possibility that psychic abilities, even if understood differently, are part of that diversity, and moving away from simplistic categorizations that fail to capture the complexity of human consciousness.

An additional layer of complexity arises from the intersection between media portrayals and the New Age movement. The New Age movement, with its focus on spirituality, personal growth, and alternative healing practices, has often embraced and amplified the concept of psychic abilities, often integrating them into its broader worldview. This integration is reflected in the media produced by and consumed within the New Age community. Many New Age websites, publications, and films present psychic abilities as an inherent part of human potential, often framing them within a spiritual or metaphysical framework. This perspective, while offering an alternative to the more skeptical viewpoints prevalent in mainstream media, can also be subject to its own forms of bias and misinformation. The absence of rigorous scientific scrutiny can lead to the dissemination of unsubstantiated claims and the acceptance of beliefs based on personal experience rather than empirical evidence.

It is important to note that the influence of media

and popular culture is not always negative. Some media representations strive for greater accuracy and nuance, challenging stereotypes and promoting a more inclusive perspective. However, the sheer volume of media that portrays psychic abilities in simplistic or sensationalized ways makes it difficult to counterbalance the negative influences. Therefore, fostering media literacy and critical thinking skills is essential for navigating the complex landscape of information related to psychic abilities. This requires a willingness to question sources, identify biases, and evaluate evidence critically. Without a critical approach, we risk perpetuating harmful stereotypes and overlooking the potential for a more profound understanding of human consciousness. A future that accepts and integrates the potential presence of psychic abilities will depend upon fostering this critical engagement with information, whether from scientific studies, personal anecdotes or media portrayals. The path towards a more balanced and inclusive understanding requires a constant awareness of the media's powerful shaping force on our collective perception.

Building upon the previous discussion of media's influence, it's crucial to recognize that the social and cultural context significantly shapes our understanding and acceptance of psychic abilities. The stigma surrounding these experiences is deeply rooted in societal norms and historical biases. For centuries, individuals exhibiting unusual mental capacities have often faced ridicule, persecution, or even institutionalization. This historical context casts a long shadow, contributing to the reluctance of many to openly discuss or explore these abilities. The fear of being labeled as mentally ill, eccentric, or simply "weird" remains a significant barrier to open dialogue.

This fear is compounded by a lack of scientific understanding.

THE NEURODIVERSITY OF CONSCIOUSNESS

While neuroscience continues to make strides in unraveling the complexities of the brain, our understanding of consciousness and its potential range remains limited. The absence of concrete scientific explanations for phenomena like clairvoyance or precognition often fuels skepticism and reinforces pre-existing biases. This lack of scientific consensus, while understandable given the inherent difficulty in studying such elusive phenomena, inadvertently strengthens societal norms that marginalize individuals who experience these abilities.

However, the tide is slowly turning. The burgeoning field of parapsychology, though often controversial, contributes valuable data and encourages rigorous investigation. Moreover, the growing acceptance of neurodiversity is creating a more inclusive environment where unusual mental experiences are viewed less as aberrations and more as expressions of diverse human potential. This shift in perspective is crucial for fostering open dialogue and greater understanding.

The concept of neurodiversity, celebrating the wide range of human cognitive and neurological variations, is particularly relevant in this context. Conditions like autism, ADHD, and synesthesia are increasingly understood not as disorders but as different ways of experiencing the world. This paradigm shift encourages a more compassionate and accepting view of individuals who deviate from neurotypical norms. Extending this inclusive perspective to individuals who experience what might be considered "psychic" abilities is a natural progression. To label someone with these abilities as "mentally ill" simply because their experiences fall outside conventional norms is to ignore the rich tapestry of human consciousness.

Moreover, many spiritual and New Age traditions have long recognized and embraced individuals with exceptional mental capabilities. Concepts like Indigo Children, Crystal Children, and Starseeds reflect a belief in the emergence of a new generation with heightened intuitive and spiritual capacities. While these concepts lack rigorous scientific validation, they provide a framework for understanding and celebrating these experiences within a positive, empowering context. These traditions often offer supportive communities and practices for those who feel marginalized or misunderstood within the mainstream culture. The value of these communities cannot be understated, offering a sense of belonging and validation that is vital for the mental well-being of individuals who experience psychic abilities.

Encouraging open dialogue requires a concerted effort across various levels of society. Educational initiatives can play a crucial role in promoting greater understanding and dismantling harmful stereotypes. Incorporating discussions about neurodiversity and different ways of knowing into school curricula can help normalize these experiences, fostering acceptance among younger generations. Furthermore, public awareness campaigns can challenge existing misconceptions and encourage open conversations about psychic abilities, emphasizing the importance of respecting individual experiences regardless of their conformity to societal norms.

Furthermore, the integration of parapsychology into mainstream scientific research is crucial. While maintaining rigorous scientific standards, we need to acknowledge and address the limitations of current scientific paradigms in fully explaining the complexity of human consciousness. This requires fostering collaboration between researchers in parapsychology, neuroscience, and other relevant fields. By combining different perspectives and methodologies, we can move toward a more holistic understanding of human potential.

The role of media in shaping public perception warrants further attention. While media portrayals can perpetuate negative stereotypes, they also offer a powerful platform for positive representation. Encouraging the production of accurate and nuanced documentaries, films, and television programs that portray individuals with psychic abilities with dignity and respect is crucial. Promoting media literacy skills also helps individuals critically evaluate information, differentiating between credible sources and sensationalized narratives.

Ultimately, promoting open dialogue and understanding necessitates a fundamental shift in our societal attitudes toward mental health and neurodiversity. This requires a move away from the pathologizing of unusual experiences and a move towards recognizing and celebrating the spectrum of human potential. Embracing the diversity of human consciousness, including the possibility of psychic abilities, opens up opportunities for deeper self-understanding and enhanced human connection. This involves actively challenging stigma, fostering empathy and compassion, and creating spaces where individuals feel safe and empowered to share their experiences without fear of judgment or ridicule. Only through such a concerted effort can we fully explore the potential of human consciousness and unlock the benefits of integrating diverse mental experiences into a more inclusive and harmonious society. This journey requires patience, persistence, and a commitment to understanding the complexities of the human mind, transcending the limitations of conventional scientific thought and incorporating broader perspectives on consciousness and human potential. It is a path toward a future that not only accepts but celebrates the spectrum of human experience.

CHAPTER 11: THE POTENTIAL BENEFITS OF EMBRACING NEURODIVERSITY

The traditional medical model often focuses on deficits and pathologies when addressing mental illness. This approach, while offering valuable diagnostic and treatment tools, can inadvertently stigmatize individuals and limit their potential. It often emphasizes what someone *cannot* do rather than celebrating their unique strengths and capabilities. A paradigm shift is necessary – one that embraces a strengths-based approach, recognizing that individuals with mental health conditions possess unique talents and perspectives that can be harnessed for personal growth and societal benefit. This shift requires a fundamental re-evaluation of how we define "mental illness" itself. Instead of viewing it solely as a deficit, we can view it as a form of neurodiversity, acknowledging that different brain structures and functions lead to varied ways of experiencing the world. This doesn't diminish the challenges individuals face, but it reframes the narrative to one of empowerment and potential.

For example, consider the case of individuals diagnosed with autism spectrum disorder (ASD). While challenges in social interaction and communication are often prominent features of ASD, many individuals with ASD demonstrate exceptional abilities in areas such as pattern recognition, memory, or visual-spatial reasoning. Instead of focusing solely on the difficulties they face in social situations, a strengths-based approach would emphasize these strengths and create supportive environments that allow them to flourish in areas where they excel. This might involve specialized educational programs tailored to their learning styles, career paths that leverage their unique skills, or social support groups that foster a sense of belonging and understanding. Similarly, individuals with schizophrenia, often stigmatized for their hallucinations or delusions, may exhibit enhanced creativity, imaginative thinking, or intense focus in specific domains. Focusing on these strengths can foster self-esteem and provide opportunities for meaningful engagement, potentially leading to greater independence and fulfillment.

The concept of "superpowers" associated with some neurodiverse conditions is gaining traction. This doesn't trivialize the challenges, but instead emphasizes that these "differences" can translate into exceptional abilities under the right circumstances. For example, the hyperfocus often experienced by individuals with ADHD can be a powerful tool for deep work and achieving remarkable productivity when channeled effectively. The intense sensory sensitivity common in autism can lead to exceptional levels of observation and detail-oriented perception, valuable skills in fields such as art, science, or engineering. Recognizing and fostering these strengths can lead to significant positive outcomes for both the individual and society.

This strengths-based approach necessitates a move away from diagnostic labels as the primary focus. While diagnoses are important for accessing support services, they should not define the individual's identity or limit their potential. The emphasis should shift towards understanding the individual's unique profile of strengths and challenges, creating personalized support plans that cater to their specific needs and foster their growth. This approach requires collaboration between mental health professionals, educators, employers, and the individuals themselves, fostering a collaborative partnership to achieve positive outcomes.

A significant aspect of embracing neurodiversity is promoting inclusion and acceptance within society. Creating environments where individuals with different ways of thinking and being are valued and respected is crucial. This includes challenging the prevalent stigma associated with mental illness, promoting open dialogue and understanding, and fostering empathy and compassion towards those who may experience the world differently. Inclusive educational settings, workplaces that embrace neurodiversity, and social communities that celebrate individual differences are crucial in creating a supportive society where everyone can thrive.

The benefits of embracing neurodiversity extend beyond individual well-being. Harnessing the unique talents and perspectives of individuals with diverse neurological profiles can lead to significant societal benefits. The innovative thinking, creativity, and unique problem-solving approaches often associated with neurodiversity can be invaluable assets in various fields. By creating environments that support and encourage the participation of neurodiverse individuals, we can unlock a wealth of untapped potential, leading to advancements in science, technology, art, and many other areas. Companies that actively promote neurodiversity often report increased creativity, innovation, and improved problem-solving capabilities.

Educational strategies must adapt to meet the needs of neurodiverse learners. One-size-fits-all approaches to education often fail to cater to the unique learning styles and needs of neurodiverse children and adults. Implementing individualized learning plans, utilizing alternative teaching methods, and creating inclusive classroom environments are essential to supporting their educational success. This includes providing appropriate accommodations, fostering a sense of belonging, and celebrating their unique strengths and talents. Flexible learning environments, tailored to individual learning styles and needs, create opportunities for all to engage actively and reach their full potential.

Moreover, the power of diversity in problem-solving is undeniable. Diverse teams bring together different perspectives, experiences, and ways of thinking, leading to more innovative and robust solutions. A neurodiverse workforce, with its varied cognitive styles and abilities, can lead to enhanced creativity and the capacity to tackle complex problems more effectively. Encouraging diversity in the workplace, including employing individuals with diverse neurological profiles, can drive greater innovation and ultimately contribute to greater success.

The integration of strengths-based approaches in mental health requires a fundamental shift in mindset, moving away from a deficit-focused model to one that celebrates the unique strengths and capabilities of individuals with diverse neurological profiles. It is a journey that requires collaborative efforts from mental health professionals, educators, employers, and society as a whole, fostering a culture of acceptance, inclusivity, and understanding. By embracing neurodiversity, we not only improve the lives of individuals with mental health conditions, but also enrich society as a whole, unlocking a wealth of untapped potential and paving the way for a more inclusive and fulfilling future for everyone. The ultimate goal is to move beyond simply managing symptoms and towards a holistic approach that promotes individual well-being, enhances personal growth, and celebrates the full spectrum of human potential. This requires ongoing research, education, and advocacy, ensuring that neurodiversity is recognized, valued, and celebrated as a source of strength and innovation.

The previous chapter highlighted the potential benefits of reframing our understanding of mental health conditions as manifestations of neurodiversity, moving away from a deficit-focused model to one that embraces individual strengths. This shift, however, is not merely a theoretical exercise; it necessitates tangible changes in societal attitudes and structures. True inclusivity requires a proactive and multifaceted approach, one that moves beyond mere tolerance and embraces the richness and potential that neurodiversity brings.

This necessitates a dismantling of the deeply ingrained stigma surrounding mental health. For too long, individuals exhibiting traits associated with conditions like autism, schizophrenia, or ADHD have been marginalized, often facing misunderstanding, prejudice, and limited opportunities. This stigmatization stems from a lack of understanding and empathy, a failure to recognize the unique perspectives and talents these individuals often possess. Education plays a crucial role in combatting this stigma. By disseminating accurate information about neurodiversity, dispelling common misconceptions, and promoting positive narratives, we can foster a more informed and compassionate society. This educational effort should start early, integrated into school curricula to ensure children grow up with a foundational understanding of neurodiversity and its positive aspects.

Beyond formal education, community-based initiatives are essential. Support groups, workshops, and public awareness campaigns can provide crucial platforms for sharing experiences, building empathy, and fostering a sense of belonging. These initiatives should actively involve individuals with neurodiverse conditions, ensuring their voices are heard and their perspectives are valued. Their lived experiences are invaluable in shaping effective strategies for inclusion and challenging harmful stereotypes.

The workplace presents another crucial arena for promoting neurodiversity. Many neurodivergent individuals possess exceptional skills and talents, such as meticulous attention to detail, strong analytical abilities, and innovative thinking. However, traditional workplace structures often fail to accommodate their unique needs and preferences, hindering their ability to contribute their full potential. Creating inclusive workplaces requires a comprehensive approach, encompassing adjustments to working environments, flexible scheduling, and accommodations for sensory sensitivities. This also involves training managers and colleagues to understand and appreciate neurodiversity, fostering an environment of mutual respect and support.

Furthermore, accessible and inclusive design principles need to be applied across various sectors. From public spaces to digital platforms, accessibility considerations should be central to design and development. This means ensuring that environments and technologies are user-friendly for individuals with a wide range of neurological profiles, taking into account factors such as sensory sensitivities, cognitive differences, and communication styles. This principle extends beyond physical accessibility to encompass digital accessibility, making information and services readily available to all, regardless of their neurological makeup. This could mean the development of user-friendly interfaces, accessible technology, and appropriate assistive technologies.

The media also plays a significant role in shaping perceptions of neurodiversity. While there have been some positive strides in recent years, there's still a long way to go to ensure fair and accurate representation. Often, neurodivergent individuals are portrayed in stereotypical ways, reinforcing harmful misconceptions and perpetuating negative stigma. Promoting diverse and nuanced representations in media, including film, television, and literature, is crucial in challenging these stereotypes and showcasing the richness of neurodiverse experiences. The stories of neurodivergent individuals should be told by neurodivergent individuals themselves, ensuring authentic and empowering narratives that celebrate their strengths and resilience.

Beyond individual actions and societal initiatives, systemic changes are necessary to create truly inclusive environments. Legislation and policies play a critical role in protecting the rights of neurodivergent individuals and ensuring equal opportunities. This includes enacting laws that prohibit discrimination based on neurological differences and promoting inclusive practices in education, employment, and healthcare. Furthermore, funding for research into neurodiversity is essential, furthering our understanding of these conditions and informing the development of effective support and intervention strategies. This necessitates a commitment from governments and research institutions to allocate resources to research projects that are inclusive and collaborative, involving neurodivergent individuals and their families as active partners in the research process.

Moreover, promoting a holistic approach to health care is vital. This necessitates a shift from a purely medical model that primarily focuses on pathology and deficits to an approach that acknowledges and supports the individual's strengths and unique talents. This integrated approach would incorporate alternative healing modalities, recognizing that these methods can provide complementary support for neurodivergent individuals, addressing aspects of well-being that may not be fully encompassed by traditional medical interventions. This could encompass practices like mindfulness, meditation, art therapy, music therapy, and other holistic approaches. Such an approach respects the person's individual needs and preferences, incorporating their unique viewpoints on healing and well-being.

The concept of neurodiversity, when truly embraced, can transform not only the lives of neurodivergent individuals but also the fabric of society as a whole. By celebrating the unique strengths and perspectives of individuals with diverse neurological profiles, we unlock a wealth of untapped potential. This potential manifests in various forms – in innovation, creativity, and problem-solving, in diverse talents and perspectives that enrich our communities and workplaces. Neurodiversity isn't simply about accommodating differences; it's about recognizing that these differences are, in fact, sources of strength and innovation. Embracing neurodiversity leads to a more vibrant and resilient society, one that is more adaptable, more creative, and ultimately, more fulfilling for everyone. It is a journey that requires collective effort, continuous learning, and a steadfast commitment to building a truly inclusive and accepting society where every individual has the opportunity to thrive and reach their full potential. The goal is not merely tolerance, but genuine celebration of the extraordinary spectrum of human experience. This paradigm shift is crucial not only for the well-being of neurodivergent individuals, but also for the overall health and advancement of humanity as a whole. The world needs the unique contributions that neurodivergent people offer. By fostering an environment of understanding, acceptance, and support, we not only uplift individuals, but we enrich society itself. The future lies in embracing the full spectrum of human potential, recognizing that what may appear as a "difference" is often a remarkable source of strength and creativity.

The previous chapter established the framework for understanding neurodiversity as a spectrum of human potential, moving beyond the limitations of a purely deficit-based model. Now, we delve into the practical implications of this paradigm shift, exploring how individuals possessing exceptional abilities – whether traditionally considered "psychic" or simply unconventional – can harness their gifts for positive social impact. This isn't about exploiting or commodifying these abilities; rather, it's about fostering an environment where these individuals can flourish and contribute meaningfully to the world, guided by ethical considerations and a deep respect for their unique experiences.

One significant avenue for positive change lies in utilizing these abilities for creative expression. Many individuals with neurodivergent profiles demonstrate exceptional artistic talent, often expressing themselves through unconventional mediums and exhibiting unique perspectives that resonate deeply with others. For example, individuals with autism spectrum disorder (ASD) often possess remarkable attention to detail and a capacity for focused concentration, leading to exceptional proficiency in areas such as visual art, music, or writing. Their unique sensory experiences and processing styles can translate into art that transcends conventional boundaries, offering fresh insights and perspectives to the wider community. Similarly, individuals with synesthesia, a condition where sensory experiences blend, may produce works that evoke multi-sensory responses in others, enriching the artistic experience beyond the limitations of a single sense. Supporting and promoting these artistic endeavors not only empowers these individuals but also enhances the cultural landscape, fostering a more inclusive and creative environment for all.

Beyond artistic expression, the unique cognitive strengths associated with neurodiversity can be harnessed in fields demanding innovative problem-solving and critical thinking. Individuals with ADHD, for instance, often exhibit hyper-focus and lateral thinking capabilities, enabling them to approach challenges from unconventional angles and generate creative solutions. Their ability to think outside the box can be invaluable in fields such as software development, scientific research, or even entrepreneurship. Similarly, individuals with ASD's meticulous attention to detail and capacity for pattern recognition can be highly beneficial in fields like data analysis, cybersecurity, and engineering. The key is to create inclusive workplaces that recognize and value these unique abilities, providing appropriate support and accommodations that allow these individuals to thrive. This includes designing tasks that leverage their strengths while mitigating potential challenges posed by sensory sensitivities or social communication differences. Furthermore, fostering a culture of understanding and acceptance within the workplace is crucial, promoting collaboration and creating a sense of belonging that is essential for maximizing these individuals' contributions. Training programs focused on neurodiversity awareness can equip colleagues with the knowledge and tools to effectively work alongside neurodivergent individuals, creating a synergistic environment that benefits everyone.

The application of these abilities extends to fields beyond the arts and sciences. Individuals possessing what some might consider "psychic" abilities—such as heightened intuition, empathy, or clairsentience—can contribute to areas such as alternative healing, counseling, and conflict resolution. However, a cautious and ethically-minded approach is paramount here. These abilities should never be used to exploit or manipulate others, and rigorous training and ethical guidelines should be implemented to ensure responsible practice. It is essential to differentiate between genuine abilities and potential misinterpretations arising from mental health conditions. Proper diagnosis and psychological evaluation are crucial to prevent the conflation of genuine gifts with symptomatic manifestations. While acknowledging the potential benefits, it is vital to maintain scientific rigor and to avoid promoting unsubstantiated claims. The focus should be on developing ethical frameworks and support structures that enable individuals with these abilities to use them beneficially within a safe and regulated context. This could involve creating certified training programs, establishing professional organizations, and implementing ethical codes of conduct to ensure responsible and transparent practice.

The potential for positive social change extends to the societal impact of embracing and celebrating neurodiversity. By acknowledging and valuing the unique perspectives and contributions of neurodivergent individuals, we can foster a more inclusive and understanding society. This means moving beyond simply tolerating differences to actively celebrating and incorporating the rich tapestry of human experience into our collective consciousness. Neurodiversity isn't simply about making accommodations; it's about recognizing the inherent strengths and innovative capabilities of individuals with different neurological profiles, creating a world where everyone feels a sense of belonging and purpose. This shift requires systemic changes in education, employment, and healthcare, ensuring that these systems are designed to accommodate and support the needs of all individuals, regardless of their neurological differences.

Furthermore, recognizing the potential benefits of embracing neurodiversity prompts a reevaluation of our understanding of mental illness. Rather than viewing mental health conditions solely through a deficit-based lens, we can begin to see them as diverse manifestations of human consciousness, each with unique strengths and vulnerabilities. This requires a paradigm shift in mental healthcare, moving towards a more holistic and person-centered approach that values individual strengths and fosters personal growth. Therapy and support should be tailored to the individual's unique needs and strengths, rather than solely focusing on addressing perceived deficits. A holistic approach might incorporate alternative healing modalities alongside traditional therapeutic methods, acknowledging the potential benefits of various approaches and adapting them to the individual's specific circumstances.

The integration of neurodiversity into societal structures requires a conscious effort to challenge societal biases and stereotypes. Negative perceptions surrounding neurodivergent individuals often stem from a lack of understanding and a failure to acknowledge the diversity of human experience. Educational programs targeting the general public can play a vital role in promoting greater understanding and empathy. By fostering greater awareness of neurodiversity, we can challenge misconceptions, reduce stigma, and create a more inclusive and supportive society for neurodivergent individuals and their families. This includes promoting positive portrayals of neurodiversity in the media, highlighting the contributions of neurodivergent individuals, and sharing personal stories that humanize these experiences and challenge preconceived notions.

The concept of "Indigo Children," "Crystal Children," and related New Age terms often associated with exceptional abilities further highlights the need for a nuanced approach. While lacking a firm scientific basis, these concepts reflect a growing awareness of individuals with unconventional strengths and perspectives. Instead of dismissing these concepts outright, it may be more fruitful to explore the underlying experiences and phenomena they represent, examining the potential neurological, psychological, and spiritual factors at play. This could involve investigating reported experiences of heightened intuition, empathy, and spiritual awareness in these individuals, exploring the underlying neural mechanisms and psychological processes associated with these experiences. This approach requires a careful balance between scientific rigor and an open-minded exploration of unconventional phenomena, avoiding both dismissal and unsubstantiated claims.

Ultimately, harnessing unique abilities for positive change hinges on creating a society that values diversity, inclusivity, and ethical practice. It's not about exploiting or commodifying these abilities; it's about fostering an environment where individuals with exceptional skills can thrive, contribute to society, and live fulfilling lives. This requires a multifaceted approach, encompassing educational initiatives, systemic changes in healthcare and employment, and a shift in societal attitudes towards neurodiversity. By embracing this new paradigm, we unlock a wealth of untapped potential, not only benefitting individuals with exceptional abilities but also enriching society as a whole and fostering a brighter future for all. The journey towards this future necessitates continuous learning, ongoing dialogue, and a steadfast commitment to creating a truly inclusive and equitable world.

Educating neurodiverse learners requires a fundamental shift in pedagogical approaches. Traditional, one-size-fits-all methods often fail to recognize and accommodate the unique learning styles and cognitive strengths of individuals with diverse neurological profiles. Instead of focusing solely on deficits, we need to identify and leverage their exceptional abilities. This necessitates a move towards individualized education plans (IEPs) that are not merely remedial but rather proactively design learning experiences to nurture their specific talents and mitigate challenges in a supportive and empowering way.

For instance, children exhibiting heightened sensitivity, often associated with what some might term "psychic" abilities like clairsentience (increased sensitivity to emotions and energies), might benefit from sensory-sensitive classrooms. This could involve minimizing visual clutter, using calming colors, and providing noise-canceling headphones or quiet spaces for breaks when sensory overload becomes overwhelming. The curriculum itself could be adapted to incorporate kinesthetic learning activities, allowing them to express and process information through movement and physical engagement, mitigating potential anxiety associated with traditional classroom settings. These students might thrive in project-based learning, allowing them to explore their interests independently, potentially channeling their heightened sensitivities into creative projects that benefit from their unique perceptive abilities.

Students with strong intuitive abilities, sometimes perceived as precognitive or possessing heightened intuition, might excel in open-ended inquiry-based learning environments. Instead of rote memorization and standardized testing, they should be encouraged to ask questions, explore their curiosity, and delve deeply into subjects that resonate with their intrinsic motivations. Their capacity for insightful connections and pattern recognition can be nurtured through complex problem-solving tasks and creative projects that allow for divergent thinking and original solutions. Providing opportunities for collaborative projects can encourage them to contribute their unique insights to group endeavors and develop valuable teamwork skills.

For learners who demonstrate exceptional memory or information processing capabilities, often associated with savant syndrome or other forms of neurodiversity, a curriculum designed to accelerate their learning pace may be appropriate. This doesn't necessarily mean pushing them through the material faster, but rather providing more challenging and stimulating content that keeps them engaged and prevents boredom. These students might flourish in advanced courses or programs tailored to their advanced skills, allowing them to pursue their intellectual passions deeply and meaningfully. Their potential for innovation and contribution can be unlocked by providing them with access to mentors and resources that support their advanced cognitive abilities.

Furthermore, incorporating mindfulness and meditation practices into the educational setting can be profoundly beneficial for neurodiverse learners. These practices can help regulate emotional responses, enhance focus and concentration, and cultivate self-awareness—essential skills for navigating the challenges of a potentially overwhelming environment. Mindfulness-based stress reduction (MBSR) techniques, for instance, can provide tools to manage sensory overload and emotional dysregulation, enabling learners to better regulate their responses and participate more fully in the learning process. The development of self-regulation skills is not merely an accommodation but an empowerment, allowing neurodiverse individuals to harness their strengths more effectively.

The integration of technology also holds significant potential. Adaptive learning software can personalize the educational experience, offering individualized support based on a student's specific learning needs and pace. Assistive technologies, such as text-to-speech software or speech-to-text programs, can help overcome challenges related to reading, writing, or communication. The strategic use of technology can create a more inclusive and accessible learning environment for neurodiverse learners, enhancing their access to information and fostering independence.

However, it's crucial to acknowledge that the concept of "psychic" abilities, as traditionally understood, raises complex ethical considerations in an educational context. While we should celebrate and support unique cognitive strengths, we must avoid exploiting or commodifying these abilities. It's essential to foster an environment of respect, where individuality is valued, and exceptional abilities are seen as strengths to be developed ethically and responsibly. This includes prioritizing the well-being of the student, ensuring they feel safe, supported, and empowered to express their unique gifts in a way that aligns with their personal values and aspirations.

Moving beyond childhood education, adult neurodiverse individuals also require tailored support to succeed. Workplaces and professional development opportunities need to be adapted to their unique learning styles and cognitive preferences. This includes flexible work arrangements, alternative communication strategies, and access to mentors who understand and appreciate neurodiversity. Flexible work arrangements, such as remote work options or adjusted schedules, can significantly improve the quality of life and productivity of neurodiverse adults. By acknowledging their strengths and providing appropriate support, we unlock their potential to contribute meaningfully to the workforce and society at large.

Furthermore, the development of social skills and emotional intelligence is crucial for neurodiverse adults navigating social and professional environments. Social skills training can help them develop strategies for effective communication, conflict resolution, and building healthy relationships. By equipping them with these skills, we can facilitate their integration into society and enhance their overall well-being. Emotional intelligence training can similarly empower them to understand and manage their emotions, improving interpersonal interactions and fostering greater self-awareness and empathy.

Creating supportive communities is also crucial. Support groups and peer mentoring programs can provide valuable opportunities for neurodiverse individuals to connect with others who share similar experiences, fostering a sense of belonging and mutual understanding. These communities provide a space for sharing knowledge, exchanging strategies for coping with challenges, and celebrating successes, fostering resilience and reducing feelings of isolation. Moreover, the creation of accessible resources, including information on effective coping mechanisms, employment strategies, and social support networks, is critical for the well-being and empowerment of neurodiverse adults.

Ultimately, the education and support of neurodiverse learners requires a paradigm shift, moving away from a deficit-based model toward a strengths-based approach. By recognizing and celebrating their unique abilities, fostering inclusive environments, and providing tailored support, we unlock their potential to thrive, contribute meaningfully to society, and live fulfilling lives. This holistic approach, encompassing educational initiatives, systemic changes, and a societal shift in attitudes, will not only benefit neurodiverse individuals but will enrich society as a whole, fostering a more inclusive and equitable future for everyone. This requires ongoing research, open dialogue, and a committed effort to understand and support the diverse tapestry of human experience, embracing the full spectrum of neurological expression. Only then can we truly unlock the vast potential inherent in neurodiversity, enriching both individual lives and the collective human experience.

The remarkable capacity of the human brain to solve complex problems is often underestimated. While traditional models of intelligence focus on convergent thinking—arriving at a single, "correct" solution—the reality is far more nuanced. Truly innovative solutions, the breakthroughs that reshape our understanding of the world, often arise from divergent thinking, a process characterized by exploring multiple perspectives and approaches. This is where the power of neurodiversity truly shines. Individuals with diverse neurological profiles bring unique cognitive strengths to the table, offering a kaleidoscope of perspectives that can unlock creative solutions previously unimaginable. The notion of a "standard" or "average" brain, against which neurodivergent individuals are measured, is a limiting and ultimately inaccurate framework.

Consider the well-documented phenomenon of "groupthink," where the desire for conformity within a homogeneous group stifles dissent and inhibits creative problem-solving. A team composed of individuals with similar backgrounds, educational experiences, and cognitive styles may reach consensus quickly, but that consensus may lack the robustness and originality needed to address complex challenges effectively. They may fall prey to confirmation bias, seeking out information that supports pre-existing beliefs while ignoring contradictory evidence. The introduction of neurodivergent perspectives disrupts this homogeneity, introducing a crucial element of critical analysis and challenging assumptions that may have otherwise remained unquestioned.

Individuals with autism spectrum disorder (ASD), for instance, often demonstrate exceptional attention to detail and an ability to identify patterns that might escape neurotypical observers. Their focus can be laser-like, allowing them to dissect complex problems with meticulous precision and uncover hidden connections. Similarly, individuals with ADHD, often characterized by hyperactivity and impulsivity, can bring a unique energy and spontaneity to brainstorming sessions, generating a prolific stream of ideas that might spark innovative solutions. Their capacity for rapid association and lateral thinking can transcend conventional limitations.

This isn't to say that neurodiversity guarantees effortless problem-solving; indeed, challenges remain. Differences in communication styles can create barriers, and the unique cognitive strengths of neurodivergent individuals may require careful facilitation to be effectively integrated into a team dynamic. However, the potential rewards significantly outweigh the challenges. By fostering inclusive environments where individuals feel safe to contribute their unique perspectives, we can unlock a synergistic effect, where the combined cognitive strengths of neurotypical and neurodivergent individuals create a powerful force for innovation.

The benefits extend beyond individual problem-solving. Consider the advancements in technology and the arts driven by neurodivergent individuals. Many groundbreaking technological innovations can be traced to individuals with ASD, whose meticulous attention to detail and ability to identify patterns have led to breakthroughs in areas ranging from software design to scientific research. The unique perspectives of neurodivergent artists have also enriched the world, challenging conventional aesthetics and offering innovative expressions of creativity. Their contributions often challenge societal norms and expand our understanding of artistic expression itself.

The key lies in recognizing and valuing the diverse cognitive styles that characterize neurodiversity. This requires a shift in mindset, moving away from a deficit-based model that seeks to "fix" neurodivergent individuals and towards a strengths-based model that celebrates their unique abilities. It necessitates creating workplaces and educational environments that are truly inclusive, accommodating the diverse needs and communication styles of individuals with different neurological profiles. This might involve providing visual aids, offering flexible work arrangements, encouraging different communication methods, and creating spaces where individuals feel comfortable expressing themselves authentically.

Moreover, fostering a culture of respect and understanding is paramount. This means educating both neurotypical and neurodivergent individuals about the strengths and challenges associated with different neurological profiles, promoting empathy and collaboration. It involves actively challenging biases and stereotypes and fostering an environment where differences are celebrated rather than stigmatized. This requires a conscious effort at every level, from individual interactions to institutional policies.

The impact of embracing neurodiversity extends far beyond the workplace and classroom. Consider the implications for social innovation and the development of solutions to global challenges such as climate change, poverty, and inequality. The ability to approach problems from multiple perspectives, to challenge assumptions, and to identify creative solutions is essential to addressing these complex issues. By harnessing the cognitive diversity of the human population, we can generate more resilient, sustainable, and equitable solutions.

One particularly promising area of exploration is the application of neurodiversity principles to the development of artificial intelligence (AI). The current generation of AI systems often lacks the creativity and adaptability of the human brain. By incorporating the diverse cognitive strengths of neurodivergent individuals into the design and development of AI, we may be able to create systems that are more creative, resilient, and better able to adapt to complex and evolving situations. This could lead to breakthroughs in various fields, from medicine and engineering to art and entertainment.

Furthermore, the study of neurodiversity offers valuable insights into the nature of consciousness itself. The unique cognitive experiences of neurodivergent individuals challenge our conventional understanding of how the brain processes information and creates subjective experience. By exploring these differences, we can gain a deeper understanding of the mechanisms underlying human consciousness and the vast potential of the human mind. This research has implications not only for neuroscience but also for fields such as philosophy, psychology, and even spirituality.

Ultimately, embracing neurodiversity is not merely a matter of social justice or inclusivity; it is a strategic imperative. It is about unlocking the full potential of the human brain, harnessing the diverse cognitive strengths of our population to address the complex challenges of our time and create a more innovative, equitable, and sustainable future. By shifting our focus from deficits to strengths, from conformity to diversity, we can unleash a wave of creativity and innovation that will benefit individuals, communities, and society as a whole. The future belongs to those who embrace the full spectrum of human experience, recognizing and celebrating the unique gifts that each individual brings to the table. This is not merely a matter of tolerance; it's a matter of recognizing that neurodiversity is a source of strength, a wellspring of innovation, and a key to unlocking the boundless potential of the human spirit. The integration of these diverse perspectives isn't simply a matter of inclusion, but a pathway to a richer, more innovative, and ultimately more human future.

CHAPTER 12: ALTERNATIVE HEALING AND SPIRITUAL PRACTICES

Energy healing, a broad term encompassing various techniques aiming to manipulate purported energy fields within and around the body, has garnered increasing interest, despite a lack of robust scientific evidence within conventional medical frameworks. Proponents suggest these methods can address physical and emotional imbalances, promoting well-being and even facilitating healing from illness. While the underlying mechanisms remain largely unexplained, exploring the potential neurological effects of energy healing offers a fascinating lens through which to view its potential impact.

One prominent approach is Reiki, a Japanese technique involving the practitioner channeling universal life force energy (often referred to as

ki or *prana*) to the recipient. The process typically involves gentle touch or hovering hands above the body, with the practitioner focusing intention on promoting healing and balance. While subjective reports of relaxation, reduced pain, and improved well-being are common, objective neurological studies remain limited. Some researchers propose that Reiki might influence the autonomic nervous system, potentially reducing stress responses through decreased sympathetic activity and increased parasympathetic activity. This could manifest as lower heart rate, reduced blood pressure, and a sense of calm. Electroencephalography (EEG) studies could potentially reveal changes in brainwave patterns during Reiki sessions, indicating alterations in states of consciousness similar to those observed during meditation. However, rigorous, controlled studies comparing Reiki to placebo treatments are necessary to determine the extent of its specific effects.

Therapeutic Touch (TT) is another energy healing modality, characterized by the practitioner's hands passing over the patient's body without physical contact. Practitioners claim to sense energy fields and manipulate them to promote healing. Similar to Reiki, the purported effects include relaxation, pain reduction, and improved well-being. The lack of robust evidence supporting TT's efficacy has led to its criticism within the scientific community. However, from a neuroscientific perspective, the placebo effect cannot be discounted. The belief and expectation of healing, along with the ritualistic nature of the practice, might trigger endogenous opioid release and other neurochemical changes associated with pain relief and improved mood. Furthermore, the calming effect of human touch, even without direct physical contact, can activate the vagus nerve, promoting relaxation and potentially reducing stress hormone levels. Further research employing sophisticated neuroimaging techniques like fMRI could help identify specific brain regions involved in the experience of TT and potentially uncover any measurable changes in brain activity related to purported energy field manipulation.

Beyond Reiki and TT, various other energy healing modalities exist, including Qi Gong, Pranic Healing, and others. These practices often involve specific movements, visualizations, and intentions aimed at manipulating energy flow. The common thread amongst these approaches lies in their purported impact on subtle energy fields, influencing the body's physiological processes. From a neuroscientific perspective, this warrants consideration of the brain's intricate network of neurotransmitters, hormones, and electrical impulses. The mind-body connection is well-established, with bidirectional communication between the brain and body constantly occurring. It's conceivable that the focused intention and mental imagery employed during energy healing practices might modulate brain activity, leading to physiological changes, albeit through indirect pathways.

The potential neurological effects are complex and multifaceted. Energy healing practices might influence:

The Autonomic Nervous System: As mentioned earlier, energy healing may affect the balance between the sympathetic (fight-or-flight) and parasympathetic (rest-and-digest) nervous systems, leading to a more relaxed state. This could be associated with reduced cortisol levels (a stress hormone) and increased levels of neurotransmitters associated with relaxation, such as GABA.

The Endocrine System: The endocrine system, responsible for hormone regulation, could be influenced indirectly through the autonomic nervous system. Changes in hormone levels could impact various bodily functions, including mood, sleep, and immune function.

Pain Perception: Energy healing practices are often reported to alleviate pain. This could be attributed to the placebo effect, the release of endogenous opioids (the body's natural painkillers), or a combination of both. Further research using neuroimaging could potentially reveal the specific neural pathways involved in pain reduction.

Brainwave Activity: Changes in brainwave patterns, particularly an increase in alpha and theta waves associated with relaxation and meditation, might be observed during energy healing sessions. This could be detected through EEG recordings.

Immune Function: While the mechanisms are unclear, some proponents suggest that energy healing may positively influence the immune system. This could potentially be linked to stress reduction, as chronic stress is known to suppress immune function.

Despite the lack of conclusive scientific evidence, the growing popularity of energy healing suggests a significant unmet need for alternative approaches to health and well-being. The subjective experiences reported by practitioners and recipients warrant further investigation, employing both rigorous scientific methodology and an open mind towards the complexities of the mind-body connection. Future research must address methodological limitations, ensuring controlled studies, appropriate control groups, and objective measures of neurological and physiological changes. Furthermore, incorporating qualitative research methods, such as in-depth interviews with practitioners and recipients, could offer valuable insights into the lived experiences and subjective understanding of these healing modalities. The interdisciplinary nature of this field calls for collaboration between neuroscientists, parapsychologists, and practitioners of energy healing to unravel the potential benefits and mechanisms behind these intriguing practices. This open and collaborative approach is crucial to advance our understanding of both the neurological and spiritual dimensions of healing, and to responsibly integrate alternative healing modalities into a holistic approach to well-being. Ultimately, the goal should be to provide evidence-based information to empower individuals to make informed choices regarding their health and well-being, regardless of their belief systems or preferred healing modalities. The path forward requires a balance of scientific rigor and a respectful appreciation for the subjective experiences that drive the popularity of energy healing modalities.

The exploration of energy healing naturally leads us to consider the powerful tools of meditation and mindfulness. While seemingly disparate from the energetic manipulations discussed previously, these practices share a common thread: the profound impact they can have on the brain and its capacity for self-regulation and healing. Meditation and mindfulness, far from being mere relaxation techniques, are potent neurological interventions, capable of reshaping brain structure and function in ways that correlate with improved mental and physical health.

One of the key mechanisms through which meditation exerts its influence is its impact on the autonomic nervous system (ANS). The ANS, responsible for regulating involuntary bodily functions like heart rate, breathing, and digestion, operates largely unconsciously. Chronic stress and anxiety often lead to a state of ANS dysregulation, manifesting as elevated heart rate, shallow breathing, digestive problems, and a heightened state of physiological arousal. Studies using neuroimaging techniques, such as EEG and fMRI, reveal that regular meditation practice can significantly reduce ANS activity, shifting the balance towards the parasympathetic nervous system—the "rest and digest" system—and promoting a state of physiological calm. This reduction in sympathetic nervous system activity translates to lower levels of cortisol, the stress hormone, and a decreased risk of stress-related illnesses.

Beyond its impact on the ANS, meditation demonstrably alters brain structure and function. Longitudinal studies have shown increases in grey matter density in brain regions associated with attention, emotional regulation, and self-awareness, including the prefrontal cortex, hippocampus, and insula. These changes are particularly pronounced in individuals practicing mindfulness-based meditation, which emphasizes cultivating present moment awareness without judgment. The increased grey matter density suggests a strengthening of neural connections in these regions, reflecting enhanced cognitive function and emotional resilience. Conversely, areas of the brain linked to stress and anxiety, such as the amygdala, often show reduced activity following consistent meditation practice. This dampening of amygdala activity can translate to a lessened emotional reactivity and a decreased susceptibility to anxiety and fear.

The benefits extend beyond the neurological realm. Studies have linked regular meditation to improvements in sleep quality, pain management, immune function, and even cardiovascular health. The mechanisms underlying these effects are complex and multifaceted, likely involving the interplay of neurochemical changes, hormonal modulation, and improved stress coping mechanisms. For instance, improved sleep quality is likely related to the reduction in stress hormones and the promotion of a more relaxed physiological state, making it easier to fall asleep and stay asleep. Pain management, on the other hand, may be influenced by changes in brain regions involved in pain perception and processing, as well as the activation of endogenous opioid systems that contribute to natural pain relief.

Furthermore, the integration of mindfulness techniques into various therapeutic approaches has shown promising results in managing conditions such as depression, anxiety, PTSD, and addiction. Mindfulness-based cognitive therapy (MBCT), for example, combines elements of cognitive behavioral therapy (CBT) with mindfulness practices, helping individuals become more aware of their thoughts and emotions without judgment, thus reducing their tendency to engage in maladaptive coping mechanisms. This approach has demonstrated significant efficacy in preventing relapse in individuals with recurrent depression and improving overall mental well-being.

The types of meditation and mindfulness techniques are diverse, offering a range of approaches to suit different preferences and needs. Transcendental Meditation (TM), a popular technique involving the repetition of a mantra, is known for its ability to induce deep relaxation and reduce stress. Mindfulness meditation, on the other hand, focuses on cultivating present moment awareness of thoughts, feelings, and bodily sensations without judgment. Other practices, such as Vipassanā meditation, emphasize the observation of bodily sensations and mental phenomena to gain insight into the nature of reality and achieve liberation from suffering. Yoga, with its combination of physical postures, breathing exercises, and meditation, also provides a holistic approach to cultivating mindfulness and promoting physical and mental well-being.

The specific benefits experienced from each technique can vary, depending on individual factors such as personality, practice style, and the specific condition being addressed. However, the common thread among these practices is their ability to cultivate a greater sense of self-awareness, emotional regulation, and overall mental clarity. This improved self-regulation can have cascading positive effects on various aspects of life, including relationships, productivity, and overall life satisfaction. Moreover, the accessibility of these practices, requiring minimal equipment or specialized training, makes them an appealing option for individuals seeking to enhance their well-being.

It is crucial to recognize that meditation and mindfulness are not quick fixes for complex mental or physical health issues. While they offer substantial benefits, they are most effective when practiced consistently and integrated into a holistic approach to well-being that may include other therapies, lifestyle changes, and potentially conventional medical treatments. Furthermore, the initial experience of meditation can be challenging for some individuals, with the mind often wandering and focusing on distracting thoughts or sensations. Perseverance and patience are crucial, and seeking guidance from experienced instructors or meditation groups can significantly enhance the learning process and provide support along the way.

The exploration of meditation and mindfulness within the broader context of neurodiversity and exceptional human potential reveals a fascinating synergy. Individuals with certain neurological conditions, such as autism spectrum disorder, may exhibit a natural predisposition towards focused attention and heightened sensory awareness, characteristics that can be harnessed and enhanced through meditation practices. Moreover, the heightened sensory sensitivity often associated with neurodiversity can be perceived as a disadvantage, but mindfulness practices can offer tools for managing sensory overload and developing strategies for coping with heightened sensory input. This suggests that meditation and mindfulness can be particularly valuable in supporting neurodivergent individuals in achieving greater self-regulation, emotional resilience, and overall well-being.

Similarly, the reported experiences of individuals identifying as Indigo, Crystal, or Rainbow Children, often characterized by heightened intuition, empathy, and spiritual awareness, can be understood as a form of neurodiversity expressing itself in unconventional ways. Mindfulness and meditation practices may serve to amplify these innate abilities by fostering a deeper connection to inner wisdom and intuitive insights. The focused attention and enhanced self-awareness cultivated through meditation can facilitate the development of intuitive skills and strengthen the connection to one's inner world. This integration of spiritual perspectives with neuroscientific findings highlights the potential for these practices to enhance the unique capabilities of neurodivergent individuals and further support their personal growth and integration into society.

The lack of extensive research specifically examining the interaction between meditation, mindfulness, and the purported abilities of individuals identifying as Starseeds or Lightworkers does not negate the potential benefits of these practices. Anecdotal evidence suggests that meditation can enhance their spiritual experiences, enabling a deeper connection to their perceived spiritual gifts and facilitating a more harmonious integration of these abilities into their daily lives. The potential for self-reflection and emotional regulation offered by meditation practices could be particularly beneficial for individuals who experience heightened sensitivity or emotional intensity, traits sometimes associated with these groups. Further research is needed to explore these possibilities systematically, applying rigorous methodology to investigate potential correlations between specific meditation practices and subjective experiences related to enhanced intuitive capacities, heightened spiritual awareness, or other unique attributes often described in the literature on Starseeds and Lightworkers.

Ultimately, the integration of meditation and mindfulness techniques into a holistic approach to well-being aligns perfectly with the overarching message of this book. It emphasizes the importance of recognizing and respecting individual differences, celebrating unique abilities, and harnessing human potential for positive change. Meditation and mindfulness offer powerful tools for self-discovery, self-regulation, and self-healing, fostering a greater understanding of the complex interplay between the mind, body, and spirit. By embracing these practices, we can unlock untapped potential within ourselves and contribute to a future that values neurodiversity and fosters the growth of human consciousness. The path forward requires an interdisciplinary approach, integrating neuroscientific research with spiritual perspectives to fully grasp the transformative power of meditation and mindfulness in enhancing both physical and mental health, and potentially even unlocking exceptional human capabilities.

The exploration of alternative healing modalities naturally leads us to delve into the fascinating world of spiritual practices and their profound influence on consciousness. Many spiritual traditions utilize practices designed to alter states of consciousness, often with the intention of achieving enhanced self-awareness, spiritual insight, or healing. These practices, far from being mere rituals, can be understood as powerful tools for reshaping brain activity and fostering profound physiological and psychological changes. The mechanisms by which these practices achieve their effects remain a subject of ongoing scientific inquiry, but a growing body of research suggests a complex interplay between neurological processes, psychological states, and subjective experience.

One of the most widely practiced and researched spiritual techniques is meditation. Numerous studies employing neuroimaging techniques, such as EEG and fMRI, have shown that meditation can induce significant changes in brainwave patterns. For instance, prolonged meditation practice is associated with increased activity in the prefrontal cortex, a region associated with executive functions, attention, and self-regulation. Conversely, it often reduces activity in the amygdala, a brain region implicated in fear and anxiety responses. These neurological changes correlate with improvements in mood, stress reduction, and enhanced emotional regulation, suggesting a tangible link between spiritual practice and neural plasticity. Different forms of meditation, such as mindfulness meditation, transcendental meditation, and vipassanā meditation, may elicit distinct neural responses, highlighting the nuanced relationship between practice type and neurological outcome. The variations in technique and the individual's response to these techniques underscore the importance of personalized approaches to meditation practice, tailored to individual needs and preferences.

Beyond meditation, other spiritual practices also demonstrably alter consciousness. Yoga, for example, combines physical postures (asanas), breathing techniques (pranayama), and meditation to promote physical and mental well-being. Studies suggest that yoga can enhance neuroplasticity, improve mood, reduce stress hormones like cortisol, and positively influence brain structure and function. The coordinated movement and breath control in yoga may stimulate the parasympathetic nervous system, inducing a state of relaxation and promoting a sense of calm and centeredness. The integration of mindful movement with meditative focus enhances the overall impact on the nervous system, suggesting a synergistic effect that transcends the simple sum of its individual components.

Similarly, breathwork practices, often employed in various spiritual traditions, can profoundly impact consciousness. Controlled breathing techniques can alter oxygen levels in the blood, influencing brain chemistry and promoting changes in brainwave patterns. Specific breathing patterns, such as hyperventilation or slow, deep breathing, can induce altered states of consciousness ranging from feelings of euphoria to profound relaxation. These effects are not solely subjective; they are demonstrably measurable through physiological indicators such as heart rate variability, blood pressure, and oxygen saturation levels. The ability to consciously manipulate breathing patterns to induce specific states of consciousness offers a powerful example of the mind-body connection and the potential for self-regulation through spiritual practices.

Certain spiritual traditions involve the use of entheogens— naturally occurring substances with psychoactive properties —as tools for inducing altered states of consciousness. Substances such as psilocybin mushrooms, ayahuasca, and ibogaine have been used in indigenous cultures for centuries in spiritual and healing ceremonies. While the use of these substances carries risks, controlled research studies are now exploring their potential therapeutic applications in treating conditions such as depression, anxiety, and addiction. These studies suggest that entheogens may act by facilitating neural plasticity, promoting emotional processing, and fostering a sense of self-transcendence, leading to beneficial changes in mental health. However, it's crucial to emphasize the need for caution and responsible use, particularly given the potential for adverse effects and the importance of a safe and supportive setting under experienced guidance. The ethical considerations and legal ramifications surrounding entheogens necessitate rigorous research and careful regulation to ensure both safety and responsible therapeutic use.

The concept of near-death experiences (NDEs) offers another avenue for exploring the intersection of spiritual practices and altered states of consciousness. NDEs, often reported after critical medical events such as cardiac arrest, frequently involve vivid out-of-body experiences, feelings of peace and transcendence, and encounters with deceased loved ones. Although the neurological mechanisms underlying NDEs remain a subject of debate, some researchers suggest that they may result from oxygen deprivation in the brain or the release of endorphins and other neurochemicals. Others posit that NDEs reflect a fundamental aspect of consciousness that transcends the physical body and brain. Regardless of the underlying mechanism, the subjective experiences reported by individuals undergoing NDEs often have a profound impact on their worldview and spiritual beliefs. This suggests a potential pathway of spiritual transformation and altered states of consciousness that deserve further investigation, particularly in the context of how such experiences correlate with subsequent mental and emotional wellbeing.

Furthermore, spiritual practices often incorporate elements of ritual, symbol, and narrative to facilitate altered states of consciousness. Rituals, whether simple or complex, provide a structured framework for engaging in spiritual practices, promoting focus and intentionality. Symbols, imbued with meaning and cultural significance, can evoke powerful emotions and enhance the subjective experience of spiritual practices. Narratives, particularly those found in religious and mystical texts, provide a framework for understanding the world and one's place within it, fostering a sense of connection and belonging. The interplay of ritual, symbol, and narrative creates a rich tapestry of meaning and experience, contributing to the overall effectiveness of spiritual practices in inducing altered states of consciousness.

Understanding the role of spiritual practices in inducing

altered states of consciousness requires a multidisciplinary approach, integrating insights from neuroscience, psychology, anthropology, and religious studies. By employing rigorous scientific methods while acknowledging the subjective and personal nature of spiritual experience, researchers can shed light on the complex interplay between brain function, psychological states, and the profound transformative potential of spiritual practices. The growing body of research in this area underscores the importance of integrating spiritual practices into a holistic approach to well-being and healing, recognizing their potential to enhance mental health, promote emotional regulation, and foster a deeper understanding of the human condition. The exploration of this intersection offers a pathway to a more comprehensive understanding of human consciousness and its potential for growth and transformation. The integration of these diverse fields of knowledge is crucial for developing a more comprehensive and nuanced understanding of the human experience, particularly in relation to the transformative power of spiritual practices. As research continues to advance, we can anticipate a more sophisticated understanding of how these practices shape our brains, our minds, and ultimately, our lives. This integration will be crucial for developing effective therapeutic interventions and facilitating a more holistic approach to human well-being. The future of understanding human potential likely lies in embracing the convergence of science and spirituality, fostering a richer appreciation of the extraordinary capabilities inherent in the human experience.

The exploration of spiritual practices and their impact on consciousness naturally leads us to consider their potential synergy with complementary and alternative medicine (CAM). While conventional medicine focuses on addressing the physical symptoms of illness through pharmaceuticals and surgical interventions, CAM encompasses a broader range of practices aimed at promoting overall well-being and addressing the root causes of disease. This includes modalities such as acupuncture, herbal medicine, homeopathy, chiropractic care, massage therapy, and various mind-body techniques like meditation and yoga. The integration of these approaches holds significant promise for enhancing healthcare and fostering a more holistic approach to patient care.

One of the key principles underlying CAM is the interconnectedness of mind, body, and spirit. This holistic perspective acknowledges the profound influence of emotional, psychological, and spiritual factors on physical health. Chronic stress, for example, is a well-established risk factor for numerous physical ailments, including cardiovascular disease, autoimmune disorders, and gastrointestinal problems. CAM therapies often address these underlying psychological and emotional stressors through techniques that promote relaxation, stress reduction, and emotional regulation. Mindfulness meditation, for instance, has shown promising results in reducing stress, improving mood, and enhancing overall well-being. Similarly, yoga combines physical postures, breathing techniques, and meditation to promote physical flexibility, reduce stress, and cultivate a sense of inner peace.

The efficacy of CAM therapies is often supported by anecdotal evidence and testimonials from patients who have experienced positive outcomes. However, the scientific evidence base for many CAM practices remains limited, and rigorous clinical trials are needed to establish their efficacy and safety. Nevertheless, a growing body of research suggests that certain CAM modalities hold significant therapeutic potential. Acupuncture, for example, has been shown to be effective in relieving pain and managing nausea and vomiting, while herbal medicine offers a rich source of bioactive compounds with potential therapeutic benefits. The challenge lies in conducting well-designed, randomized controlled trials to objectively assess the efficacy of these treatments, while also acknowledging the subjective and individualized nature of CAM practices.

The integration of CAM into mainstream healthcare presents both opportunities and challenges. One significant challenge is the need for standardized training and certification for CAM practitioners to ensure quality and safety. Another challenge is the need for improved communication and collaboration between conventional and CAM practitioners to facilitate a more integrated approach to patient care. However, the potential benefits of this integration are substantial. By combining the precision of conventional medicine with the holistic perspective of CAM, we can create a more comprehensive and personalized approach to healthcare that addresses the unique needs of each patient.

This integrated approach requires a shift in the prevailing medical paradigm, moving away from a purely reductionist view of illness and towards a more systems-based approach that acknowledges the complex interplay of physical, psychological, and spiritual factors. This requires a reassessment of the traditional healthcare model, which often treats symptoms rather than addressing underlying causes. The integration of CAM can provide tools for addressing these root causes, fostering a more preventative and holistic approach to health.

Consider the example of chronic pain management. Conventional treatments often rely heavily on pharmaceuticals, which can have significant side effects. CAM therapies such as acupuncture, massage therapy, and mindfulness-based stress reduction can provide complementary approaches to pain management, reducing reliance on medications and improving overall quality of life. The combined approach, tailored to the individual patient, can offer a more effective and less invasive treatment strategy.

Furthermore, the integration of CAM can enhance the patient experience. Many patients value the personalized attention, patient-centered approach, and holistic perspective that CAM therapies often provide. This can foster a stronger therapeutic alliance between the patient and healthcare provider, leading to improved adherence to treatment plans and better overall outcomes. The empowering aspect of many CAM practices, enabling patients to take an active role in their own healing process, is a key element in their appeal and potential therapeutic value.

However, it's crucial to address potential pitfalls. The lack of regulation in some CAM fields can lead to ineffective or even harmful treatments. Misinformation and unsubstantiated claims must be carefully addressed to protect patients. The integration process needs to ensure rigorous standards, emphasizing evidence-based practices while acknowledging the complexities of the human experience beyond solely biological factors. A critical, yet open-minded approach is paramount, balancing scientific rigor with a recognition of the subjective and often profound personal experiences associated with CAM therapies.

The growing interest in mind-body medicine further exemplifies this integration. Techniques like biofeedback and neurofeedback demonstrate the powerful connection between mental states and physiological processes. These approaches aim to empower individuals to consciously regulate their physiological responses, thereby impacting their health. These technologies offer a fascinating avenue to further explore the mind-body connection and their potential therapeutic applications, suggesting a future where technology and consciousness intersect to create novel healing approaches.

The exploration of the mind-body connection also raises the question of the role of the placebo effect. While often dismissed as merely psychological, the placebo effect highlights the remarkable power of belief and expectation in shaping physiological outcomes. This emphasizes the importance of the patient-practitioner relationship and the role of hope and positive expectation in healing. Understanding the mechanisms underlying the placebo effect and harnessing its power therapeutically holds significant potential for enhancing the efficacy of both conventional and CAM treatments. A deeper understanding of this phenomenon requires a convergence of scientific and humanistic perspectives, integrating both neuroscientific and psychological insights to understand the role of expectation and belief in modulating bodily functions.

The integration of CAM into mainstream healthcare isn't merely about adding alternative treatments to existing practices. It represents a paradigm shift towards a more holistic and patient-centered approach. It's about creating a more nuanced understanding of health and illness that acknowledges the complex interplay of biological, psychological, and spiritual factors. This will require collaborative efforts among healthcare professionals, researchers, policymakers, and patients to develop appropriate guidelines, educational programs, and research initiatives. The future of healthcare may very well lie in this integrative model, where the strengths of both conventional and complementary medicine are combined to optimize patient outcomes and enhance overall well-being. This holistic model also aligns with the broader understanding of neurodiversity and expanded human potential, recognizing individual differences in both susceptibility to illness and response to treatment. The personalized approach facilitated by this integration ensures tailored therapies that best address the individual's unique needs, fostering a future where healthcare is as unique as the individuals it serves. The challenge, and the exciting opportunity, lies in navigating this integration with both scientific rigor and a genuine appreciation for the richness and complexity of the human experience.

The exploration of alternative healing modalities and their potential connection to neurodiversity and expanded consciousness necessitates a profound discussion on ethical considerations. While the allure of unconventional therapies and spiritual practices can be compelling, particularly for individuals seeking relief from conditions not adequately addressed by conventional medicine, the paramount importance of ethical practice cannot be overstated. This involves a multifaceted approach, with informed consent forming the cornerstone of any responsible interaction between practitioner and client.

Informed consent goes beyond a simple signature on a form. It represents a genuine, informed understanding on the part of the client regarding the nature of the treatment, its potential benefits and risks, and the alternatives available. This requires clear, transparent communication from the practitioner, using language that the client can readily comprehend, regardless of their educational background or familiarity with the specific modality. The practitioner must avoid technical jargon and ensure the client fully grasps the process involved, the potential outcomes (both positive and negative), and the limitations of the treatment. It's crucial to manage expectations realistically, avoiding overpromising or creating unrealistic hopes. For example, if a practitioner is offering energy healing, they must clearly articulate that this is not a replacement for conventional medical treatment for a diagnosed condition, but might serve as a complementary therapy to support overall well-being. The client should be empowered to ask questions, express concerns, and withdraw their consent at any point without pressure or coercion.

This principle of informed consent extends to the use of spiritual practices within the healing context. Many alternative healing techniques incorporate spiritual elements, whether through prayer, meditation, visualization, or connection to a higher power. The practitioner must respect the client's beliefs and values, while also being transparent about their own spiritual framework, avoiding any attempt at proselytization or imposition of beliefs. If a particular technique draws on a specific spiritual tradition, the practitioner should explain this clearly, ensuring the client understands and agrees to participate in the context of that tradition. This transparency prevents misunderstanding and fosters a therapeutic alliance built on mutual respect and trust. For instance, if a shamanic healing practice is involved, the practitioner should clearly explain the spiritual dimensions of the healing process and ensure the client feels comfortable and respected throughout the experience. The client should never be subjected to any practice that violates their personal beliefs or values.

The ethical responsibilities of practitioners extend beyond informed consent to encompass a range of professional standards. These include maintaining appropriate professional boundaries, avoiding conflicts of interest, and adhering to confidentiality. The therapeutic relationship must be strictly professional, with clear boundaries defined to safeguard against exploitation or harm. This is particularly crucial in therapies involving personal disclosure and emotional vulnerability. For example, a therapist practicing energy healing should avoid blurring professional and personal boundaries by establishing clear guidelines for communication and interaction outside of therapy sessions.

Furthermore, practitioners should be honest and transparent about their qualifications, training, and experience. They should avoid making unsubstantiated claims or promises of cures. This is especially crucial given the prevalence of misinformation and exaggerated claims surrounding alternative therapies. Practitioners should only use modalities for which they have received adequate training and supervision, and they must adhere to relevant professional codes of conduct. For instance, a practitioner offering Reiki should clearly state their certification level and any relevant professional affiliations, ensuring they are operating within the ethical guidelines set by their governing body. They should never represent themselves as qualified to diagnose or treat medical conditions unless they possess the appropriate medical qualifications.

The ethical framework also necessitates robust mechanisms for addressing complaints and resolving conflicts. Clients should feel empowered to voice concerns or complaints without fear of reprisal. Practitioners should have a clear process in place for handling complaints, providing a fair and impartial avenue for resolution. This might involve internal review processes, mediation, or referral to relevant professional bodies. This transparency fosters accountability and ensures that the profession maintains high ethical standards. The presence of a robust complaint system instills confidence in clients and maintains the integrity of alternative healing practices.

Beyond individual practitioners, the ethical framework must also extend to the broader context of research and public discourse. Research investigating the effectiveness of alternative healing modalities must adhere to the highest standards of scientific rigor, including properly designed randomized controlled trials and peer review. Claims about the efficacy of a particular treatment should be supported by robust evidence, rather than anecdotal reports or testimonials. This ensures that information presented to the public is accurate and avoids misleading or misinforming potential clients.

Furthermore, the public discourse surrounding alternative healing should encourage open dialogue and a balanced approach, acknowledging the complexities of the subject matter. It should encourage critical thinking and discourage unqualified claims, pseudoscientific beliefs and harmful practices. The goal should be to foster a climate where individuals can access reliable information about alternative healing modalities, making informed decisions based on a solid understanding of both their benefits and limitations. The integration of alternative healing into mainstream healthcare requires a collective commitment to ethical practice, both at the individual practitioner level and at the level of research and public discourse.

The development of ethical guidelines specifically tailored for alternative healing practices is an ongoing process, reflecting the diverse range of modalities involved. These guidelines must be informed by ethical principles from the fields of medicine, psychology, spirituality, and related disciplines. They should also reflect cultural sensitivities and recognize the unique needs of diverse populations. The ongoing dialogue and development of these ethical guidelines should involve practitioners, researchers, ethicists, and representatives from the broader community, promoting a holistic and nuanced approach to ethical considerations within alternative healing. This continuous process of refinement and review will ensure the long-term integrity and responsible development of this evolving field. Ultimately, the commitment to ethical practice is not merely a safeguard against harm, but a vital component of ensuring the genuine benefit and positive impact of alternative healing on individuals and society as a whole. The ethical integration of these modalities with conventional healthcare will pave the way for a more comprehensive and holistic approach to wellness, acknowledging the complex interplay of physical, mental, and spiritual dimensions of human experience.

CHAPTER 13: ETHICAL CONSIDERATIONS IN RESEARCH AND PRACTICE

Responsible research practices are paramount when exploring the intersection of neuroscience, parapsychology, and neurodiversity. The very nature of the subject matter —examining phenomena often considered outside the mainstream scientific paradigm—demands a heightened awareness of ethical considerations. This section outlines key principles for conducting responsible research in this sensitive area, ensuring the protection of participants and the integrity of the findings.

Firstly, informed consent is absolutely crucial. Participants must be fully informed about the nature of the research, the potential risks and benefits, and their right to withdraw at any time without penalty. This is especially vital when working with individuals who may have pre-existing mental health conditions or who hold strong beliefs about their abilities. The language used in the informed consent process must be clear, concise, and easily understandable, avoiding jargon or technical terms that might confuse or intimidate participants. Furthermore, researchers should ensure that participants understand the limitations of the study and what the results might—and might not—reveal. This includes explicitly addressing the uncertainties inherent in researching areas such as psychic abilities, acknowledging the lack of conclusive scientific evidence and avoiding any implications of guaranteed outcomes. The informed consent process should be documented meticulously, and researchers must actively demonstrate respect for participants' autonomy and choices.

Protecting vulnerable populations is another crucial ethical consideration. Individuals with certain neurodiverse conditions or mental illnesses may be particularly vulnerable to exploitation or harm within a research setting. Therefore, researchers must adhere to stringent ethical guidelines designed to safeguard their well-being. This may involve working closely with ethic review boards and obtaining additional consents or approvals where necessary. It also necessitates a heightened sensitivity to the potential psychological impact of the research, providing access to appropriate support services and ensuring that participants are not subjected to undue stress or pressure. The anonymity and confidentiality of participants must be strictly maintained, protecting their personal information from unauthorized access or disclosure. Data must be handled securely and stored in accordance with relevant regulations, ensuring both the privacy and dignity of individuals involved in the study.

The avoidance of misinformation and misrepresentation is paramount. Research findings must be presented accurately and responsibly, avoiding any exaggeration or distortion of the results. Researchers must avoid sensationalism or making claims that are not supported by the evidence. Transparency is key—clearly stating the limitations of the study and acknowledging areas of uncertainty. Any claims about psychic abilities or neurodiversity must be presented cautiously and avoid any misleading statements or conclusions that may be misinterpreted by the public. Researchers have a responsibility to communicate their findings clearly and accurately, avoiding language that could be construed as promoting or endorsing pseudoscience. The potential for misinterpretation of findings is high in this field, and researchers must proactively mitigate this risk by using precise language and ensuring that their conclusions are clearly stated and supported by the evidence.

Transparency and openness in research are equally vital. Researchers should make their data and methodologies readily accessible to the wider scientific community, encouraging scrutiny and replication of their work. Openness promotes trust and allows for independent verification of the findings. It also fosters collaboration and facilitates the development of a more comprehensive understanding of the phenomena under investigation. This may involve sharing data sets, research protocols, and analytical methods with other researchers, contributing to the collective body of knowledge in the field. By being transparent about their methods and findings, researchers can encourage further investigation and ultimately lead to a more accurate and nuanced understanding of these complex issues.

Addressing potential bias and prejudice is a crucial ethical responsibility. The research area often carries historical and cultural baggage associated with stigma and misunderstanding related to both mental illness and purported psychic abilities. Researchers must be acutely aware of potential biases that might influence their interpretations and conclusions. This requires a conscious effort to avoid stereotypes and generalizations, ensuring that participants are treated with respect and dignity, regardless of their perceived abilities or condition. Researchers should employ rigorous methodological approaches to minimize bias in data collection and analysis, ensuring that their findings are not influenced by pre-conceived notions or personal beliefs. Furthermore, they must strive to represent the diversity of human experience within their research, avoiding language or framings that might perpetuate existing biases or stigmas. The inclusion of diverse perspectives—including from individuals with lived experience—within research teams can help to mitigate potential biases and ensure a more nuanced and inclusive approach.

Furthermore, the ethical responsibilities extend beyond the conduct of the research itself. Researchers must consider the wider societal impact of their findings and how they might be interpreted by the public. This involves being mindful of the potential for their work to be misused or misinterpreted. They have a duty to communicate their results responsibly and avoid making claims that are not supported by the evidence. In the case of findings suggesting a potential link between neurodiversity and psychic abilities, for example, researchers must be careful to avoid pathologizing neurodiversity or suggesting that these abilities are inherently problematic. Instead, the focus should be on promoting a more inclusive and accepting approach to understanding the spectrum of human experience.

Moreover, the ethical landscape concerning research in this

---

field needs continual evaluation and adaptation. As our understanding of the brain and consciousness evolves, so too must our ethical guidelines. A dynamic and reflexive approach is necessary, incorporating ongoing feedback and adjustments to ensure that research practices remain responsible, ethical, and respectful of all involved. This includes engaging with ethic review boards, participating in relevant professional forums, and staying abreast of current best practices in research ethics. The ongoing dialogue and refinement of ethical standards are critical to maintaining integrity and promoting responsible investigation within this intriguing and often controversial field. The goal is not just to produce scientifically sound research but to ensure that this research is carried out in a manner that respects individual dignity, promotes inclusivity, and contributes to a more holistic understanding of human consciousness and potential. In the end, ethical considerations are not merely an addendum to the research process but its essential foundation.

The unique challenges presented by research into psychic abilities and neurodiversity necessitate a particularly rigorous approach to protecting vulnerable populations. Individuals with conditions such as schizophrenia, autism spectrum disorder, or other neurodevelopmental differences may be disproportionately represented in studies exploring exceptional mental capacities. This is not to suggest a causal link, but rather to acknowledge the potential overlap between certain neurological conditions and experiences that might be interpreted as psychic. Therefore, safeguards must be in place to prevent exploitation or misinterpretation.

One key concern is the potential for stigmatization. Participants, particularly those with pre-existing mental health diagnoses, might be vulnerable to further stigmatization if their participation in research exploring "paranormal" abilities is misunderstood or misrepresented. Researchers have a responsibility to ensure that participation in the study does not reinforce existing social biases or lead to negative labeling. This requires careful consideration of language used in recruitment materials, informed consent processes, and data dissemination. Studies must explicitly address the potential for stigma and actively work to counter it. For instance, research reports should emphasize the diversity of human experience and avoid language that could pathologize unusual abilities.

Informed consent is paramount, especially when dealing with vulnerable populations. This necessitates a meticulous process that goes beyond simply obtaining a signature on a form. Researchers must ensure that participants fully understand the nature of the study, including the potential risks and benefits. This is particularly important when dealing with individuals who may have cognitive or communication difficulties. The informed consent process should be adapted to the individual's needs, utilizing accessible language and methods that promote genuine comprehension. This might include using visual aids, providing multiple opportunities for questions and clarifications, and offering support from trusted individuals like family members or caregivers. Furthermore, participants should be given the freedom to withdraw from the study at any time without penalty.

Beyond informed consent, researchers must be particularly attuned to the potential for emotional distress. Exploring psychic experiences can be emotionally intense, and individuals with pre-existing vulnerabilities might be more susceptible to negative emotional consequences. Therefore, access to appropriate mental health support services is crucial.

This should be incorporated into the study design, with clear pathways for participants to access counseling or other forms of support, both during and after their participation. Researchers should have a clear plan in place for managing any instances of emotional distress that arise during the study. This could involve pre-arranged consultations with therapists experienced in working with individuals who have reported psychic experiences or who struggle with pre-existing mental health conditions.

The protection of privacy and confidentiality is another crucial ethical consideration. Data collected during research in this sensitive area must be handled with the utmost care. Researchers must employ stringent data protection measures to prevent unauthorized access or disclosure of sensitive personal information. This includes adhering to relevant data privacy regulations and using anonymization techniques to protect participants' identities. Researchers should be transparent about how data will be stored, managed, and used, both in the informed consent process and in the final research report. The potential for misinterpretation or misuse of personal information is particularly high in this field, emphasizing the importance of meticulous data protection strategies. The use of pseudonyms, secure data storage systems, and limiting access to data to only authorized personnel are necessary precautions.

The issue of potential exploitation is particularly pertinent. Vulnerable individuals might be more susceptible to exploitation, particularly if the research involves promises of healing, enhanced abilities, or financial gain. Researchers must ensure that their study design and methods are free from any element of coercion or undue influence. Participants should never feel pressured to participate or to continue participating if they feel uncomfortable. Researchers should be aware of the power imbalance that may exist between themselves and participants, and should actively work to mitigate this imbalance. Transparency in funding sources and potential conflicts of interest should also be openly disclosed.

In the realm of treatment, the ethical considerations are equally complex. The integration of parapsychological concepts into therapeutic practices raises specific concerns. Therapists must be cautious not to make unsubstantiated claims or offer treatments that lack scientific evidence. The use of alternative healing modalities alongside conventional treatments requires careful consideration of potential risks and interactions. In cases involving individuals with established mental health conditions, it's critical to ensure that any alternative therapies are complementary to, and not a replacement for, evidence-based treatments prescribed by a qualified professional. Informed consent is essential, with a focus on the potential benefits and risks of integrating alternative approaches into the treatment plan.

Researchers and practitioners working with vulnerable populations must prioritize ongoing self-reflection and ethical deliberation. This involves a commitment to continuous learning and a willingness to adapt practices in response to emerging ethical challenges. Regular consultation with ethics committees, participation in professional development workshops, and engagement in open dialogue with colleagues are crucial aspects of maintaining ethical integrity in this field. A robust ethical framework is not a static entity; it requires ongoing adaptation and refinement to reflect evolving understanding and societal values.

Moreover, the broader societal context needs to be considered. The intersection of neuroscience, parapsychology, and neurodiversity operates within a framework of societal beliefs and prejudices. Researchers must be mindful of these societal influences and avoid perpetuating harmful stereotypes or biases. For example, attributing unusual abilities solely to individuals from specific neurodiverse populations could reinforce existing societal inequalities. It's crucial to emphasize the spectrum of human experience and avoid essentializing or generalizing about any group.

The pursuit of knowledge in this field should not come at the cost of human dignity. Respect for individual autonomy, privacy, and well-being must remain the cornerstone of all research and practice. The ultimate goal is not merely to expand scientific understanding but to utilize this understanding to benefit humanity, ensuring that all individuals, irrespective of their abilities or challenges, are treated with fairness, compassion, and respect. The integration of rigorous scientific methods with ethical principles and a deep appreciation for the inherent worth of each individual will ultimately shape the progress of this fascinating and complex field. The potential for positive outcomes—from improved mental health care to a more inclusive and understanding society—is immense, but only if achieved with unwavering commitment to ethical conduct. The responsibility rests upon each researcher and practitioner to actively safeguard the vulnerable, fostering a research environment where ethical considerations guide every step of the process. Only then can we truly unlock the transformative potential of this unique intersection of science and human experience.

The potential for misinterpretations and the spread of misinformation in the field of parapsychology and neurodiversity is significant, demanding a heightened awareness of responsible communication strategies. Our exploration into the intersection of these fields, particularly when examining seemingly paranormal abilities within neurodiverse populations, treads a delicate line between scientific inquiry and the potential for sensationalism. The temptation to overstate findings, to draw premature conclusions, or to present anecdotal evidence as irrefutable fact is ever-present. Resisting these temptations is paramount for maintaining the integrity of our research and for protecting the individuals whose experiences form the basis of our studies.

One of the primary concerns is the potential for misrepresenting correlations as causations. For instance, observing a higher incidence of reported psychic experiences within a specific neurodiverse population does not automatically imply a direct causal link. Such a correlation could be influenced by various factors, including societal biases, differing levels of self-reporting, or the specific social and environmental contexts experienced by these individuals. Furthermore, the very definition of "psychic experiences" is highly subjective and prone to biases in interpretation. What one individual perceives as a precognitive dream, another might dismiss as coincidence or simply a vivid imagination. The lack of universally accepted operational definitions for these phenomena adds to the difficulty in conducting robust and replicable research.

To mitigate these risks, we must employ rigorous methodological standards. This includes meticulous data collection, thorough statistical analysis, and a critical evaluation of all findings. Transparency in methodology is crucial, allowing other researchers to scrutinize our work and replicate our studies. Openly acknowledging limitations and uncertainties inherent in the research process is equally important. Presenting research findings solely as definitive truths without qualifying statements and acknowledgements of potential biases can mislead the public and contribute to the spread of inaccurate information.

Beyond the scientific rigor of the research process itself, responsible communication extends to the dissemination of findings. This involves careful consideration of the language used in reports, publications, and public presentations. Avoiding sensationalist or overly dramatic language is crucial. We must strive to represent our research findings accurately, avoiding generalizations or oversimplifications that could be misinterpreted. The use of precise and unambiguous terminology is essential, ensuring that our conclusions are easily understood and not susceptible to misinterpretation. Complex statistical concepts should be explained in a clear and accessible manner, avoiding jargon that could obscure their meaning to a wider audience.

The challenge of communicating complex scientific findings to a non-specialist audience, particularly on topics with established social and cultural narratives, necessitates an even more cautious approach. The popular media frequently sensationalizes stories about paranormal phenomena, often distorting the nuances of the research. Therefore, researchers need to be proactive in correcting misinterpretations and providing accurate context. Engaging with the media responsibly, providing clear and concise explanations of our findings, and correcting any inaccuracies that arise are critical responsibilities.

Moreover, the ethical considerations extend beyond the accuracy of scientific communication. The vulnerability of individuals with neurodiversity must always be a primary concern. Our research should never exploit or endanger them. It is imperative that participants' privacy and confidentiality are strictly protected, their informed consent obtained and maintained throughout the study, and that all research protocols are aligned with relevant ethical guidelines and regulations. The potential benefits of our research must outweigh any potential risks to participants, necessitating careful consideration of study designs and data-handling procedures.

Another crucial aspect of responsible communication lies in acknowledging the existing cultural and spiritual beliefs surrounding psychic abilities and neurodiversity. While our research strives to adopt a scientific approach, we should not disregard or dismiss the lived experiences and beliefs of the individuals involved in our studies. Respectful engagement with these perspectives is crucial, recognizing that many individuals ascribe meaning and significance to their experiences that extend beyond purely scientific explanations. Dismissing these subjective experiences as irrelevant or simply "incorrect" is not only ethically questionable but also risks alienating the very individuals whose participation is crucial to our research.

Furthermore, we must be wary of the potential for our research to be misused or misinterpreted by groups promoting potentially harmful practices or beliefs. Some individuals and organizations might attempt to exploit our findings to legitimize unfounded claims, promote pseudoscientific therapies, or justify discriminatory practices. Researchers have a responsibility to be vigilant against such misappropriations and to actively counter misleading interpretations of our work. This could involve publishing critical analyses of such misuses, engaging in public discourse to clarify misunderstandings, and actively participating in educational initiatives to promote accurate understanding of our findings within wider society.

In conclusion, ethical considerations are not merely an addendum to the research process; they are an integral and inseparable component of it. Avoiding misinformation and misrepresentation requires a multifaceted approach: methodological rigor, responsible data handling, transparent communication, respect for participants' vulnerability, and critical engagement with diverse perspectives. Our ultimate aim should be not only to advance scientific understanding but also to utilize that understanding to benefit humanity, fostering a more inclusive and informed society, built upon a foundation of mutual respect and ethical integrity. The pursuit of knowledge in this fascinating area requires a constant vigilance in protecting against misinterpretation and misuse, ensuring the ethical safeguarding of all involved. The potential benefits are vast, but only if we commit to the highest ethical standards. The responsibility lies with each of us to uphold these principles at every stage of the research process, from conception to dissemination, to ensure the responsible and beneficial exploration of this extraordinary intersection of science and human experience.

Transparency, in the context of our investigations into

the nexus of neurodiversity and purported psychic abilities, transcends mere data sharing; it represents a commitment to intellectual honesty and a recognition of the inherent complexities involved. The very nature of our subject matter—abilities that lie outside the conventionally accepted boundaries of science—demands an even higher level of scrutiny and openness. We must actively strive to avoid the pitfalls of confirmation bias, the allure of sensationalism, and the potential for misinterpretations that can arise when exploring phenomena that are often shrouded in mystery and misconception. This necessitates a multi-pronged approach to transparency, encompassing data accessibility, methodological rigor, and a commitment to open dialogue.

Firstly, data accessibility is paramount. Raw data, along with detailed methodological descriptions, should be made available to the wider scientific community for scrutiny and replication. This is not simply a matter of adhering to ethical guidelines; it is essential for building trust and fostering a collaborative environment. The inherent skepticism surrounding research into psychic phenomena necessitates a level of transparency that goes beyond what is typically expected in more established scientific fields. Hiding data or employing opaque methodologies only serves to fuel skepticism and hinder the progress of the field. By making our data publicly accessible, we invite critical evaluation and contribute to the collective effort of verifying or refuting our findings. This open-data approach also allows for independent researchers to build upon our work, potentially identifying patterns or insights that may have eluded us. For instance, data regarding the EEG patterns of individuals reporting clairsentience could be shared through open-access repositories, allowing others to analyze the data using different analytical techniques or to compare it with data from other neurological studies. Furthermore, the detailed description of participant selection criteria, experimental protocols, and data analysis techniques must be meticulously documented and readily available, fostering the reproducibility of our research.

Secondly, methodological rigor is undeniably crucial. The methodologies employed in studying phenomena at the fringe of science must be exceptionally robust to withstand critical scrutiny. This means employing well-established research methodologies, controlling for confounding variables, and utilizing appropriate statistical analyses. In the case of investigating potential links between neurodiversity and psychic abilities, we need to employ rigorous diagnostic tools to accurately identify and characterize the neurodiverse populations involved. This necessitates collaboration with qualified clinicians and specialists in neurodevelopmental disorders. Moreover, the experimental designs employed must account for the subjective nature of many of the phenomena being investigated. This could involve utilizing blind or double-blind studies to minimize bias and employing control groups to rule out alternative explanations. For example, in studying alleged precognitive abilities, using randomized stimulus presentation and independent judges to evaluate the results would be essential in mitigating the risk of confirmation bias. Quantitative data, whenever possible, should be the mainstay of our approach; while qualitative data such as anecdotal accounts can provide valuable context, it should not form the sole basis for conclusions. Rigorous qualitative research methodologies such as thematic analysis should be employed to ensure objectivity and minimize the risk of interpretative bias. Transparency in methodology allows other researchers to assess the validity of our findings and the strength of our conclusions.

Thirdly, open communication is the bedrock of ethical research. This encompasses transparent reporting of findings, both positive and negative, and active engagement with critique and counterarguments. It also includes proactive dissemination of findings through peer-reviewed publications, presentations at scientific conferences, and accessible public communication formats. Suppressing negative findings or selectively highlighting only positive results would be a serious breach of ethical responsibility. A commitment to open communication extends beyond simply publishing research findings; it also involves actively participating in public discussions and engaging with critics and skeptics in a respectful and constructive manner. This is particularly important when dealing with topics that are subject to considerable public interest and potential misunderstanding, as is the case with research into psychic abilities and neurodiversity. For example, if a study fails to find a statistically significant correlation between a specific neurodevelopmental condition and a particular claimed psychic ability, this negative result should be reported transparently and discussed openly. Ignoring or suppressing such results only damages the credibility of the research. We have a responsibility to engage with the broader public and to correct any misinterpretations or misrepresentations of our findings. This involves communicating the complexities of our research in an accessible and understandable manner, avoiding sensationalism and maintaining scientific accuracy. Openness to constructive criticism is vital for growth and ensuring that the scientific process serves its purpose of advancing knowledge rather than justifying pre-existing beliefs.

Transparency also necessitates acknowledging limitations

and uncertainties. No research is perfect, and it is ethically responsible to acknowledge the limitations of our methods, the scope of our findings, and the potential for alternative interpretations. Acknowledging these limitations strengthens the credibility of our work, as it demonstrates an understanding of the complexities involved and a commitment to intellectual humility. For instance, in research on the correlation between specific neurological conditions and psychic abilities, it is important to acknowledge the possibility of confounding variables or alternative explanations for observed correlations. Overstating the certainty of our findings or neglecting to discuss potential limitations could lead to misinterpretations and even harm the individuals involved in the study. Furthermore, recognizing the potential for bias in our own perspectives is essential. Our pre-existing beliefs and assumptions can inadvertently shape our research design, data analysis, and interpretation of results. Consciously striving for objectivity and acknowledging our potential biases is crucial for maintaining the integrity of our research.

Ultimately, transparency and openness in research are not simply ethical considerations; they are the foundations upon which scientific progress is built. In the field of exploring the intersection of neurodiversity and purported psychic abilities, where the potential for misinterpretation is high, these principles are even more critical. By adhering to these principles—data accessibility, methodological rigor, open communication, and acknowledgement of limitations —we can contribute to a more responsible and reliable body of knowledge, fostering a greater understanding of human consciousness and the remarkable diversity of human experience. This commitment to transparency strengthens not only the scientific validity of our work but also its ethical integrity and social impact. It builds trust with the scientific community, the public, and, crucially, with the neurodiverse individuals whose experiences are at the heart of our investigations. This trust is essential for ensuring that our research benefits humanity and fosters a more inclusive and understanding society. A commitment to full transparency enables other researchers to replicate our findings, validate our conclusions, or even to identify flaws and suggest improvements. This collective effort is the essence of the scientific process, and its absence hinders the pursuit of knowledge and the advancement of understanding in this complex and fascinating field.

The exploration of neurodiversity and purported psychic abilities necessitates a rigorous examination of potential biases, particularly those surrounding mental illness. The very terminology we employ can inadvertently reinforce stigmatizing perceptions. For instance, the historical association of phenomena like clairvoyance or clairsentience with mental illness, specifically schizophrenia, has created a pervasive bias where these abilities are often dismissed as mere symptoms of pathology rather than potentially distinct neurological variations. This bias impacts both research methodologies and clinical practice.

In research, the selection of participants can inadvertently skew results. If studies predominantly focus on individuals diagnosed with mental illness who also report psychic experiences, the findings may incorrectly conflate the two. A more nuanced approach requires careful consideration of control groups, ensuring that comparisons are made not just between individuals with and without a mental illness diagnosis, but also between individuals with and without reported psychic experiences, regardless of diagnostic status. This stratified approach helps to isolate the effects of each variable and avoids the spurious correlation of psychic experiences solely with mental illness.

Furthermore, the diagnostic criteria themselves are subject to biases. The DSM-5, for example, relies heavily on subjective reporting and clinical observation, leaving room for interpretive bias. A clinician with pre-existing biases against the possibility of psychic abilities might be less inclined to consider alternative explanations for a patient's experiences, potentially leading to misdiagnosis. Conversely, a clinician with a strong belief in these abilities might over-interpret ambiguous symptoms, potentially leading to an inaccurate diagnosis of a psychic phenomenon when a different neurological or psychological condition might be more appropriate. The lack of objective, universally accepted diagnostic criteria for psychic abilities further exacerbates this issue.

The use of standardized assessment tools is crucial to mitigate bias in research. However, even these tools are not immune to influence. The phrasing of questions, the format of the test, and the very context of the assessment can all unconsciously shape responses. For example, a test designed to detect deception might inadvertently penalize individuals with highly developed intuition or empathy, who might struggle to "lie" in the conventional sense, even if they're not attempting deception. Developing culturally sensitive and neurodiversity-aware assessment tools is therefore paramount. This might involve the development of entirely new assessment paradigms that move beyond traditional binary measures of "true" and "false" or "normal" and "abnormal," embracing the spectrum of human experience.

Another critical area to address is the researcher's own biases. Researchers, like clinicians, are not immune to preconceived notions. Conscious or unconscious biases can influence every stage of the research process, from the formulation of the hypothesis to the interpretation of the results. To mitigate this, rigorous methodology, including blinding techniques and peer review, is essential. Blinding procedures, where researchers are unaware of the participant's diagnostic status or reported experiences, help minimize subconscious influences on data collection and analysis. Similarly, peer review by a diverse panel of experts with varying perspectives can help identify and challenge potential biases in research design and interpretation.

Beyond research, clinical practice requires careful consideration of these biases. Mental health professionals need training to approach reported psychic abilities with an open yet critical mind. This means avoiding immediate dismissal or pathologization, while simultaneously engaging in a thorough investigation that considers various diagnostic possibilities, including the potential for neurodiversity-related differences in cognitive functioning. The focus should shift from labeling individuals based on perceived deviations from the norm to understanding the underlying neurological mechanisms that contribute to their experiences.

The integration of alternative healing modalities, often associated with New Age spirituality, further complicates ethical considerations. While some alternative therapies might offer therapeutic benefits, the lack of rigorous scientific evidence for their efficacy warrants caution. The line between genuine healing and exploitation can be blurred, particularly for vulnerable populations. It's crucial that clinicians and researchers approach these modalities with a critical lens, evaluating their effectiveness and safety based on robust empirical evidence rather than anecdotal reports or faith-based beliefs. Transparency with patients regarding the limitations and potential risks associated with such therapies is vital.

Addressing the potential for exploitation is equally crucial. Individuals who report psychic abilities, especially those who identify with groups like Indigo, Crystal, or Rainbow Children, might be particularly vulnerable to manipulation and financial exploitation. Charlatans and unscrupulous individuals might prey on their beliefs and vulnerabilities, offering unproven treatments or promising miraculous cures. Ethical practitioners must actively work to protect these individuals from such exploitation, ensuring that they are not subjected to harmful practices or financial scams in the name of spiritual healing or psychic development.

Further complicating the ethical landscape is the potential for stigmatization and discrimination. Individuals who report psychic abilities or identify with neurodiverse groups might experience prejudice and social exclusion. Research and clinical practice must be conducted in a manner that respects their dignity and autonomy, avoiding the perpetuation of harmful stereotypes. Confidentiality and informed consent are paramount. Participants and patients must be fully informed about the nature and purpose of the research or treatment, including any potential risks or benefits. Their participation must be voluntary and based on a full understanding of the process.

The challenge, therefore, lies in navigating the complex interplay between scientific skepticism, ethical responsibility, and the lived experiences of individuals who report psychic abilities or identify with neurodiverse groups. It necessitates an approach that embraces inclusivity and avoids reducing complex human experiences to simplistic labels. Developing a more nuanced and holistic understanding of consciousness requires both rigorous scientific inquiry and a deep respect for the diversity of human experience, fostering a future where exceptional abilities are understood, celebrated, and harnessed for the benefit of humanity. This requires not only an ethical framework for research and practice but also a societal shift in perspective, one that moves beyond outdated biases and embraces the potential for human consciousness to transcend our current understanding. The journey towards this future requires ongoing dialogue and collaboration among researchers, clinicians, and the communities whose lived experiences are central to this exploration. The ultimate goal is not to prove or disprove the existence of psychic abilities, but to understand the neurobiological and psychological underpinnings of these experiences within the broader context of human consciousness and neurodiversity. This demands a radical shift in perspective, away from a binary understanding of normal versus abnormal, towards a more holistic acceptance of the diverse tapestry of human experience.

CHAPTER 14: A NEW PARADIGM FOR UNDERSTANDING HUMAN CONSCIOUSNESS

The preceding chapters have explored the fascinating intersection of neuroscience, parapsychology, and neurodiversity, challenging conventional understandings of the brain and consciousness. We've examined the neurological underpinnings of purported psychic abilities, comparing them to manifestations of psychosis to identify potential genetic or epigenetic overlaps. We've also delved into the New Age concepts of Indigo, Crystal, and Rainbow children, Starseeds, and Lightworkers, proposing that these groups may represent a form of neurodiversity, showcasing unique cognitive and perceptual capacities. This exploration leads us to a crucial juncture: how do we reconcile these seemingly disparate fields – the rigorous methodology of science with the intuitive wisdom of spirituality? The answer lies in a paradigm shift, a new way of thinking about human consciousness that embraces both the tangible and the intangible.

This integration is not about dismissing scientific rigor in favor of unsubstantiated spiritual claims. Instead, it's about recognizing the limitations of a purely materialistic worldview and acknowledging the existence of phenomena that currently lie outside the scope of conventional scientific explanation. The history of science is replete with examples of phenomena initially dismissed as impossible or supernatural, only to be later understood through the lens of new scientific discoveries. Psychic abilities, altered states of consciousness, and the purported experiences of groups like Indigo children might represent such phenomena.

One key element in bridging the science-spirituality gap is recognizing the limitations of reductionist thinking. While neuroscience has made tremendous strides in understanding the brain's intricate workings, reducing consciousness solely to neurochemical processes risks neglecting the subjective experience of individuals. Spiritual practices, such as meditation and mindfulness, have been shown to induce measurable changes in brain activity, suggesting a profound interplay between the inner world of subjective experience and the physical reality of the brain. Neuroimaging studies, for example, have revealed alterations in brainwave patterns, increased grey matter density in certain regions, and changes in functional connectivity during and after meditative practices. These observable, measurable changes lend credence to the idea that spiritual practices can have a tangible impact on the brain.

Furthermore, the placebo effect, often dismissed as purely psychological, underscores the potent influence of belief and intention on physical and mental health. The very act of believing in a treatment, regardless of its objective efficacy, can elicit physiological changes. This highlights the power of the mind-body connection, a connection often explored in depth within spiritual traditions. The placebo effect is not merely a psychological trick; it suggests an intricate interaction between belief systems, emotional states, and physiological processes. It suggests a level of mind-body interaction that extends beyond currently understood neurological pathways.

The concept of quantum physics offers another potential bridge. Quantum phenomena, such as entanglement and non-locality, challenge our classical understanding of cause and effect, suggesting interconnectedness and non-linearity at a fundamental level. Some researchers have explored parallels between quantum physics and consciousness, suggesting that the universe itself may be far more interconnected and less deterministic than previously thought. This perspective aligns with many spiritual traditions that emphasize the interconnectedness of all things and the inherent unity of consciousness. Of course, the connection between quantum physics and consciousness remains a topic of ongoing debate and investigation. However, the very possibility of such a link suggests a realm beyond purely material explanations.

The integration of science and spirituality also requires a reassessment of "normalcy" and "exceptionality." Neurodiversity challenges the very notion of a single, standard model of human functioning. What we typically consider "abnormal" or "pathological" might simply represent different expressions of human potential. Individuals reporting psychic abilities or belonging to groups like Indigo children might not be suffering from mental illness; they might simply possess cognitive or perceptual capacities that lie outside the conventionally defined norms. This doesn't mean that we should disregard mental health challenges, but it does suggest that we need a more nuanced and holistic understanding of the spectrum of human experience. We need a paradigm that values and celebrates individual differences, fostering environments that support a wide range of abilities, both within the "normal" and "exceptional" realms.

This approach calls for a radical shift in how we conduct research. It requires embracing interdisciplinary collaboration between neuroscientists, parapsychologists, spiritual practitioners, and other experts. Traditional scientific methods must be adapted to incorporate the subtleties of subjective experience. Qualitative research methods, such as in-depth interviews and phenomenological studies, can provide valuable insights that complement quantitative data. Furthermore, ethical considerations must be paramount, ensuring the respectful and responsible treatment of all participants, regardless of their reported abilities or beliefs.

The goal isn't to prove or disprove the existence of psychic abilities or the validity of specific New Age concepts. Instead, it's to foster a more open-minded and inclusive approach to understanding human consciousness. This means acknowledging the limitations of current scientific knowledge and recognizing that there are dimensions to human experience that transcend purely materialistic explanations. By integrating scientific rigor with spiritual insights, we can unlock a deeper understanding of the vast potential within each individual and the collective human consciousness.

This new paradigm requires a willingness to embrace uncertainty and explore unconventional possibilities. It demands a questioning of established paradigms, a willingness to reconsider long-held assumptions, and a recognition of the complex interplay between mind, body, and spirit. The ultimate goal is not simply to understand the intricacies of consciousness, but to utilize this knowledge to create a more compassionate, equitable, and fulfilling world for all. This includes creating supportive environments for individuals with neurodiverse conditions, and fostering respectful dialogue about experiences that lie outside the conventional understanding of the human mind. A society that values all expressions of human potential, embracing both the scientific and spiritual dimensions of existence, will be a far more vibrant and enriched society. The journey towards this holistic understanding is a collective one, requiring the collaboration of individuals from diverse fields and perspectives. The path forward requires openness, curiosity, and a profound respect for the richness and complexity of human experience. By embracing this path, we unlock the potential not only for a deeper understanding of consciousness but for a future where the unique abilities and experiences of every individual are valued and celebrated.

The preceding chapters have laid the groundwork for a radical reimagining of human consciousness, suggesting a profound interconnectedness between seemingly disparate phenomena: psychic abilities, neurodiversity, and the spiritual practices of various New Age communities. We've explored the neurological substrates of experiences often categorized as "paranormal," highlighting potential overlaps with neurological conditions while simultaneously acknowledging the unique perceptual and cognitive strengths of individuals identified as Indigo, Crystal, Rainbow children, Starseeds, and Lightworkers. Now, we must confront a fundamental question: how do we redefine "normalcy" in light of this expanding understanding?

The very concept of "normalcy" is a social construct, a

statistical average derived from a limited and often biased sample of the human population. Historically, societal norms have been used to categorize individuals, often leading to the marginalization and pathologization of those who fall outside the bell curve. This has been particularly detrimental to individuals with neurodiverse conditions, whose unique cognitive profiles have been misinterpreted as deficits rather than alternative forms of intelligence and perception. Consider, for example, the historical treatment of autism spectrum disorder, once viewed solely as a debilitating condition. Now, an increasingly nuanced understanding recognizes the remarkable strengths and unique talents possessed by many individuals on the autism spectrum. Their exceptional focus, attention to detail, and innovative thinking are increasingly valued in fields requiring specialized skills and creative problem-solving.

Similarly, the dismissal of psychic abilities as delusion or fantasy reflects a narrow definition of normalcy. For centuries, individuals reporting experiences of clairvoyance, clairsentience, or telepathy have been labeled as mentally ill, their experiences dismissed as hallucinations or fabrications. Yet, the increasing body of parapsychological research, albeit controversial, suggests that these experiences may represent genuine extensions of human perception, potentially linked to advanced states of consciousness or untapped neurological capabilities. Instead of viewing these experiences as exceptional or aberrant, we might consider them as variations within the spectrum of human potential, representing different ways of perceiving and interacting with reality.

The New Age descriptions of Indigo, Crystal, and Rainbow children, and concepts like Starseeds and Lightworkers, offer further challenges to conventional definitions of normalcy. These concepts propose that certain individuals possess heightened intuitive abilities, spiritual awareness, and an empathetic connection to others. While often lacking rigorous scientific validation, these descriptions resonate with many individuals who identify with these labels, finding community and understanding within these frameworks. To dismiss these experiences as mere social constructs or delusional beliefs ignores the profound personal meaning and transformative power these concepts have for countless individuals. Instead of pathologizing these experiences, we must consider the possibility that they reflect a genuine diversity of human consciousness, expressions of heightened sensory perception and intuitive understanding that lie outside the boundaries of our current scientific understanding.

A crucial element of redefining normalcy lies in recognizing the limitations of our current scientific models. While neuroscience has made extraordinary advancements in understanding the brain, our current understanding remains incomplete. The reductionist approach of focusing solely on neurochemical and anatomical structures neglects the holistic nature of consciousness, the profound influence of experience, intention, and belief. To fully appreciate human consciousness, we must integrate insights from both scientific observation and subjective experience. This calls for a more nuanced and holistic approach, integrating quantitative data from neuroscience with qualitative data from personal accounts and spiritual practices.

This shift necessitates a paradigm change in how we view mental health. The current diagnostic model, based on the Diagnostic and Statistical Manual of Mental Disorders

(DSM), often pathologizes experiences that may simply represent variations in cognitive functioning or perceptual experiences. This can lead to misdiagnosis, stigmatization, and inappropriate treatment. A more compassionate and nuanced approach would recognize the spectrum of human experience, acknowledging that some "symptoms" might represent unique abilities rather than deficits. For instance, heightened sensory sensitivity, often associated with autism or other neurological conditions, could be viewed as a form of heightened awareness, potentially offering advantages in certain contexts. Similarly, experiences described as hallucinations or delusions might be viewed as alternative modes of perception, deserving of careful exploration rather than immediate dismissal as pathological.

Redefining normalcy also requires embracing a broader definition of intelligence. Traditional measures of intelligence, such as IQ tests, focus on narrow cognitive abilities, often overlooking other forms of intelligence such as emotional intelligence, social intelligence, and spiritual intelligence. Individuals identified as neurodiverse, or those with purported psychic abilities, may not excel in traditional measures of intelligence, yet they may demonstrate remarkable abilities in other areas. Recognizing and valuing this diverse range of intelligences is essential to creating a society that embraces and supports all its members.

Moreover, the redefinition of normalcy extends beyond individuals to encompass society as a whole. A truly inclusive society embraces and celebrates diversity in all its forms – neurodiversity, cultural diversity, and spiritual diversity. This means creating supportive environments that accommodate individual needs, recognize unique abilities, and foster respectful dialogue. Such a society would not only reduce stigma and discrimination but also actively encourage the development and exploration of all forms of human potential. It fosters collaboration and integration, not separation and judgment.

This shift also requires a significant change in educational practices. Current educational systems often prioritize conformity and standardization, leaving little room for the unique talents and learning styles of neurodiverse individuals. A more inclusive approach would recognize and adapt to individual differences, providing customized learning experiences that cater to the diverse needs and strengths of all students. This would necessitate a move away from standardized testing, focusing instead on personalized assessments that measure a wider range of abilities and talents.

The journey toward a redefinition of normalcy and the celebration of human diversity is ongoing. It requires ongoing dialogue, collaboration between scientists, spiritual practitioners, educators, and policymakers. It demands a paradigm shift, not just in our understanding of the human mind but in the structure of our society. It requires a conscious effort to dismantle ingrained biases and prejudices, to create a world where everyone feels valued, respected, and empowered to live authentically and express their unique potential. The ultimate goal is not just to understand human consciousness in its multifaceted glory, but to create a more compassionate and equitable society that celebrates the inherent richness and diversity of the human experience. Only by embracing this path, with openness and acceptance, can we truly unlock the boundless potential of human consciousness and create a world that is truly inclusive and harmonious.

The path forward necessitates a fundamental shift in perspective, a conscious decision to embrace the unknown rather than recoil from it. For too long, the scientific community has operated within a rigid framework, prioritizing quantifiable data and demonstrable evidence while relegating phenomena that defy easy explanation to the fringes of acceptability. This approach, while seemingly rigorous, has inadvertently limited our understanding of human consciousness, excluding a wealth of experiences and abilities that lie beyond the confines of conventional scientific paradigms.

The exploration of psychic abilities, neurodiversity, and the spiritual experiences of groups like Indigo, Crystal, and Rainbow children demands a willingness to confront our own biases and preconceived notions. We must acknowledge the limitations of our current models and embrace a more holistic, inclusive approach that recognizes the interconnectedness of seemingly disparate phenomena. The very act of labeling something as "paranormal" or "abnormal" often stems from a deeply ingrained fear of the unknown, a reluctance to grapple with complexities that challenge our established worldview.

This fear is understandable. The human brain, with its intricate network of neural pathways and complex cognitive processes, remains largely a mystery. We are only beginning to unravel the intricate tapestry of consciousness, and our current understanding is undoubtedly incomplete. To dismiss phenomena that fall outside our current comprehension as mere fantasy or delusion is not only intellectually lazy but also potentially harmful. It shuts down avenues of inquiry, stifles innovation, and prevents us from accessing a potentially vast reservoir of human potential.

Consider the experiences of individuals who report vivid extrasensory perceptions. While some of these accounts might be attributable to misinterpretations, coincidence, or even psychological factors, many remain unexplained. To simply dismiss these experiences as hallucinations or fabrications is to ignore a potentially valuable source of information about the workings of the human mind and the nature of reality itself. Instead, we should approach such accounts with a sense of scientific curiosity, seeking to understand the underlying mechanisms rather than dismissing them outright.

Similarly, the unique cognitive abilities and spiritual orientations of individuals identified as Indigo, Crystal, and Rainbow children, or Starseeds and Lightworkers, deserve serious consideration. These individuals often exhibit exceptional creativity, empathy, intuition, and a deep connection to the spiritual realm. Their experiences, while often difficult to quantify using conventional scientific methods, offer valuable insights into the breadth and depth of human consciousness. To dismiss them as mere social constructs or manifestations of mental illness is to disregard a potentially transformative source of understanding.

The integration of these diverse perspectives – the rigorous methodology of science, the experiential knowledge of spiritual practitioners, and the lived realities of neurodiverse individuals – is crucial for forging a new paradigm. This paradigm will not be a simple synthesis of existing models but rather a radical reimagining of human consciousness, a framework that acknowledges the interconnectedness of the physical, mental, and spiritual realms. It will embrace the unknown not as a threat but as an opportunity for discovery and growth.

This requires a significant shift in the way we conduct research. We must move beyond a purely reductionist approach, which seeks to break down complex phenomena into their smallest components, and embrace a more holistic perspective that considers the emergent properties of complex systems. This necessitates interdisciplinary collaboration, bringing together neuroscientists, psychologists, parapsychologists, spiritual practitioners, and other relevant experts to create a more comprehensive and nuanced understanding of human consciousness.

Such collaboration will require overcoming significant obstacles. The scientific community, traditionally wary of anything that smacks of the paranormal, must overcome its inherent skepticism and embrace a more open-minded approach to research. Spiritual communities, in turn, must be willing to engage in rigorous scientific inquiry, subjecting their beliefs and practices to scrutiny. This reciprocal process of investigation and validation is essential for building a truly integrated understanding of human consciousness.

Beyond the scientific realm, this new paradigm requires a fundamental shift in societal attitudes. We must move beyond a simplistic notion of normalcy that prioritizes conformity and homogeneity, and instead embrace the richness and diversity of human experience. Neurodiversity, once viewed as a deficit, must be recognized as a source of strength and innovation. The unique abilities and perspectives of individuals who fall outside the conventional norms should be celebrated and supported rather than marginalized or pathologized.

Creating a society that genuinely embraces neurodiversity and celebrates the spectrum of human potential necessitates systemic changes. Educational institutions must adapt their curricula to accommodate diverse learning styles and abilities. Healthcare systems must provide accessible and inclusive services for individuals with a wide range of mental and physical needs. Workplace environments must foster a culture of inclusivity and understanding, recognizing the valuable contributions that neurodiverse individuals can make.

This is not a utopian vision, but a realistic goal that requires concerted effort and unwavering commitment. It demands a fundamental shift in consciousness – not only in the scientific and spiritual communities, but within society as a whole. We must cultivate a collective willingness to question our assumptions, challenge our biases, and embrace the unknown with curiosity and compassion. Only then can we truly unlock the boundless potential of human consciousness and create a world that is truly inclusive, equitable, and harmonious. This is not merely about understanding the mysteries of the mind, but about creating a future where every individual has the opportunity to thrive.

The journey will not be easy. Resistance to change is inevitable. The integration of seemingly disparate fields of knowledge – science, spirituality, and the lived experiences of neurodiverse individuals – will require navigating complex philosophical and methodological challenges. But the potential rewards are immense. By embracing the unknown and fostering a more inclusive and holistic understanding of human consciousness, we can unlock a deeper appreciation for the richness and complexity of human experience, creating a world that celebrates individuality, nurtures potential, and promotes a more compassionate and harmonious existence for all. This requires not just intellectual understanding, but a fundamental shift in our collective consciousness, a movement toward empathy, acceptance, and a genuine celebration of the extraordinary diversity of the human spirit.

The process of embracing the unknown necessitates a willingness to step outside our comfort zones, to challenge our ingrained beliefs, and to engage in meaningful dialogue with those who hold different perspectives. This requires both intellectual humility and a deep commitment to truth-seeking. We must be prepared to confront uncomfortable truths, to acknowledge our own limitations, and to approach the mysteries of human consciousness with both curiosity and respect. It is a journey that requires courage, openness, and a deep faith in the inherent goodness and potential of humanity. The journey towards a deeper understanding of ourselves and our place in the universe is a lifelong endeavor, one that demands constant learning, adaptation, and a willingness to embrace the unknown with open arms.

Ultimately, the goal is not just to understand the mysteries of consciousness, but to utilize this understanding to create a more just and compassionate world. By embracing neurodiversity and recognizing the unique strengths of all individuals, regardless of their perceived abilities or differences, we can build a society that is not only more inclusive but also more innovative, resilient, and ultimately, more humane. The path forward lies in cultivating a collective consciousness that values diversity, celebrates individuality, and embraces the unknown as a source of wonder, inspiration, and endless possibilities. The exploration of the unknown, far from being a threat, offers an incredible opportunity for growth, understanding, and the creation of a brighter future for all.

The limitations of current neuroimaging techniques hinder a complete understanding of the brain's intricate processes. While fMRI and EEG provide valuable insights into brain activity, they offer a relatively coarse-grained view of the complex interplay of neural networks. These technologies primarily measure aggregate activity, revealing broad patterns of activation but failing to capture the subtle, nuanced interactions occurring at the level of individual neurons or even smaller components like synaptic connections. To truly understand the mechanisms underlying phenomena like clairvoyance or clairsentience, we need technologies capable of resolving activity at a much finer scale. This calls for further development in areas like advanced microscopy, allowing for real-time visualization of neuronal activity in vivo, and possibly even the creation of novel neuroimaging techniques that move beyond the limitations of current methodologies. For example, imagine a technology that could directly map the flow of information across different brain regions, visualizing the complex pathways and networks involved in higher cognitive functions and potentially paranormal experiences.

Furthermore, our understanding of consciousness itself remains deeply incomplete. The dominant materialistic paradigm, while providing a solid foundation for understanding the physical aspects of the brain, falls short in explaining the subjective experience of consciousness – qualia – the "what it's like" aspect of sensations, emotions, and thoughts. The "hard problem of consciousness," as philosopher David Chalmers famously termed it, remains a significant challenge. Bridging the gap between the physical processes in the brain and the subjective experience of consciousness requires a multidisciplinary approach, integrating insights from neuroscience, philosophy, psychology, and even physics. Exploring theories of quantum consciousness, for example, which posit a role for quantum phenomena in the brain's operation, could offer valuable new perspectives. These theories, while speculative, open the door to considering mechanisms that might explain experiences outside the realm of conventional neuroscience. Similarly, further research into the brain's plasticity and its ability to adapt and reorganize itself throughout life, termed neuroplasticity, is crucial. This capacity may hold the key to understanding the development of unusual abilities, or even the potential for the human brain to evolve beyond its presently understood capabilities.

The very definition of "normal" brain function needs reconsideration. Our current understanding of neurological and psychiatric conditions often relies on a narrow definition of normalcy, based on statistical averages of behavioral and cognitive patterns. This approach can overlook individual differences and unique variations in brain function that are not necessarily indicative of pathology. Instead of focusing solely on deviations from an arbitrary norm, we should embrace neurodiversity as a spectrum of human potential. The purported unique abilities associated with individuals identified as Indigo, Crystal, or Rainbow children, or even those labeled as Starseeds or Lightworkers, may not represent an aberration but rather a different expression of human consciousness. These individuals might exhibit unusual patterns of brain activity, possibly involving unique connectivity between brain regions, or even the activation of neural pathways that remain largely dormant in the broader population. Studying these individuals through rigorous scientific methods, while respecting their unique experiences and perspectives, can significantly expand our understanding of the brain's plasticity and its capacity for extraordinary function.

The challenges in studying these phenomena lie in the difficulty in establishing robust experimental designs that can account for potential confounding factors. The very nature of psychic abilities, if they are indeed real, makes controlled experimentation difficult, as these abilities are often subtle, difficult to replicate, and highly dependent on subjective experiences. Developing reliable methodologies for assessing and quantifying these abilities is a critical step towards validating their existence and understanding their underlying mechanisms. This necessitates the development of new experimental designs that incorporate aspects of both quantitative and qualitative research methods. For instance, combining neuroimaging techniques with qualitative data obtained through interviews and subjective experience reports could provide a richer and more comprehensive understanding of the phenomena under investigation. Furthermore, the development of rigorous statistical methods capable of analyzing non-linear and complex data sets is essential.

Technological advancements will play a significant role in advancing our understanding. The development of more sophisticated neuroimaging techniques, as mentioned earlier, will allow for a more precise and detailed mapping of brain activity, potentially revealing patterns of neural activity that are currently invisible to us. Advances in artificial intelligence (AI) could also play a crucial role in data analysis. AI algorithms can be trained to identify subtle patterns in complex datasets that might be missed by human researchers. Furthermore, the development of wearable sensors that can continuously monitor brain activity throughout a subject's daily life could help us to understand the correlation between specific mental states and patterns of neural activity. Longitudinal studies using these technologies could reveal how brain activity evolves over time, shedding light on the development and expression of potentially unusual abilities.

The ethical considerations involved in studying these phenomena are equally important. The potential for misinterpretation and stigmatization of individuals with unusual abilities is a significant concern. Researchers must ensure that their studies are conducted with the utmost respect for the dignity and autonomy of participants. Informed consent is paramount, and rigorous safeguards are needed to prevent any potential harm or exploitation of individuals involved in the research. Furthermore, it's crucial to avoid perpetuating stereotypes or reinforcing societal biases. The goal is to understand and appreciate the diversity of human consciousness, not to categorize or label individuals based on their abilities. The focus should remain on promoting inclusivity and celebrating the unique strengths of all individuals, regardless of their perceived differences.

Moving forward requires a paradigm shift in our approach to research. We need to embrace a more holistic and integrated approach, bringing together diverse perspectives and methodologies from across the scientific and spiritual landscape. This involves fostering collaborations between researchers from different disciplines – neuroscience, psychology, parapsychology, philosophy, and even spiritual traditions. By working together, we can develop a more comprehensive and nuanced understanding of human consciousness and its potential. Openness to exploring unconventional hypotheses and interpretations is essential. This does not mean abandoning scientific rigor, but rather expanding our definition of what constitutes valid evidence. We must be willing to consider alternative explanations, to challenge existing paradigms, and to embrace the unknown, for it is within the unknown that we may uncover the most profound insights into the nature of human consciousness. A truly comprehensive approach would acknowledge the limitations of current scientific paradigms and embrace the insights offered by diverse perspectives, including those traditionally excluded from the mainstream scientific community. This requires a willingness to engage in open dialogue and to consider the possibility that our current understanding is incomplete and may even be fundamentally flawed in its assumptions.

Ultimately, expanding our understanding of the brain and human consciousness is not merely an intellectual pursuit; it holds profound implications for the future of humanity. By acknowledging and embracing neurodiversity, we can create a more just and equitable society that celebrates the unique contributions of all individuals. By harnessing the potential of the human brain, we can unlock new possibilities for innovation, creativity, and positive social change. This is not simply about uncovering the mysteries of consciousness; it is about building a better world for all. The pursuit of knowledge, in this context, becomes a path towards greater understanding, empathy, and social harmony. The path lies not just in unraveling the intricacies of the brain, but in applying this knowledge to create a more compassionate and inclusive society that values and respects the unique gifts of every individual. This integration of scientific inquiry with a holistic, humanistic approach is crucial for building a future that embraces human potential in all its multifaceted forms. The journey towards this future requires not only scientific breakthroughs but also a shift in societal attitudes, a recognition of the inherent value and potential in every individual, irrespective of their neurotype or perceived abilities.

The implications of a neurodiversity-inclusive understanding of consciousness extend far beyond the laboratory and the clinic. It necessitates a fundamental shift in how we structure our societies, educate our children, and approach healthcare. Currently, our systems are largely built upon a narrow definition of normalcy, often pathologizing what might be considered unique variations in cognitive processing and perception. This creates barriers for individuals who don't neatly fit into pre-defined boxes, potentially hindering their personal growth and contribution to society. Imagine a future where educational systems are designed to embrace diverse learning styles, recognizing that individuals may process information and express their creativity in vastly different ways. This might involve moving away from standardized testing that prioritizes rote memorization and toward assessments that evaluate critical thinking, problem-solving skills, and creative expression – abilities that might be particularly pronounced in individuals exhibiting traits often associated with "neurodiversity."

Such a shift requires educators to be trained to recognize and support a wide spectrum of cognitive styles and sensitivities. This includes understanding sensory processing differences, emotional regulation challenges, and alternative ways of communicating and learning. It requires creating inclusive learning environments that are flexible, adaptable, and responsive to individual needs. This isn't merely about accommodating disabilities; it's about recognizing and celebrating the diverse strengths and perspectives that neurodiversity brings to the table. Consider, for instance, the potential contributions of individuals with heightened sensory perception or intuitive abilities in fields like art, music, design, or even scientific research. Their unique perspectives might lead to breakthroughs that wouldn't be possible within a system that prioritizes conformity.

In the realm of healthcare, a neurodiversity-inclusive approach demands a radical re-evaluation of diagnostic criteria and treatment strategies. The current diagnostic systems often focus on identifying deficits and pathologies, neglecting the potential strengths and adaptive strategies that individuals may develop. A more holistic approach would involve recognizing the unique strengths alongside challenges, fostering resilience and self-acceptance. It would necessitate the development of personalized interventions tailored to the specific needs and abilities of each individual, rather than applying a one-size-fits-all approach. This would require a greater emphasis on collaborative care models that involve not only medical professionals but also family members, educators, and support networks. Imagine a future where individuals with experiences typically classified as "psychosis" are supported in harnessing their unique cognitive abilities, perhaps in creative endeavors or fields requiring deep intuition and insight, rather than being solely defined by their perceived deficits.

Beyond education and healthcare, this paradigm shift extends into all aspects of societal organization. Work environments could be designed to accommodate diverse communication styles, sensory sensitivities, and cognitive preferences, fostering a more inclusive and productive atmosphere. This might involve flexible work arrangements, noise-reduction strategies, and opportunities for individuals to leverage their unique skills and talents. Consider how a more inclusive workplace might benefit from the enhanced intuition and creativity often associated with certain forms of neurodiversity. The inclusion of diverse perspectives and cognitive styles can foster innovation and problem-solving capabilities that would be impossible in a homogeneous environment.

Furthermore, a holistic understanding of consciousness challenges our existing notions of mental health and well-being. It suggests that the current focus on symptom reduction may be insufficient and perhaps even counterproductive in many cases. A more comprehensive approach would involve fostering self-acceptance, promoting self-awareness, and empowering individuals to develop strategies for managing challenges and leveraging their unique strengths. This might involve integrating alternative healing modalities, such as mindfulness practices, meditation, energy healing, and other holistic approaches, alongside traditional medical interventions. The integration of these approaches acknowledges the interconnectedness of mind, body, and spirit, promoting a more balanced and comprehensive approach to well-being.

This new paradigm also necessitates a significant shift in

societal attitudes and values. We need to move away from a culture that stigmatizes difference and towards one that celebrates and embraces diversity in all its forms. This requires challenging deeply ingrained biases and prejudices, promoting education and awareness, and fostering a culture of empathy and understanding. The media, education systems, and other influential institutions have a critical role to play in shaping public perception and promoting a more inclusive society. By portraying neurodiversity as a source of strength and creativity, rather than a deficit, we can help break down stereotypes and create a more equitable society.

The journey toward this more holistic and inclusive future is not without its challenges. There are significant obstacles to overcome, including resistance to change, lack of resources, and the need for further scientific research to fully understand the complexities of neurodiversity and human consciousness. However, the potential benefits are immense. By embracing neurodiversity, we can unlock a vast reservoir of untapped human potential, fostering innovation, creativity, and social progress. It is a call to build a society that not only tolerates but celebrates difference, valuing the unique contributions of every individual and fostering a world where everyone can thrive.

This requires a collaborative effort involving scientists, healthcare professionals, educators, policymakers, and the community at large. It demands a willingness to question established norms, embrace new perspectives, and challenge the status quo. The path forward requires ongoing dialogue and collaboration across disciplines, fostering a more interconnected and interdisciplinary approach to the study of consciousness. This may involve integrating insights from neuroscience, psychology, parapsychology, anthropology, and spiritual traditions to develop a more nuanced and comprehensive understanding of the human experience.

The integration of spiritual and holistic perspectives is crucial in this new paradigm. Many spiritual traditions emphasize the interconnectedness of all things, the importance of self-awareness, and the potential for human beings to transcend limitations. These perspectives offer valuable insights that can complement and enrich scientific investigations of consciousness. For example, practices like meditation and mindfulness have been shown to have positive effects on brain function and mental well-being, suggesting a potential link between spiritual practices and neurological processes. By integrating scientific rigor with a holistic, humanistic approach, we can move towards a more comprehensive and nuanced understanding of human potential.

Ultimately, the goal is to create a society that values and respects the unique gifts of every individual, regardless of their neurotype or perceived abilities. This includes those who experience phenomena often associated with "paranormal" abilities, recognizing their experiences as potentially valid expressions of human consciousness rather than dismissing them as aberrant or pathological. The shift toward a more holistic and inclusive approach requires a fundamental re-evaluation of our values, beliefs, and societal structures. It is a journey that requires patience, perseverance, and a deep commitment to fostering a more equitable and just world. This future is not simply a utopian ideal; it is a tangible possibility that can be achieved through collaborative effort and a shared vision of a society that celebrates the full spectrum of human consciousness. The journey requires a paradigm shift – a move from a narrow, reductionist view of consciousness to one that embraces complexity, diversity, and the potential for extraordinary human experience.

CHAPTER 15: CONCLUSION: THE FUTURE OF NEUROSCIENCE AND PARAPSYCHOLOGY

This book has embarked on a journey to explore the fascinating intersection of neuroscience and parapsychology, a territory often considered the realm of fringe science and spiritual exploration. We began by establishing a foundation, bridging the historical and philosophical chasm that separates the scientific and spiritual perspectives on consciousness. The initial chapters laid the groundwork by defining psychic abilities—such as clairvoyance and clairsentience—through a neurological lens, examining potential brain regions involved, the role of synaptic plasticity, and the influence of genetic and epigenetic factors. This exploration wasn't simply about cataloging alleged abilities; it was about situating them within a broader context.

A crucial element of this context was the exploration of neurodiversity. We examined the often-overlooked parallels between reported psychic experiences and manifestations of psychosis in conditions like schizophrenia. This comparison was not intended to pathologize psychic abilities, but rather to highlight the potential for a spectrum of neurological experiences, ranging from those considered within the bounds of "normal" functioning to those associated with clinical diagnoses. The question posed—and partially answered—was whether these abilities represent an extreme expression of human potential or a manifestation of a misunderstood aspect of the human brain. The evidence strongly suggests a spectrum, not a binary.

Further exploration delved into the New Age concepts of Indigo, Crystal, and Rainbow children, along with Starseeds and Lightworkers. These groups, often characterized by purported unique abilities and a heightened spiritual focus, were analyzed through the lens of neurodiversity. The argument presented is that these individuals may represent a form of neurodiversity, potentially employing different brain regions and exhibiting unusual cognitive and perceptual abilities. The book didn't shy away from acknowledging the lack of robust scientific evidence for many of these claims, but it did emphasize the importance of exploring these phenomena with open minds and rigorous methodologies.

The core thesis of this work rests on the interconnectedness of seemingly disparate phenomena. We argued that clairvoyance, clairsentience, the experiences of Indigo children, and the spiritual practices of Lightworkers are potentially linked by common underlying neurological mechanisms, reflecting a broader spectrum of human potential. This unifying theme challenges conventional paradigms in neuroscience, psychology, and spiritual studies, pushing for a more integrative, holistic approach to understanding human consciousness.

The investigation extended to various altered states of consciousness, such as those experienced during meditation, near-death experiences, lucid dreaming, and under the influence of certain substances. The neurological underpinnings of these states were examined, highlighting their potential relevance to heightened perception and unconventional experiences. Intuition and empathy, often considered less tangible aspects of human experience, were also analyzed within this neurological framework, exploring their potential links to extrasensory perception and shared emotional experiences.

The book incorporated multiple case studies of individuals who report experiencing exceptional abilities. These case studies, though not definitive proof, serve as illustrative examples of the diversity of human experience and the challenges of categorizing such experiences within existing models. We acknowledge the limitations of case studies, highlighting the need for more rigorous research, but also emphasizing the potential insights that individual narratives offer.

The social and cultural context of psychic abilities is vital to understanding their interpretation and acceptance. We examined historical perspectives, societal attitudes, the influence of cultural beliefs, and the role of media portrayals in shaping public perception. The prevailing stigma associated with both psychic abilities and mental illness was addressed, emphasizing the urgent need for greater acceptance and understanding of the spectrum of human experiences.

Building upon this foundation, the book advocated for the benefits of embracing neurodiversity, promoting strengths-based approaches to mental health, and fostering inclusive environments that value and support individual differences. Alternative healing practices and spiritual methods were also explored, acknowledging their potential role in improving well-being but also stressing the importance of ethical and informed consent in these practices.

The ethical considerations surrounding research and practice in this field are paramount. The book highlighted the importance of responsible research practices, protecting vulnerable populations, avoiding misinformation, and promoting transparency and openness in research findings. It emphasized the crucial need to mitigate potential biases related to mental illness and psychic abilities to ensure fairness and avoid perpetuating harmful stereotypes.

Finally, the book concluded by presenting a new paradigm for understanding human consciousness. This paradigm integrates scientific and spiritual perspectives, challenges traditional notions of normalcy and exceptionality, and embraces the unknown. It emphasizes the need for continued research into the complexities of the brain and human consciousness, promoting a future that celebrates individual differences and promotes well-being for all. The overarching message is one of acceptance, understanding, and a willingness to explore the full spectrum of human potential, even those aspects that lie outside the boundaries of currently accepted scientific understanding. The future lies not in dismissing the unconventional, but in integrating diverse perspectives to achieve a more complete picture of the human experience. This holistic perspective may unlock not only a deeper understanding of the mind, but also new avenues for personal growth, societal advancement, and ultimately, a richer understanding of the human condition. The journey into the unexplored intersections of neuroscience and parapsychology has only just begun, and the possibilities are vast. The integration of these fields may lead to innovations in mental health treatment, educational approaches, and our very understanding of what it means to be human. The potential benefits are profound, extending far beyond the realm of the "paranormal" to encompass a fundamental shift in how we perceive and interact with the world around us. A new era of understanding awaits, one built on open-mindedness, scientific rigor, and a profound respect for the amazing diversity of the human experience.

The exploration undertaken in this book has only scratched the surface of a vast and largely unexplored territory. The convergence of neuroscience and parapsychology presents a wealth of opportunities for future research, demanding a multidisciplinary approach that transcends traditional boundaries. The initial findings, while suggestive, require rigorous validation through larger-scale, well-controlled studies. This necessitates a shift away from anecdotal evidence and towards robust experimental designs capable of minimizing bias and confounding variables.

One critical area for future investigation involves refining our understanding of the neurological correlates of purported psychic abilities. While we've touched upon potential brain regions involved—such as the anterior cingulate cortex, the parietal lobe, and the temporal lobes—more sophisticated neuroimaging techniques, like advanced fMRI and MEG, are crucial for achieving higher resolution and a more nuanced understanding of the neural networks implicated in phenomena like clairvoyance and clairsentience. Longitudinal studies tracking brain activity over extended periods are needed to understand the developmental trajectories of these abilities, examining whether they are innate or learned, and how they might be influenced by environmental factors and training.

Furthermore, the genetic and epigenetic underpinnings of these abilities deserve far more attention. Genome-wide association studies (GWAS) could help identify specific genes or gene variants associated with an increased likelihood of displaying psychic abilities or heightened sensitivity to subtle energetic cues. Epigenetic research could explore the impact of environmental factors, such as stress, trauma, or even spiritual practices, on gene expression and the development of these capabilities. This line of inquiry could potentially reveal mechanisms that influence both the development of these abilities and their expression. Understanding the interplay of genetics, epigenetics, and environment could unlock strategies for enhancing or modulating these abilities in a safe and ethical manner. It also raises questions about the potential inheritance of psychic traits, which requires extensive investigation involving family studies across multiple generations.

The link between psychic abilities and neurodiversity requires deeper exploration. The potential connection between conditions like autism spectrum disorder (ASD) and synesthesia, and the reported experiences of individuals identifying as Indigo, Crystal, or Rainbow children, warrants further investigation. Comparative studies analyzing the neurological profiles of individuals with these conditions and those who report extraordinary mental capabilities could reveal shared neural mechanisms or functional patterns. This might help differentiate between abilities that are genuinely unique and those that are simply manifestations of existing conditions. The objective should be to determine whether these are distinct phenomena or aspects of a broader spectrum of human cognitive diversity.

Another area needing significant attention is the development of standardized assessment tools for measuring psychic abilities. Currently, assessing these phenomena relies heavily on subjective reporting and anecdotal accounts, lacking objectivity and precision. The development of standardized tests, incorporating both quantitative and qualitative data, is crucial for improving the reliability and validity of research findings. This also raises ethical considerations. For example, how do we ensure that such tests do not inadvertently pathologize or stigmatize individuals who report such experiences? Establishing appropriate ethical guidelines and ensuring appropriate safeguards are paramount.

Moreover, the integration of subjective experiences with objective data is crucial. Qualitative research methods, such as in-depth interviews and phenomenological studies, can provide rich insights into the lived experiences of individuals reporting psychic abilities. Integrating these qualitative findings with quantitative data from neuroimaging and genetic studies can create a more comprehensive understanding of these phenomena. This approach could potentially move beyond simply quantifying abilities and delve into their meaning and impact on the individual's life.

The role of consciousness in the manifestation of psychic

abilities needs further examination. The exploration of consciousness itself remains a frontier in neuroscience, with various theories attempting to explain its nature and function. Integrating these theories with the study of purported psychic abilities may reveal new insights into the relationship between consciousness, the brain, and the external world. Exploring altered states of consciousness, through practices like meditation, mindfulness, or even through the use of psychedelics under strictly controlled environments, could provide further insights into the neural mechanisms underpinning expanded states of awareness that may facilitate psychic experiences. However, such research necessitates rigorous ethical oversight and strict safety precautions.

Finally, the potential therapeutic applications of psychic abilities and neurodiversity must be thoroughly explored. If specific individuals possess heightened sensitivity to subtle energetic cues or possess unusual cognitive abilities, how can this be harnessed for therapeutic purposes? This research avenue could potentially lead to innovative approaches in mental health treatment, alternative therapies, and even educational methodologies. For instance, individuals with highly developed intuition or empathic abilities could potentially contribute to therapeutic settings, providing a unique perspective that complements traditional approaches. These abilities, previously considered marginal, could contribute significantly to healing and well-being.

In conclusion, the future of neuroscience and parapsychology hinges upon a collaborative, open-minded approach that embraces both scientific rigor and a respectful consideration of subjective experiences. This requires interdisciplinary

THE NEURODIVERSITY OF CONSCIOUSNESS

collaboration involving neuroscientists, parapsychologists, geneticists, psychologists, and ethicists, working together to establish rigorous research methodologies, develop standardized assessment tools, and address the ethical considerations inherent in this field. The potential benefits of this research are immense, extending beyond simply understanding unusual mental phenomena to potentially revolutionizing our understanding of consciousness, the brain, and the therapeutic potential inherent within the full spectrum of human cognitive diversity. This integrated approach will not only advance scientific knowledge but also enhance our ability to support and empower individuals with unique cognitive and sensory experiences, fostering a more inclusive and equitable future for all. The journey has only just begun, and the potential discoveries promise to reshape our understanding of human potential and the very nature of reality itself.

The potential for a truly transformative understanding of consciousness lies in the synergistic collaboration of seemingly disparate fields. Neuroscience, with its rigorous methodologies and focus on the physical substrates of the mind, provides the empirical foundation. Parapsychology, often marginalized by mainstream science, offers a wealth of anecdotal and, in some cases, statistically significant data on phenomena that defy conventional explanations. However, it is the inclusion of spiritual practitioners and those with lived experience of altered states of consciousness who can bridge the gap between the objective measurements of neuroscience and the subjective realities reported by individuals with exceptional abilities.

This collaboration isn't simply about combining datasets; it's about a fundamental shift in perspective. For too long, the scientific community has approached the study of consciousness through a reductionist lens, attempting to dissect the mind into its component parts without fully appreciating its emergent properties. The richness and complexity of consciousness, particularly when considering individuals who report experiences outside the accepted norms, cannot be fully captured by fMRI scans and EEG readings alone. The subjective experiences of these individuals —their qualitative descriptions of clairvoyance, clairsentience, precognitive sensations, or other phenomena—are invaluable data points that often hold the key to unlocking a deeper understanding of the brain's potential.

Spiritual practitioners, with their profound understanding of altered states of consciousness and their ability to guide individuals through meditative practices and other techniques for accessing expanded awareness, offer a unique contribution. Their expertise complements the objective measurements of neuroscientists, providing context and enriching the interpretation of findings. For instance, a neuroscientist might observe specific brainwave patterns during a meditative state associated with heightened intuition or psychic abilities. A spiritual practitioner could then provide insight into the subjective experience of that state, explaining the accompanying sensations, emotions, and cognitive shifts that may be associated with the observed neural activity. Such a collaborative approach moves beyond the limitations of either discipline alone, revealing a more comprehensive picture of the mind-body connection and the nature of consciousness itself.

This interdisciplinary approach must be carefully structured to ensure both scientific rigor and respect for the subjective experiences of participants. Ethical considerations are paramount. The potential for misinterpretation, stigmatization, or exploitation of individuals with exceptional abilities must be addressed proactively. Clear guidelines for informed consent, data privacy, and the responsible dissemination of research findings are crucial. This collaboration needs to be founded on principles of mutual respect, open communication, and a commitment to ethical research practices.

One promising avenue for collaboration lies in the study of neurodiversity. The exploration of conditions like autism spectrum disorder (ASD), where individuals often exhibit heightened sensory sensitivities or unusual cognitive abilities, presents a natural bridge between neuroscience and parapsychology. Studies exploring the correlation between specific genetic markers associated with ASD and the reported incidence of psychic abilities could reveal important insights into the neurological basis of these phenomena. Similarly, examining the brain structures and functional connectivity in individuals with ASD who report psychic experiences could illuminate the neural correlates of these abilities.

Beyond ASD, the concept of "neurodiversity" itself can expand our understanding of human potential. The New Age perspectives on Indigo, Crystal, and Rainbow children, as well as Starseeds and Lightworkers, suggest a population of individuals with unique cognitive and spiritual abilities. While these concepts may seem outside the realm of conventional science, they offer a framework for studying individuals who report experiences that defy easy explanation. A rigorous investigation, acknowledging both the scientific and spiritual dimensions of these experiences, could lead to profound discoveries.

For example, imagine a study that combines EEG measurements of brainwave activity during meditative practices reported by individuals who identify as "Indigo children" with qualitative interviews exploring their subjective experiences. This integrated approach could reveal unique brain patterns associated with their heightened intuition or spiritual awareness, and the qualitative data could provide depth and context to these findings, leading to a richer, more nuanced understanding of their reported abilities.

Another area ripe for exploration is the intersection of altered states of consciousness (ASC) and psychic abilities. ASC, induced through meditation, psychedelic experiences (under carefully controlled and ethical conditions), or other means, often involve altered perceptions, enhanced intuition, and experiences that resemble psychic phenomena. Neuroscience can study the neural correlates of these altered states, while parapsychology can investigate the reported experiences and their potential connections to psychic abilities. By combining these approaches, we can gain a deeper understanding of the relationship between altered brain states and these extraordinary experiences.

The collaboration should not only focus on individual abilities but also on the potential for enhancing these abilities through therapeutic interventions. Techniques such as meditation, mindfulness practices, and neurofeedback training have shown promise in enhancing cognitive functions and emotional regulation. Studies exploring the potential of these techniques to enhance or develop psychic abilities could lead to the development of new therapeutic approaches for individuals seeking to cultivate their inherent potential.

Furthermore, advances in brain-computer interfaces (BCIs) offer exciting possibilities for studying and potentially even enhancing psychic abilities. BCIs can directly measure and interact with brain activity, providing a powerful tool for investigating the neural correlates of consciousness and potentially facilitating the expression of extraordinary mental capabilities. Ethical considerations surrounding BCIs and their potential for misuse must be carefully addressed, but their potential for advancing this field is immense.

The future of neuroscience and parapsychology is not about a dichotomy of science versus spirituality. It is about an integration—a synergistic relationship where the rigorous methodologies of science are combined with the deep wisdom and intuitive understanding of spiritual traditions and the lived experience of individuals with exceptional abilities. This integrative approach necessitates a shift in our societal understanding of consciousness, recognizing the full spectrum of human potential and creating a more inclusive and equitable environment for individuals with diverse cognitive and sensory experiences. This is not simply about understanding unusual phenomena; it's about embracing the full potential of the human mind and harnessing that potential for the benefit of humankind. The journey ahead is challenging, demanding significant resources and collaborative spirit, but the potential rewards are immeasurable—a deeper understanding of consciousness itself and the unlocking of human potential previously deemed impossible. This is not just a scientific endeavor; it's a journey of self-discovery for humanity as a whole.

The journey towards a more complete understanding of consciousness—one that embraces both the rigorous methodologies of neuroscience and the profound insights of parapsychology and spiritual traditions—demands more than just intellectual curiosity. It necessitates a profound shift in societal attitudes and a concerted effort to foster acceptance and understanding. This is not merely a call for tolerance; it is a call to action, a plea for empathy, and a recognition of the untapped potential residing within the neurodiverse population and those possessing what are often termed "exceptional abilities."

For far too long, individuals exhibiting traits outside the perceived norm have been marginalized, misunderstood, and even pathologized. Those experiencing heightened sensory perception, clairvoyance, clairsentience, or other seemingly paranormal experiences have often been relegated to the fringes of society, stigmatized, and denied access to support and understanding. Similarly, those identified as Indigo, Crystal, or Rainbow children—often characterized by their heightened intuition, empathy, and spiritual sensitivity—have frequently faced social challenges and a lack of acceptance. This societal bias, rooted in a narrow definition of "normalcy," not only causes significant individual suffering but also prevents us from recognizing and harnessing the immense potential represented by neurodiversity.

The implications of this narrow perspective extend far beyond the individual. By dismissing or pathologizing these abilities, we are actively limiting our collective potential. Imagine a world where the heightened sensory awareness of certain individuals could be channeled to develop early warning systems for natural disasters, where intuitive insights could revolutionize scientific discovery, or where profound empathy could guide us toward more compassionate and just social structures. Instead of fearing or suppressing these abilities, we must actively seek to understand and integrate them into our collective consciousness.

This integration requires a multi-pronged approach. Firstly, we need to invest in rigorous, unbiased research. This includes funding studies that explore the neurological correlates of exceptional abilities, conducting large-scale epidemiological studies to determine the prevalence of these traits in the population, and developing standardized assessments that accurately capture the range of human sensory and cognitive experiences. Such research should be conducted with the utmost respect for the individuals involved, ensuring their autonomy and well-being are prioritized. The collaborative nature of this research is key; scientists, spiritual practitioners, individuals with lived experience of these abilities, and ethicists need to work together.

Secondly, we must challenge the pervasive stigma associated with neurodiversity and exceptional abilities. This requires a shift in societal narratives, from one that pathologizes difference to one that celebrates it. We need to foster a culture of acceptance and inclusivity, where individuals feel safe to share their experiences without fear of judgment or ridicule. This can be achieved through public awareness campaigns, educational programs, and community initiatives aimed at promoting understanding and empathy. The media also plays a vital role in shaping societal perceptions; responsible and accurate reporting on these topics is crucial to combating misinformation and harmful stereotypes.

Thirdly, we must develop educational and therapeutic approaches tailored to the unique needs of neurodiverse individuals and those with exceptional abilities. This includes creating inclusive educational environments that cater to diverse learning styles and cognitive strengths, developing support systems that address the social and emotional challenges they may face, and creating therapeutic modalities that acknowledge and work with their unique experiences. This may involve adapting existing therapeutic techniques or developing entirely new ones based on a deeper understanding of their unique neurobiological and psychological profiles. There's also a significant opportunity to explore the potential of these abilities within therapeutic contexts, such as the application of intuitive healing modalities or the use of heightened sensory awareness in clinical settings.

Fourthly, and perhaps most importantly, we must foster a deeper understanding of consciousness itself. Our current scientific models often fall short of explaining the full range of human experience, particularly phenomena that seem to defy conventional explanations. The integration of neuroscience and parapsychology, combined with the insights gained from spiritual traditions, has the potential to revolutionize our understanding of consciousness. This new paradigm should not be seen as replacing existing scientific models but rather as expanding and refining them to encompass a wider range of phenomena. This requires a willingness to embrace uncertainty, to challenge established paradigms, and to consider the possibility that our current understanding of consciousness is incomplete. It's about opening ourselves to the possibility that reality may be far more vast and complex than we currently imagine.

The path forward demands a concerted and multidisciplinary effort. Researchers, clinicians, educators, spiritual leaders, policymakers, and most importantly, the individuals with these abilities, must work together to build a more inclusive and equitable future. We must prioritize ethical considerations at every stage of the research process and in the application of new understandings. This is not merely a scientific or spiritual pursuit; it is a matter of social justice, a recognition of the inherent value and dignity of every human being, regardless of their cognitive or sensory experiences. It is about unlocking the collective potential of humanity, embracing the full spectrum of our being, and creating a world where all individuals can flourish.

The future of neuroscience and parapsychology is not about proving or disproving the existence of psychic abilities; it is about understanding the full spectrum of human consciousness and developing a more inclusive and comprehensive model of the human mind. This requires a paradigm shift, a move away from a reductionist view of consciousness towards a more holistic and integrative approach. It's about recognizing that what was once considered "abnormal" or "paranormal" may simply represent unexplored facets of human potential.

This calls for a significant investment in research and education. We need more funding for studies investigating the neurological underpinnings of exceptional abilities, as well as more resources devoted to developing effective therapeutic approaches for individuals who may struggle with managing these abilities. Educational institutions need to incorporate this new understanding of consciousness into their curricula,

355

fostering a greater appreciation for neurodiversity and challenging outdated notions of normalcy.

Moreover, we must work towards a more equitable distribution of resources and opportunities. Individuals with exceptional abilities often face significant social and economic barriers, and we have a moral obligation to ensure that they are not disadvantaged because of their unique gifts. This necessitates not only funding for research but also the establishment of support networks, mentorship programs, and other initiatives aimed at fostering their inclusion and success.

The journey towards a truly integrative understanding of consciousness will be long and challenging. It will require overcoming ingrained biases, navigating complex ethical dilemmas, and embracing uncertainty. Yet, the potential rewards are immense. By embracing neurodiversity and understanding the full spectrum of human consciousness, we can unlock untapped potential, fostering a more compassionate, equitable, and thriving society for all. It is a call to action not just for scientists and researchers, but for each of us individually. It is a challenge to reconsider our assumptions about what is possible, to broaden our understanding of the human mind, and to create a future where all human beings, with all their unique capabilities and experiences, can truly flourish.

The integration of neuroscience, parapsychology, and spiritual practices holds the key to unlocking a profound shift in our understanding of human consciousness. This integration is not simply a theoretical exercise; it has far-reaching implications for our personal lives, our communities, and our world. It calls upon us to embrace a more holistic perspective, recognizing the interconnectedness of mind, body, and spirit, and the potential for human consciousness to transcend the limitations of our current understanding. It's a path that requires courage, curiosity, and a commitment to fostering a more compassionate and inclusive future.

The journey is not without its challenges. We will face skepticism from those entrenched in traditional views, and we must be prepared to address those concerns with careful, rigorous research and open dialogue. We must also confront our own biases and prejudices, acknowledging the limitations of our current understanding of consciousness and the need for a more inclusive and expansive perspective.

Ultimately, the goal is not simply to understand the mechanisms behind exceptional human abilities, but to harness that understanding for the benefit of humanity. This could translate into new therapies for mental health conditions, improved educational strategies for neurodiverse learners, and innovative solutions to some of the world's most pressing challenges. By embracing the full spectrum of human potential, we can unlock a future brimming with possibilities, a future where all individuals are empowered to live authentically and contribute their unique gifts to the world. This is not just a call for acceptance; it's a call for celebration – a celebration of the diversity of human consciousness and its limitless potential. The future depends on our willingness to embrace this vision and act upon it.

The convergence of neuroscience and parapsychology, once considered a fringe pursuit, is poised to revolutionize our understanding of the human mind and its potential. The journey outlined in this book—a journey from the neurological underpinnings of psychic phenomena to the unique characteristics of neurodiversity and the spiritual perspectives woven into these concepts—paves the way for a future where these seemingly disparate fields not only coexist but synergistically inform and enrich one another. This integration is not merely an academic exercise; it is a crucial step towards unlocking human potential on a scale previously unimaginable.

One of the most immediate and impactful areas where this integration can manifest is in mental health care. Current treatments for conditions like schizophrenia, often characterized by hallucinations and delusions, frequently rely on pharmaceutical interventions that suppress symptoms rather than addressing their underlying causes. A deeper understanding of the neurological mechanisms shared between these conditions and certain forms of psychic experiences could lead to more targeted and effective therapeutic approaches. Imagine a future where instead of simply silencing voices heard only by the patient, we could help them understand the origin and meaning of these experiences, potentially integrating them into a more coherent and fulfilling life narrative. This requires a shift away from the stigmatizing labels of "illness" and towards a more nuanced understanding of these experiences as expressions of a wider spectrum of human consciousness. Research might focus on identifying biomarkers, genetic predispositions, or epigenetic factors that contribute to both psychic abilities and susceptibility to specific mental health conditions. This would allow for early identification of individuals at risk, facilitating preventative interventions and personalized therapies that cater to individual needs and strengths.

Furthermore, the paradigm shift proposed in this book has profound implications for education. The recognition of neurodiversity as a source of strength, rather than a deficit, necessitates a fundamental overhaul of our educational systems. Instead of forcing all students to conform to a rigid, standardized curriculum, we should strive to create learning environments that are inclusive and adaptable to diverse learning styles and cognitive strengths. This includes creating opportunities for individuals with exceptional abilities to nurture and develop their gifts, providing them with a supportive context to explore their potential without facing societal judgment or pressure to conform. Such an approach would not only empower these individuals but would also enrich the educational experience for everyone, fostering creativity, collaboration, and a deeper appreciation for human diversity. Imagine classrooms where students with heightened intuition and empathy are valued and encouraged to participate fully, where their perspectives enrich the learning process for their peers. Imagine educational programs designed to specifically cultivate and refine these extraordinary capacities, offering guidance and support to navigate their potential while addressing any potential challenges they might encounter.

Beyond education and mental health, the insights gained from this integrated approach could be pivotal in addressing various societal challenges. The heightened empathy and intuitive abilities associated with neurodiversity could prove invaluable in conflict resolution, diplomacy, and community building. Individuals with strong clairsentience or precognitive abilities, when appropriately guided and supported, could potentially contribute to disaster preparedness, financial forecasting, or even scientific discovery. This is not a suggestion that such abilities should be exploited but rather a recognition that their integration into society could yield significant benefits, provided ethical considerations are paramount. A thoughtful approach would emphasize fostering these abilities within a framework that respects individual agency, autonomy, and the potential for misuse of such abilities. This requires robust ethical guidelines and regulatory frameworks to ensure responsible application and to safeguard against potential exploitation or manipulation.

The future envisioned here is not one of replacing established scientific methods with spiritual beliefs, but rather one of integrating both for a more comprehensive and nuanced understanding of human consciousness. Neuroscience provides the tools to investigate the biological mechanisms underlying psychic phenomena, while parapsychology and spiritual traditions offer valuable insights into the subjective experiences and broader context of these phenomena. The integration of these perspectives demands a multidisciplinary approach, bringing together neuroscientists, psychologists, parapsychologists, spiritual leaders, educators, and policymakers to collaborate on research, develop new therapies, and create policies that foster inclusivity and support for neurodiverse individuals and those with exceptional abilities. This collaborative effort would involve not only scientific investigation but also a broader societal conversation about the nature of consciousness, the meaning of human potential, and the ethical implications of harnessing extraordinary abilities.

The path towards this integrated future is not without its challenges. Overcoming deeply entrenched societal biases, scientific skepticism, and the potential for misinformation requires a concerted effort from all stakeholders. Open dialogue, rigorous research, and a willingness to challenge existing paradigms are essential. This journey necessitates a paradigm shift—a fundamental change in how we perceive mental health, neurodiversity, and exceptional abilities. We must move away from a model that pathologizes difference towards one that celebrates and nurtures diversity as a source of human strength and innovation. The exploration of human potential should be a collaborative venture, involving both scientific rigor and an open heart.

This means cultivating a culture of empathy and acceptance, one where individuals feel safe to explore their own unique abilities without fear of judgment or discrimination. It requires investing in research that investigates the neurological underpinnings of both mental illness and exceptional abilities, with the goal of developing more effective treatments and educational approaches. Crucially, it also involves fostering a greater understanding and appreciation of spiritual practices and traditions, recognizing their potential role in fostering personal growth, well-being, and the development of human potential. We must actively dismantle the barriers that separate science from spirituality, recognizing their complementary roles in understanding the human experience. The future of neuroscience and parapsychology lies in embracing their interconnectedness, allowing them to inform and enrich one another in the pursuit of a more holistic understanding of consciousness and its limitless potential.

The integration of these fields offers the promise of a future where individuals with exceptional abilities are not marginalized but celebrated for their unique contributions. It offers a future where mental health conditions are understood with greater compassion and treated with more effective interventions. It offers a future where education is personalized and inclusive, empowering all individuals to reach their full potential. This is a future where the boundaries between science and spirituality blur, creating a more holistic and integrated understanding of the human experience. It is a future that requires a collective commitment to challenging existing paradigms, embracing inclusivity, and fostering a culture of open-mindedness and empathy. The journey is challenging, but the rewards—a future where human potential is fully realized—are immeasurable. The future of humanity depends upon our willingness to embark on this transformative journey, fostering a world where all individuals can flourish and contribute their unique gifts to the tapestry of human experience. This is not simply a vision for the future; it is a call to action, a call to embrace the full spectrum of human consciousness and to unlock the extraordinary potential that resides within each of us.

GLOSSARY

Clairvoyance: The purported ability to gain information about an object, location, person, or physical event through extra-sensory perception, without using any known sensory channels.

Clairsentience: The purported ability to perceive information about an object, location, person, or physical event through extra-sensory means, specifically sensing the emotions or feelings associated with that object or event.

Neurodiversity: The concept that neurological differences are a normal part of human variation, rather than deficits. This encompasses a wide range of neurological conditions and variations in cognitive and sensory processing.

Indigo Children: A New Age term for children believed to possess heightened psychic abilities and spiritual awareness.

Crystal Children: A New Age term, often used alongside Indigo Children, to describe children believed to have even greater intuitive abilities and empathic connections.

Rainbow Children: Similar to Indigo and Crystal Children, these individuals are believed to possess unique abilities, but with a greater focus on unconditional love and harmony.

Starseeds: Individuals believed to have originated from other star systems, possessing unique spiritual gifts and knowledge.

Lightworkers: Individuals dedicated to serving humanity and bringing light to the world through their actions and intentions.

Synaptic Plasticity: The ability of synapses to strengthen or weaken over time, in response to increases or decreases in their activity. This is a fundamental mechanism of learning and memory.

Epigenetics: The study of heritable changes in gene expression that do not involve alterations to the underlying DNA sequence.

www.ingramcontent.com/pod-product-compliance
Lightning Source LLC
Chambersburg PA
CBHW051412090426
42737CB00014B/2623